THE MIND OF
A MISSIONARY

What Global Kingdom Workers Tell Us About Thriving on Mission Today

 **within reach global**

PRAISE FOR
The Mind of a Missionary

"David Joannes shapes this book through various lives who have followed Jesus from the streets of their birth to the ends of the globe. *The Mind of a Missionary* is filled with the truth and grace of the Great Commission command. Here, crucifixion and resurrection meet in the lives of real people and families who have determined to carry their cross to far away places. Joannes reminds us that the rolled-away stone—the power of the resurrection—can become all peoples' eternal possession and reality."
— Nik Ripken, Author of *The Insanity of God* and *The Insanity of Obedience*, www.nikripken.com

"In *The Mind of a Missionary*, David Joannes takes us on a virtual adventure spanning centuries and continents with his latest book. His story-telling is a feast of verbal delights as he transports you into the minds and hearts of some of the most profound risk-takers for the sake of spreading the Gospel message!" — Ron Luce, Founder of Teen Mania Ministries and Jesus Global Youth Day, www.jesusglobalyouthday.com

"*The Mind of a Missionary* is a timely reminder that if we don't learn from the past, we are doomed to repeat her mistakes. Joannes brings a helpful, new perspective on timeless lessons from missionary legends. You'll be inspired and encouraged." — Craig Greenfield, Founder of Alongsiders International and author of *Subversive Jesus*, www.alongsiders.org

"*The Mind of a Missionary* is a compelling read. This book is a must for anyone who wants to last long and finish strong in their missional calling. As much as David is a masterful storyteller, he is also a practical guide. He lays out both the triumphant highs and challenging lows of life on the mission field, while always pointing to Jesus as the enabling Source and eternal Hope. Anyone who reads this book will surely be encouraged and better equipped to fulfill the Heavenly call on their life!" — Pastor How & Pastor Lia, Senior Pastors of Heart of God Church Singapore, www.hogc.sg

"In the contemporary Church, there's little difference between having a fleeting 'burden for missions' and starry-eyed wanderlust. The call for long-term missionaries willing to lay aside their lives for the cause of Christ found in past generations are mysteriously absent today. The missions enterprise is taking on the flavor of a microwave culture aimed at scratching our consumeristic itch. David Joannes exposes the need for more missionary grit; he plunges the depths of past missionary mindsets to pull out gems for this generation to learn from. Anything written by David Joannes is a worthy read. I commend *The Mind of a Missionary* to anyone interested in cross-cultural ministry—or ministry in general." — Alex Kocman, Director of Long-Term Mobilization at ABWE, www.abwe.org

"It's been said that when it comes to missions, followers of Christ have three options: Go, send or disobey. If you are a goer, read this book. If you are a sender, read this book. If you are disobedient, read this book. I believe *The Mind of a Missionary* by David Joannes will help you find your place in the greatest movement in history." — Matthew Ellison, President of Sixteen:Fifteen and co-author of *When Everything is Missions*, 1615.org

THE MIND OF
A MISSIONARY

What Global Kingdom Workers Tell Us About Thriving on Mission Today

DAVID JOANNES

DEDICATION

To my wife, Lorna:

*Your constant encouragement and support helped make this book possible.
I am so thankful to be married to a Proverbs 31 woman like you.
Your passion for God, His Kingdom, and the people we serve inspires me.
Your prayers for me for wisdom as I wrote* The Mind of a Missionary *undergirded the message of this book. I believe these words are God-breathed—in large part because you championed the Message of the Kingdom and wanted to see me thrive in the gifts God gave me. Thank you! Your reward will be the many lives this book will touch. I love you.*

To my daughter, Cara Liana:

It is my joy to guide you in your missionary journey. I am blessed to see your missions zeal grow even from your young age. I am excited for the plans God has for you. I believe that He will use you to impact the nations with the grace and glory of His Kingdom. Thank you for encouraging me to write this book. May the examples of a life well-lived stir your spirit to join God's grand plan to redeem the world. I love you.

CONTENTS

ACKNOWLEDGMENTS

First and foremost, I am compelled to thank my wife, Lorna, for her constant prayers and support as I wrote *The Mind of a Missionary*. Writing a book is a long and arduous process, and her sacrifice is not forgotten. Not only did she allow me space and time to complete this book, but she also encouraged me throughout the process. Her reminders that *The Mind of a Missionary* encompasses much more than just the author's ideas inspired me to complete the project. I pray that she would find deep satisfaction, knowing that her support will be felt around the world as this book encourages Christians to thrive on mission today.

This project would not be possible without the expertise of Felecia Killings, my writing coach, content editor, proofreader, and friend. Her professional skills have catapulted my writing ability in more ways than I can express. In 2016, she helped me complete *The Space Between Memories: Recollections from a 21st Century Missionary*, and walked with me through *The Mind of a Missionary* as well. She helped consolidate my initial thoughts into this broad narrative of the missions endeavor. Her fingerprints reveal throughout these pages. For that, I am very grateful.

I am thankful for the professional help of Sandy and Phil Hovatter. They graciously made time to design the entire interior content of *The Mind of a Missionary*. I am blessed by their expertise and generosity in helping bring this book to fruition.

Thanks to Natalie Lam for helping to research and arrange the notes and references found at the end of this book. I appreciate her incredible attention to detail and hours of tedious work.

I am particularly thankful for the many global Kingdom workers serving in foreign fields around the world who contributed to this book by telling me their testimonies. Nearly one-hundred people took *The Mind of a Missionary Survey*; the thoughts and experiences they shared were priceless. I also interviewed dozens of missionaries serving in nearly fifty countries around the world. They told me about their difficulties and desires, frailties and triumphs. My prayer is that their thoughts shine through this book, giving voice to the many present-day missionaries who seek to articulate the often-misunderstood nuances of the mission field. In part, this book is a journey through missions history. But it is much more than that. It is the longing of scores of missional Christians who seek the advent of God's Kingdom on the earth; who wait expectantly for the consummation of Christ's kingly rule in the nations. I pray that my feeble words give justice to the many passionate global Kingdom workers highlighted in *The Mind of a Missionary*.

To our foreign and indigenous missionaries serving at Within Reach Global: may you be encouraged and inspired to pursue the call of God on your lives. Your missional efforts among the unreached people groups of the 10/40 Window are making a tremendous impact. The effects of your service may be difficult to recognize at times because you are small parts in God's grand redemption plan. Continue to press forward and reach the Gospel-deprived peoples who wait at the other end of your obedience! The Spirit of God understands the times and seasons better than you do. He delights to include you in His missionary enterprise.

I thank God for allowing me to be a small part of His story. The thoughts in this book exist to bring Him glory in the nations; to elicit "righteous deviants" who will push against the current of social influence, and who will follow the leading of the Spirit into the darkness to shine as beacons of light. Indeed, this book is less about *The Mind of a Missionary* than it is about the mind of Christ.

FOREWORD

Our family's world has been defined by Jesus' Matthew 28 command to "go into all the world" and make disciples of every people group. In the last 35 years of "going," we have met others in the Christian faith who have refused this command, ran from His command, trivialized such a foundational command, and those who have romanticized the Great Commission to dangerous extremes.

Not so with David Joannes in *The Mind of a Missionary*. Joannes highlights various people who followed Jesus from the streets of their birth to the ends of the globe. He reminds us that Christ's followers are called to be "sheep among wolves," but he never settles for foolish actions on the part of the sheep. One of my favorite biblical observations about Jesus was that He was filled with "truth and grace." Biblical obedience, balanced with the love and the example of Christ, is apparent in each story Joannes illustrates.

I almost refused to pen this foreword. It caused me to experience, once again, the faces of starved Somali children, ravaged women, hopeless fathers, and a shattered people group. Through the lives illustrated, David calls believers in Jesus to embrace a lost world with every ounce of one's mind, soul, and strength.

For years, our ministry in the Horn of Africa received many volunteers who followed Jesus to the ends of the earth. They joined us in Somalia to serve the Somali people. The country was an edgy place to be; some considered it a destination only for "radical Christians." Increasingly, the cavalier attitude of some people arriving to serve caused us concern, as the focus seemed to be more about the one going rather than the Lord who sent. We knew something must be done to address this attitude and to call forth altruistic missions motivation. One of the methods we implemented served to curb the vainglory of potential volunteers and to assist all of us who served in such a hostile environment.

Before going in-country, we asked those who joined our team to write a letter to their family and friends. This letter would remain in their file.

If the worst happened, and they did not live through their time among the Somali people, the letter would be given to their family to explain why they followed Jesus to such a hard environment. This practice of "counting the cost" and writing a letter to explain their potential death was often met with a wild-eyed response. Suddenly, the price of following Jesus to Somalia became real. Before going in-country, we gathered our teams and read each letter aloud. The written words of our volunteers crystalized the cost of following Jesus.

After serving with us in Somalia for up to six months, we would celebrate their service with a team meal, the giving of a gift, and a review of their time with our teams. Often we would hear our volunteers say something like, "You know, my time in Somalia did not bother me as much as I thought it would before I went in the first time." Their missional efforts shined the light of the Gospel in difficult places. They had served Jesus well.

Every day, they helped feed 50,000 starving people. They witnessed the burial of scores of small children who died each night. Conversations with molested women filled their days. They listened to husbands and fathers who had been made to watch their wives and daughters molested and killed. The stories of these tragedies were their common lot. Now, we were sending our volunteers back to their families and churches as spokespersons for a people group decimated by civil war and famine. They were returning home as our advocates for the Somali people; yet their common, incredulous response was "how little my time in Somalia bothered me!"

Their attitude brought our family's faith journey to the forefront of our minds. We served among a horrifically-abused people who had, by and large, been overlooked by the Christian Church for much of the 2,000 years since the death and resurrection of Jesus. We recalled the times we tried to tell family and friends in the United States what we had experienced on the mission field. It was never easy; the moment we began to describe the tragedies we encountered, a waterfall of emotions rushed over us.

With these contemplations in mind, we asked our volunteers to describe in detail their experience in Somalia. "In less than a week, you will be standing before your family, friends, and churches," we began. "What will you tell them? Tonight, you are in a safe place. Practice on us. Remember with us. What will you say to those who sent you here?"

They began to speak, to remember, to unpack their experiences.

Within minutes, sobs of emotion replaced their stoic narrative. It was normal for them to sit on the floor, broken by what they had experienced. It was exceedingly painful for them to open up the closets in their minds where they had hidden images of the children buried, the emaciated fed, and numerous young women whose innocence was stolen from them on a daily basis. During our debriefing period, we cried together at each shared memory. Our meeting culminated in rejoicing at their willing obedience to allow God to use them. We prayed for the people who had been touched by their lives, praying that we would one day see our Somali brothers and sisters standing before God's throne. The unpacking of their experiences realigned our hearts and minds with the eternal Kingdom of God.

The Mind of a Missionary by David Joannes took me back to those moments of deep introspection. This book is filled with the "truth and grace" of the Great Commission command. Here, crucifixion and resurrection meet in the lives of real people and families who have determined to carry their cross to far away places. The world knows what it means to be broken, to be crucified. David helps us to "write our letter home" so that, if we don't make it back, others will realize the lives laid down for the Gospel of Jesus. He reminds us that the rolled-away stone—the power of the resurrection—can become all peoples' eternal possession and reality.

Dr. Nik Ripken
Author of *The Insanity of God* and *The Insanity of Obedience*
July 10, 2018

INTRODUCTION

God enlarged my heart and awakened my mind to the needs of the world when I was still a child. My parents read missionary biographies to me— stories of cannibal-headhunters, orphaned children, and unreached people groups living in distant lands. The heroic narratives glimmered with romanticized hues; the valiant deeds of global Kingdom workers portrayed otherworldly courage I had never before experienced. As I learned about the radical individuals God used to advance His Kingdom on the earth, missionaries became my heroes. Their sacrificial service inspired me; their fervent passion for God left an indelible mark on my heart and mind. The portrait of a missionary—albeit both aggrandized and incomplete—propelled me to join the missionary enterprise by going overseas.

Today, I am less starry-eyed and sentimental about the nuances of the mission field as I was in childhood. Having served as a missionary in Southeast Asia for over two decades, the romanticized glimpses and fantastic encounters I once read about have become my new normalcy. I have found that the people God uses are the typical types—run-of-the-mill individuals who simply said "Yes" to God. There is little that distinguishes them from the crowd. Indeed, the missionary task force comprises of ordinary people, warts and all.

As I considered this reality, I began to ponder the makeup and mindset of Christian missionaries. What propels some believers to abandon earthly comfort and man's acclaim by going to foreign fields? How do they juggle the expectations surrounding the unique call of God on their lives? Why do they take such daring risks? What rewards do they hope to gain?

This book is an effort to uncover the thought process of past and present missionaries serving around the world. In *The Mind of a Missionary*, I hope to shed light on God's Kingdom values and His power at work in and through mere men and women. He placed eternity in our hearts and invites us to join Him in His grand redemptive plan. God's scandalous grace is the starting point of the missionary venture, and His glory is the pinnacle of this timeless narrative. What concerns us at present is the messy middle—the moments and instances we find ourselves in today.

The myopic perspective through which we see the world is strikingly different than God's eternal viewpoint. He fits every piece of the puzzle into its perfect position to reveal a portrait of His great love for humankind. We often overlook the providential purposes He employs through pain, problems, and persecution. We wonder if He does, indeed, have everything under control. Amidst the struggles of life, we question His competence and capacity to overcome evil and prove Himself the Lord of Heaven and earth.

Such carnal contemplations bother the minds of every Christian, whether at home or abroad. For those who go overseas to publicize the name of Jesus in foreign cultures of the earth, these questions compound the already difficult situations they find themselves in. Missionaries face unique physical, emotional, and spiritual challenges. What, then, causes some to triumph and others to fail in their missional endeavors? How do their examples help us to thrive on mission today?

I spent months researching the missions venture. I read dozens of books, articles, journals, and blogs to better describe the nuances that global Kingdom workers encounter. Had I not sensed the Holy Spirit's powerful prompting, I would have ditched the entire project. The truth is, on numerous occasions, I nearly gave up. Like many of the "guides" found in The Mind of a Missionary, my negative internal monologue challenged the validity of my efforts. The enemy's incessant chatter confronted my desire to awaken the Church to God's glorious mandate.

I admit that a single book does not do justice to the numerous stories and the broad spectrum of the missions enterprise. Still, I believe that God desires to gather my menial thoughts and infuse them with supernatural potential. I am confident this book will inspire you to join God's glorious plan to redeem the nations and establish His Kingdom wherever you go.

Each of the following twelve chapters highlights a missionary "guide" who gives you keys to thriving on mission today. Some are well-known; others obscure. Many are considered historical legends; others are still alive today, serving in mission fields around the world. These missionary guides are Jim and Elisabeth Elliot, C. T. Studd, Nikolaus Zinzendorf, Robert Moffat, Jackie Pullinger, David Eubank, Nik and Ruth Ripken, William Carey, Hudson Taylor, Amy Carmichael, Don Richardson, and Heidi Baker.

The thoughts and experiences of dozens of modern-day global Kingdom workers pepper the pages in *The Mind of a Missionary*, revealing the extensive account of God's past and present work in the world.

Tens of thousands of individuals crossed geographic, cultural, and linguistic boundaries over the centuries. They left family and country to publicize the name of Christ, often where the Gospel message was little known and understood. Many altruistic Christians sought to win souls and advance the Kingdom of God on the earth. Many of them triumphed by leaving their mark on eternity. Unable to overcome the unforeseen hurdles of missionary life, many more left the field bruised and battered. Others—driven by personal gain, notions of acclaim, or nationalistic ambition—tarnished the purity of the Message by preaching a gospel Christ would never affirm. For these reasons, many modern-day global Kingdom workers are still trying to rid themselves of the negative connotations surrounding the term "missionary."

I hope to highlight both the difficulties and delights of joining Jesus' Great Commission command. In the following accounts of obedient sacrifice, you may be motivated to emulate the godly examples found in *The Mind of a Missionary*. Indeed, there are many praiseworthy aspects of the people found within these pages, but they are not perfect. We do well to take the words of David Livingstone to heart: "I am a missionary, heart and soul," he said. Yet, he pointed us to the perfect missionary prototype by saying, "God had an only Son, and He was a missionary... A poor, poor imitation of Him I am or wish to be."[1]

We have, in the Person of Jesus, the ultimate example of a cross-cultural missionary. He left the glories of Heaven for the people of the earth. He gave up His claim to honor to serve the undeserving. In this manner, He raised to glory all those who call upon the name of the Lord. Beyond belief, God then gave us the mind of Christ. The supreme standard of His Son acts as a catalyst. He calls you to radical obedience and allows you to operate with a missionary mindset, making known His glory in the nations.

MOTIVATIONS

Throughout history, scores of Christians dared to cross geographic, cultural, and linguistic barriers to publish the name of Jesus where the Gospel was utterly unknown. They abandoned creature comforts and earthly acclaim for a coming Kingdom. What motivated these individuals? What led them to take such courageous steps into the unknown?

In section one of *The Mind of a Missionary*, the lives of Jim and Elisabeth Elliot, C. T. Studd, and Nikolaus Zinzendorf cause us to consider the underlying motivation of our missional efforts. You will learn about the strong sense of belief in the minds of global Kingdom workers. You will see that intrinsically-motivated people embraced a Spirit-led, Kingdom-focused perspective that ultimately surpassed the promise of worldly rewards. Jesus' compassion for the crowds that clamored for His attention transplanted into their spirit; His Great Commission call permeated their being. A passion for God's glory undergirded their compassion for the lost and obedience to the commands of Christ. Global Kingdom workers of the past and present pined for an eternal home; the temporal and tangible became secondary in their hearts and minds.

The missionary examples in section one, *Motivations*, encourage you to consider the core of your relationship with Christ and examine the degree of altruism in your Christian witness. You will learn about Edward Deci's Self Determination Theory, the mark of the Missionary Generation on today's young people, the power of prayer, and God's glory as the driving force behind Christian work. As you allow the glory of God to prompt your every move, a "peace that passes understanding" will suffuse your missional efforts and display His Kingdom power in and through your life.

CHAPTER ONE

COMPASSION FOR THE LOST

Our Orders Are the Gospel to Every Creature

Five days before the fateful hour when the sting of tragedy would be felt around the world on January 8, 1956, a Piper PA-14 airplane circled the jungles of eastern Ecuador. The humid atmosphere threatened rain from low-lying clouds. Above the thick fog, the yellow propeller plane soared in sunlight, casting its ominous shadow over a blanket of mist.

Patches between the fog revealed the serpentine Curaray River that snaked across the landscape below, splitting the thick overgrowth with its zigzagging trickle. Twenty-eight-year-old Jim Elliot surveyed the verdant rain forest in search for primitive villages: the hutted homes of the Huaorani tribespeople. This unreached people group was the focus of Elliot and his band of brothers who sought to evangelize the tribe. Their missional attempt was called *Operation Auca.*

Fellow missionaries, Ed McCully, Roger Youderian, Pete Fleming, and their pilot, Nate Saint, accompanied Jim Elliot. The "Ecuador Five," as they came to be known, had already contacted the Huaorani tribe (also called the "Auca," a pejorative word meaning "savage"). This group of Ecuadorian indigenous people were considered violent and dangerous to outsiders. There were no known Christians among the Gospel-deprived people group. For weeks, Elliot and his counterparts announced their aerial presence by loudspeaker, calling out, "I like you! I like you!" They passed out gifts (trousers, shirts, machetes, cooked fish, packets of peanuts, two squirrels, one parrot, two bananas, and a smoked monkey tail, amongst other things) in hopes that the stone-age Auca would come to welcome their regular visits.

Elliot said of their mission, "Our orders are: the Gospel to every creature."[1] But the evangelization of the unreached tribe would be a task easier hoped for than accomplished.

Countless hours of prayer, language study, strategic planning, and exploration had gone into Operation Auca. The pivotal moment came, and on January 3, 1956, before their plane took flight, the five men closed their prayer time with the hymn, *We Rest On Thee*:

> *We rest on Thee, our Shield and our Defender,*
> *Thine is the battle, Thine shall be the praise*
> *When passing through the gates of pearly splendor*
> *Victors, we rest with Thee through endless days.*

During the months leading up to Operation Auca, Jim's wife, Elisabeth, reminded him of the dangers of the mission and what they both knew it might mean if he went. "Well, if that's the way God wants it to be," was his calm reply, "I'm ready to die for the salvation of the Aucas."[2]

After they landed on a strip of sand they called "Palm Beach," the five men constructed a makeshift treehouse where they stayed for the next five days. These were not the quaint streets of Portland, Oregon where Elliot grew up. The gnats, mosquitoes, and chiggers were relentless; nearby, they found alligator and puma tracks. Elliot's counterpart, Nate Saint, wrote of the experience as follows: "Except for forty-seven billion flying insects of every sort, this place is a little paradise. With the help of smoke and repellant, we are all enjoying the experience immensely."[3]

On January 4, 1956, Elliot penned a letter to his wife: "Our hopes are up, but no signs of the 'neighbors' yet. Perhaps today is the day the Aucas will be reached."[4] But the "neighbors" were nearby as Saint's handwritten note would later describe: "All's quiet at Palm Beach. However, we feel sure we are being watched."[5]

Two days later, on January 6, the missionaries of Operation Auca met the tribe face to face. Hesitant but curious, two Auca women and one man appeared from the jungle. Their hearts thumping with wild jubilation, the missionaries called across the river, "Puinani!" ("Welcome!") to their guests. The Aucas were uneasy at the sight of white men, but Elliot gradually waded into the water, caught them by the hand, and led them across to their camp.

The afternoon passed casually and cordially, and the missionaries thrilled to see the Aucas jabbering happily to themselves. The young Auca man expressed interest in the plane, and they guessed from his talk that he desired to go to his house and introduce the missionaries to his comrades. Thrilled at the prospect of befriending more Aucas, Nate Saint took him on a quick flight. He taxied down the runway and circled Palm Beach while the young man shouted all the way. The plane landed, and the band of missionary friends expected to board and visit the Auca settlement. Perhaps this friendly encounter would open a new door of opportunity to visit the primitive tribe. But this was not to be the case. Their curiosity apparently satisfied, the three Aucas began across the river, smiling and calling to the five missionaries as they disappeared back into the jungle.

Disheartened, the Ecuador Five sat at their camp and prayed that God would open another door of opportunity to them. Elliot feared they had not taken full advantage of the opportunity while the Aucas were with them, and regretted not following them into the jungle to their homes.

As the five men gazed at the embers turning to ash in the campfire, heavy clouds rolled in from the east, blanketing the empyrean canopy above them. Darkness settled over the Ecuadorian jungle. Despite the apparent setback, their spirits were high and hopeful.

Peter Fleming reclined on a mat near the fire pit and wrote in his journal: "This is a great day for the advance of the Gospel of Christ in Ecuador." His written account went on to describe the day's joyous events but ended on a discouraging note: "We are praying that the others will come and invite us to go over to their place..." And describing the young Auca man they befriended on the beach: "This fellow has seemed reluctant whenever we mentioned the subject and it may be he lacks the authority to invite us on his own."[6]

The sun rose early the next morning, and the five men decided to survey the nearby villages by plane. As far as the eye could see, the verdant jungle spread across the horizon, divided only by the serpentine Curaray River. Circling the dense landscape, the missionaries peered down in search of Auca settlements, but to no avail. When the cumulous clouds descended low enough to impede their aerial excursion, they decided to return to their temporary dwelling at Palm Beach.

That evening, sleep eluded pilot Nate Saint. In fact, all five of the men were restless that Saturday night and wondered when the breakthrough they had long prayed for might occur. A sense of urgency filled their minds, as if in agreement with Amy Carmichael, missionary to India: "We have all eternity to tell of the victories won for Christ, but we have only a few hours before sunset to win them."[7]

"Heavy heart that they fear us," Nate Saint wrote. "Saturday night I was wide awake at 1 a.m., thinking of the many ways we might have tried to keep our visitors around on Friday. I guess the thrill of being with them and of their casualness quite disarmed us of keen constructive thinking. Perhaps it is the Lord's goodness that we had a quiet day yesterday (Saturday)." Nate Saint's note, apparently scrawled out on Sunday, January 8, 1956, was the last record made of the mission to the Aucas before disaster struck. Half an hour later, Saint spoke to the base camp over the plane's radio: "We are hoping for visitors at about 2:30," he said. "I'll call you again at 4:35."

He did not call back at 4:35. When his speared body was found in the river by the search party five days later, his watch had stopped at 3:12.[8] The bodies of Jim Elliot, Ed McCully, Roger Youderian, and Pete Fleming laid face down in the Curaray River. A broken spear protruded Youderian's right hip and back; a thrusted lance found in the sand in the river bottom lay near Elliot's pierced body.

Their Lives Have Left Their Mark on Ours

In every age and from every corner of the earth, people are in desperate need of a hero. They are looking for a man whose motives are altruistic or a woman whose purposes dwarf the status quo. People need an invitation into a heroic story, one which identifies a necessary ambition, reveals the obstacles that keep them from achieving that ambition, and one that helps them overcome those hindrances.

Thus, on January 30, 1956, *LIFE Magazine* ran a ten-page article entitled, "Go Ye and Preach the Gospel: Five Do and Die." The response revealed the striking contrast between the world's version of success and how Christians understand God's definition of triumph.

To the world at large, this was a sad waste of five young lives. *Why give the best years of youth to an intangible outcome?* many people wondered. But God's plan and purpose through the Ecuador Five far exceeded man's understanding. Countless lives were impacted by the happenings on Palm Beach on January 8, 1956. A missionary fervor birthed in young people around the world. In Brazil, for example, a group of Indians at a mission station deep in the Mato Grosso, dropped to their knees upon hearing the news of the martyrdom. They cried out to God for forgiveness for their own lack of concern for fellow Indians who did not know of Jesus Christ. From Rome, an American official wrote to one of the widows: "I knew your husband. He was to me the ideal of what a Christian should be." An air force major stationed in England, with many hours of jet flying, immediately began making plans to join the Missionary Aviation Fellowship. A missionary in Africa wrote: "Our work will never be the same. We knew two of the men. Their lives have left their mark on ours." In Des Moines, Iowa, an eighteen-year-old boy prayed for a week in his room, then announced to his parents: "I'm turning my life over completely to the Lord. I want to try to take the place of one of those five."[9]

As we commence our exploration of the missionary mind, we must first seek to understand how the mind works and how motivation powerfully affects our decisions. What prompted the Ecuador Five to take the Gospel message to stone-age Amazonian "savages"? Was Jim Elliot's missionary motivation an anomaly? Was Operation Auca completely unfounded? What propelled these five young missionaries to willfully abandon creature comforts and earthly contentment for the sake of an unreached tribe? More broadly, what is the driving motivation in the mind of a missionary that leads to such self-sacrifice? Why do some people, despite hardship, persecution, and even martyrdom, expend their lives for Kingdom purposes?

The Mindset Controlled by the Spirit

The term "mind" means different things to different people. Psychologists and cognitive scientists explain that the mind is not the brain but rather what the brain does, namely, processing information. The brain gathers data and the mind processes the information. As the brain collects information from the world through the senses, the mind then executes computations based on this information, which produces human behavior.

Dr. Caroline Leaf, author of *Switch On Your Brain: The Key to Peak Happiness, Thinking, and Health*, writes that "Our free will influences our thinking, which produces our state of mind. This is so important to human behavior and potential that I have dedicated my life to understanding the process of thought and how we can choose to think the way God wants us to think."[10] She continues: "We are not driven by forces beyond our conscious control. We are accountable for every thought and decision we make.[11] We are highly intelligent beings with free will, and we are responsible for our choices."[12] So, what leads us to make such daring, missionally-charged choices? What is the underlying motivation that propels the decision-making process of cross-cultural missionaries like Elliot, McCully, Youderian, Fleming, and Saint?

Motivation is the underlying rationale by which a person acts or behaves in a particular way. This drive can be described as a cycle in which thoughts influence behaviors, behaviors drive performance, and performance affects thoughts. The cycle then begins again. Each stage is composed of many dimensions including attitudes, beliefs, intentions, effort, and withdrawal, which can all affect the motivation that an individual experiences.

Motivation can be divided into two different theories known as extrinsic motivation and intrinsic motivation. (This is where we begin to comprehend that the rationale behind the Ecuador Five was not unfounded.) Extrinsic (external) motivation occurs when we are motivated to perform a behavior or engage in an activity to earn a reward or avoid punishment. Examples of extrinsic motivators include:

- studying because you want to get a good grade;
- cleaning your room to avoid being reprimanded by your parents;
- participating in a sport to win awards;
- or competing in a contest to win a scholarship.

In each example, the behavior is motivated by a desire to gain a reward or to avoid an adverse outcome.

Intrinsic (internal or inherent) motivation, on the other hand, involves engaging in a behavior because it is personally rewarding; essentially, performing an activity for its own sake rather than the desire for some external reward. Examples of intrinsic motivators include:

- participating in a sport because you find the activity enjoyable;
- solving a word puzzle because you find the challenge fun and exciting;
- or playing a game because you find it exciting.

In each of these instances, the person's behavior is motivated by an internal desire to participate in an activity for its own sake.[13]

In his intriguing book, *Drive: The Surprising Truth About What Motivates Us*, author Daniel H. Pink explores the extrinsic and intrinsic motivators in the human mind. "The most deeply motivated people—not to mention those who are most productive and satisfied—hitch their desires to a cause larger than themselves,"[14] he says.

This is the drive we will explore in *The Mind of a Missionary*. Global Kingdom workers link their hearts and minds to a Heavenly Kingdom, knowing that God's global plan encompasses every people on the planet. They give up their menial ideals to become a small part of God's overarching objective: the relocation of souls from the kingdom of darkness into the Kingdom of His beloved Son.

Edward Deci, who is best known for his theories of intrinsic and extrinsic motivation and basic psychological needs, revealed that human motivation operates by laws that ran counter to what most scientists and citizens believed. Rewards given for some activity operate as external motivators; but this, he argued, was not enough to engender long-lasting inspiration. Reward acquisition or punishment avoidance as extrinsic motivators can deliver a short-term boost in the same way that a jolt of caffeine can keep you stimulated for a few more hours. But the effect eventually wears off and a person loses interest in the task at hand. Human beings, Deci said, have an "inherent tendency to seek out novelty and challenges, to extend and exercise their capacities, to explore, and to learn."[15]

In his Self-Determination Theory (SDT) study published in 1971,[16] Deci was concerned with the motivations that underlie the choices people make regardless of external influence and interference. In one session during the three-day experiment, Deci tasked two groups of psychology students with solving a cube puzzle as a part of a research project on problem-solving. During the second session, one group was paid for each successfully completed puzzle, while the other group was not offered any money for their participation. In a third session with the same students, neither group was paid. When Deci announced that the time was up, he left the participants alone in each of the two rooms to obverse them through a one-way window. Because the time had expired, members of the group that had been paid for their work tended to wander away from the cube puzzle they were tasked to complete. They browsed magazines on the other side of the room while the group that had never been offered compensation for the task were more likely to continue working on the puzzles. Deci concluded that the people who were driven by extrinsic motivation (the money they were offered for their participation) no longer experienced an intrinsic motivation to complete their task. People desire to accomplish a task for pleasure's sake, Deci found. The reward itself usurped this innate enjoyment by the provision of external rewards.

The value and feelings that people place upon accomplishing a task or an overarching purpose can be dampened by extrinsic motivators. Clearly, people can be motivated externally—by anticipated rewards like money or a desire for social approval—but Deci reasoned that controlled motivation undermines intrinsic drive. When the feeling of autonomy is lost, internal compulsion lessens.

In light of these psychological discoveries, we must ask ourselves: How do global Kingdom workers thrive on mission with altruistic motives? What is the driving force in the mind of a missional Christian? What is the ultimate reward that they seek? God, of course, sees our innermost being. His light penetrates the human spirit, exposing every hidden motive.[17] How, then, must we live as pure, noble, and altruistic Christian witnesses in a world waiting for the truth of the Gospel?

The Apostle Paul, writing to the Galatian Church, expressed, "Since we are living by the Spirit, let us follow the Spirit's leading in every part of our lives."[18] Later, in his first letter to Timothy, Paul wrote, "But you, man of God, flee from all this [extrinsic motivation], and pursue righteousness, godliness, faith, love, endurance and gentleness."[19]

I contend that those who are intrinsically motivated to pursue the call of God on their lives experience the deep pleasure of willing obedience. Elliot and the Ecuador Five might never have gone to such extremes for the sake of accolades or external rewards. Can the praise of man propel us to a missional effort that ends in death? Such an external reward does not contain sufficient sway. This is true of our lives as well. We will not abandon our creature comforts and thrive on mission without the pure yearning for God's glory alone. The deepest altruistic response to the call of Christ is found in the divine marriage between intrinsic motivation and a sensitive pursuing of the Holy Spirit's guidance.

Those who are motivated by the flesh only pursue what benefits the flesh. But those who live by the impulses of the Holy Spirit are motivated to pursue spiritual realities—to discern the longings and purposes of God on the earth. For the mindset of the flesh is death, but the mindset controlled by the Spirit finds life and peace. In fact, the mindset focused on the flesh fights God's plan and refuses to submit to His direction, because it cannot![20] Only when our spirits are aligned with God's deepest desires do we cease struggling, surrender to His will, and thrive in the purpose for which He created us.

In a fair assessment of the missionary enterprise that recently appeared in *The Atlantic*, author and freelance journalist Saba Imtiaz writes,

> Christianity is shrinking and aging in the West, but it's growing in the Global South, where most Christians are now located. There are hundreds of thousands of missionaries around the world, who believe scripture compels them to spread Christianity to others, but what's changing is where they're coming from, where they're going, and why.[21]

Some, driven by Western guilt, go to fulfill an overseas duty devoid of joy. Many do not possess an intrinsic desire simply to glorify God. This is not the case with every person. However, we do well to examine the underlying motivations of our Great Commission role. Imtiaz continues to explore the drive behind this new generation of missionaries by saying,

> Christian missionaries' motivations can vary widely, in part because they come from diverse denominations... They may be driven by their faith, the wish to do good in the world, and an interest in serving a higher purpose. But their motivations, according to young Christian missionaries I've spoken to, also include everything from the desire to travel abroad to the desire for social capital. Often, these are mutually reinforcing.[22]

The world is full of desperate brokenness and hopeless need. If we desire to see long-term impact, our missionary endeavors require less superficial barnstorms and more strategically focused efforts.

The trigger of missionary motivation is not a new concept. "Why is it that some Christians cross land and sea, continents and cultures, as missionaries?" John Stott queried. "What on earth impels them? It is not in order to commend a civilization, an institution or an ideology, but rather a Person, Jesus Christ, whom they believe to be unique."[23] The love of God compels us to trust His sovereignty, dare the impossible, and walk in the power of the Holy Spirit.

So, back to the question of Jim Elliot's missionary motivation. His compassion for the lost and obedience to the commands of Christ could not have been a one off. Had not his many years of experiencing the heart of God compelled him to share God's love with the Auca?

Elliot's example begs us to question our own ministry motivations. Are we externally motivated by the accolades of men and a version of success that they promise? Are we driven by wanderlust and adventure? Or are we internally compelled by the love of Christ and an understanding of our identity in Him? For what we say and do is based on what we have already built into our minds. We evaluate this information and make our choices based on this information. Then we choose to build a new thought, and this is what drives what we say and do.[24]

We Died Before We Came Here

The ministry of Jesus was marked by compassion for the lost. He traveled through all the towns and villages, teaching in the temples and announcing the good news about the Kingdom. As the throngs of people pressed in toward Him, He suddenly paused in the midst of the pandemonium. When He saw the demon-possessed, the sick, the poor, and the multitudes in the valley of decision, He had compassion on them because they were confused and helpless, like sheep without a shepherd. He said to His disciples, "The harvest is great, but the workers are few. So, pray to the Lord who is in charge of the harvest; ask Him to send more workers into His fields."[25]

Amy Carmichael, missionary to India, poignantly echoed the compassion of Jesus: "Does it not stir up our hearts, to go forth and help them, does it not make us long to leave our luxury, our exceeding abundant light, and go to them that sit in darkness?"[26] Carmichael did just that. She abandoned her homeland and shined the light of Jesus in India for fifty-five years. Global Kingdom workers around the world prove the value of Christ's suffering through radical obedience. Their lives are examples to us even today, role models who help us thrive on mission in our own contexts.

This call to action, though, requires sacrifice, and few external motivators are powerful enough to compel an individual to such extreme measures. Externally-motivated people will experience empathy for others. Even from a distance, they are aware of other people's feelings. But empathy does not demand action. Compassion, however, is completely different. It is a sympathetic consciousness of others' distress linked with a desire to alleviate it. You can view the evening news and feel empathetic, but you cannot love the Lord your God with all your heart, soul, mind, and strength without participating in His redemptive mission. When compassion is divorced from action, we operate simply out of empathy, and this is not what Jesus had in mind. Jesus' call to compassion for the lost is essentially a call to self-denial and even to death.

The Apostle Paul was a prominent first-century voice for the Christian missions endeavor. At the height of his missionary service he said,

> My old identity has been crucified with the Messiah and no longer lives; for the nails of His cross crucified me with Him. And now the essence of this new life is no longer mine, for the Anointed One lives His life through me—we live in union as one! My new life is empowered by the faith of the Son of God who loves me so much that He gave Himself for me, and dispenses His life into mine.[27]

This idea must be the starting point of all Christian ministry: God's indwelling power in me prompts my every action for Him.

The words of James Calvert, a missionary to the cannibals of the Fiji Islands in 1838, are a living example of this scripture. As they arrived at the islands, the ship's captain tried to turn Calvert back, saying, "You will lose your life and the lives of those with you if you go among such savages." To that, Calvert replied, "We died before we came here."

A sacrificial laying-down of one's life precedes every altruistic missional effort. In God's "upside-down Kingdom," death comes before life; a smoldering altar precipitates godly exaltation. True worship commences when you die to your fleshly desires, surrender your rights, and grant the Holy Spirit access into every facet of your being.

It should be stated, however, that not all missionary service begins with such selflessness. One can appreciate the honesty of the following missionary rumination:

It would feel incredible to say unequivocally that my motivation is purely about doing God's work and loving other people. As much as I want to be selfless, in all honesty I am not. My decision to serve as a missionary is as much fueled by a hope of adventure and excitement as it is by altruism. So, the question remains. Am I selfless or selfish?

> This is good work, God's work, that I will be doing. Right now, my heart may be wicked and desire its own gain from my service. However, it is still good work that I will be doing. If others believe that my service will accomplish something worthy of investing in, I will accept their aid with joy and thanksgiving, but I will not accept it with guilt or fear. I am sinful now, but if I ask God, He will work to change my heart so that my motivation is pure. So, I will pray and seek this personal growth, but in the meantime, there are needs to be met. I am willing that God might use me to meet them, and I will go.[28]

Motivations in the mind of a missionary are extremely multifarious. These motives include a strong desire to take part in something bigger than yourself, a drawing toward the distant exotic, pleasure-imbued altruism, a compassion for people, and a passion for God's glory to be known.

"So, what is the right motivation, the right passion we must ever keep before us to stay healthy in our pursuits?" David Frazier asked in his book, *Mission Smart.*

> Our motivation is the Lord Himself. He must be our joy, our passion, our satisfaction, and ultimate fulfillment. His complete forgiveness and acceptance of us must be the foundation of all we do. No 'high vocation' or spiritual achievements in life can ever fill that vacuum in our hearts.[29]

We were made to worship, and worship is more than Sunday morning singing. It is our whole selves surrendered to God's will. Our active participation in His work is simply the outcome of a life abandoned to the service of God.

During his first expedition to Ecuador in 1952, Jim Elliot wrote a letter to a friend in America. His words gave an idea of his goals at that time:

You wonder why people choose fields away from the States when young people at home are drifting because no one wants to take time to listen to their problems. I'll tell you why I left: because those Stateside young people have every opportunity to study, hear, and understand the Word of God in their own language and these [Auca] indians have no opportunity whatsoever. I have had to make a cross of two logs and lie down on it to show the indians what it means to crucify a man. When there's that much ignorance over here and so much knowledge and opportunity over there, I have no question in my mind why God sent me here. Those whimpering Stateside young people will wake up on the day of judgment condemned to worse fates than these demon-fearing indians. Because having a Bible, they were bored with it while these never heard of such a thing as writing.[30]

Elliot's response to the overwhelming need of the unreached Auca tribe drove him to extreme measures and ultimately led to his own martyrdom. But his zeal for the stone-age people was founded upon an abiding bedrock of Spirit-led obedience and self-denial. He was intrinsically motivated by the example of Christ's compassion.

Just over six years earlier, in his October 28, 1949 journal entry, Elliot expressed his belief that work dedicated to Jesus was more important than his life. He wrote, "He is no fool who gives what he cannot keep to gain that which he cannot lose." His words paralleled the promise of Jesus in Luke 9:24: "For whoever wishes to save his life will lose it, but whoever loses his life for My sake, he is the one who will save it."

The Spirit of God both usurps extrinsic motivators and undergirds intrinsic motivation. He fills us with all-surpassing power and propels us toward an altruistic missional lifestyle. He strengthens weak wings so that we fly like eagles. He empowers feeble knees so that we run without weariness. He gives us the grace to die to our own desires so that the life of Jesus might be evident in us; that we, like Jim Elliot, might give up what we cannot keep so that we may gain what we cannot lose.

We Have Become His Poetry

It should be noted that the role of identity plays a paramount part in the mind of a missionary. This underlying reality affects the success or failure of every global Kingdom worker. When your identity is fused with your role as a missionary, the tendency is to prove your inherent worth by works and human effort. This, in turn, affects the integrity of your missions motivation, the basis of your ministry expectations, and your response to such risky endeavors; it even alters the quality of the rewards you hope to reap.

Amidst the busyness and pressures of missional outreach, you must remember to pause and find refreshment in God's presence. In this posture of worshipful adoration, you come to find that your identity lies not in your performance but in your connection to Christ. When you come to understand that your identity is found in Jesus, the natural outcome is to joyfully walk out your destiny.

Writing to the church in Ephesus, Apostle Paul expressed, "For we are His workmanship, created in Christ Jesus for good works, which God prepared beforehand, that we should walk in them."[31] The Passion Translation states it this way:

> We have become His poetry, a re-created people that will fulfill the destiny He has given each of us, for we are joined to Jesus, the Anointed One. Even before we were born, God planned in advance our destiny and the good works we would do to fulfill it![32]

The Apostle Peter articulates your God-given identity and destiny by saying: "But you are a chosen race, a royal priesthood, a holy nation, a people for God's own possession, that you may proclaim the excellencies of Him who has called you out of darkness into His marvelous light."[33] The foundation of your identity is in God. Your value is not dependent upon the things you do but rather in sonship—the fact that you are His child. He has given you your identity so that His excellent character might be proclaimed through you. God made you who you are so that you could reveal who He is.

Considering the role of identity in the missions call, Deanna Fraser, a former missionary to China told me,

> Missionaries often think they need to always be on the go. Their 'being' is often fused with their 'doing.' A shift took place when I realized that not everything depends on me. I have a part to play and it's an important part, but that also includes finding time to rest, understanding my identity in Christ, and joyfully fulfilling my destiny.[34]

We are all integral parts in God's global mission. He desires each part of the body of Christ—no matter how big or small—to be healthy and whole and to operate at its fullest potential.

But the staggering needs of the mission field compound the problem. At one point in her missionary service, Deanna wondered, "Why should I spend so much time on myself when the world is the one in need?" She was driven by a sincere love for the lost. But, as we will see in chapter eight, the story of her missionary service came to an abrupt end when she failed to recognize the source of her identity in Christ.

Jim Elliot and his missionary counterparts were not immune to the precarious nature of role identity. Weeks before Operation Auca launched, pilot Nate Saint told Roger Youderian about the plan and asked him to go along as the badly-needed additional man. "Roger agreed immediately," Elisabeth Elliot wrote in *Through Gates of Splendor*. Then she reveals the inner turmoil in Youderian's mind: "But all unknown to the others, he was, at that time, passing through a deeply personal spiritual struggle and he began to wonder if he should join the others in the physical venture when not with them completely in spirit."[35]

Youderian thought about the meager effect of his missionary service and wrote, "About ready to call it quits." He goes on,

> The reason: Failure to measure up as a missionary and get next to the people. As far as my heart and aspirations are concerned, the issue is settled. It's a bit difficult to discern just what is the cause of my failure and the forces behind it... and I'm not going to try to fool myself. I wouldn't support a missionary such as I know myself to be, and I'm not going to ask anyone else to.[36]

His inner turmoil remained for some time until December 19, 1955, when his journal entry revealed he was ready to "die to self" and "be alive unto God." "He was cleansed through the Spirit for the task that lay ahead of him," his wife, Barbara, later said, "and went with a happy, expectant mind and his heart full of joy."[37]

Just before he joined the other four, he penned this poem in his journal:

"There is a seeking of honest love
Drawn from a soul storm-tossed,
A seeking for the gain of Christ,

To bless the blinded, the beaten, the lost.
Those who sought found Heavenly Love
And were filled with joy divine,
They walk today with Christ above
. . . ."[38]

The last line eluded him. He set down his pencil and said, "Barb, I'll finish it when I get home."

Their Compulsion was from a Different Source

"I know my daddy is with Jesus, but I miss him, and I wish he would just come down and play with me once in a while," said three-year-old Stevie McCully. Several weeks later, back in the United States, Stevie's little brother, Matthew, was born. One day, while the baby was crying, Stevie said, "Never you mind; when we get to Heaven I'll show you which one is our daddy."[39] This was the reality of life after the murder of the five missionary men who sought to reach the Auca tribe.

On January 16, 1956, the five widows—still trying to adjust themselves to the use of the word—sat together at a kitchen table at Shell Mera, the base of Operation Auca. Elisabeth Elliot, Marilou McCully, Barbara Youderian, Olive Fleming, and Marjorie Saint were anxious to hear the details of the findings of their husbands' bodies. The search party had just returned from Palm Beach, and weary as they were, hesitated to tell the wives about the horrific scene.

It was evident that all five of the men's deaths were caused by lance wounds and machetes. The search party deduced that it must have been an ambush. A first group of Aucas must have succeeded in convincing the men of their peaceful intentions. This group may have walked peacefully onto the beach while a second party, carrying spears, moved up under cover of the jungle foliage to carry out a surprise attack.[40]

The Piper plane revealed the true aggression of that fateful day. Strips of fabric shreds floated in the river nearby, and the plane was completely denuded. Some of the framework was bent beyond repair, and the landing gear had been battered and thrashed. The dented yellow remains of the airplane sat skewed and distorted by the "savages." Recalling the confusion and bewilderment of the moment, Elisabeth Elliot wrote,

In the kitchen we sat quietly as the reports were finished, fingering the watches and wedding rings that had been brought back, trying for the hundredth time to picture the scene. Which of the men watched the others fall? Which of them had time to think of his wife and children? Had one been covering the others in the tree house, and come down in an attempt to save them? Had they suffered long? The answers to these questions remained a mystery.[41]

At this point, one must pause and ask, *What would I have done in the widows' situation?* Packing up and leaving the mission field seems an appropriate response. And who would have blamed them? The lance-bearing Aucas stole five of their most beloved earthly treasures, and indeed Ecuador herself was the foreign land upon which the horrible event transpired. Would it not be forgivable to return to America and try to forget all that had happened? However, driven by a transcendent, Spirit-led motivation, the story of Operation Auca and the tribe's salvation had not yet reached its pinnacle.

Elisabeth Elliot expressed her thoughts of understanding and forgiveness in *Through Gates of Splendor*, writing, "The prayers of the widows themselves are for the Aucas. We look forward to the day when these savages will join us in Christian praise."[42] She prayed, in her own words, "an absurd prayer" that God would show her if there was anything she might do to reach the tribe who murdered her husband. He answered, and she obliged.

Over the next two years, she renewed contact with the tribe, and in 1958, accompanied by her three-year-old daughter and Rachel Saint, martyr Nate Saint's sister, Elliot moved in with the Huaoranis. She ministered to them and remained in their settlement for three years in the foothills of the Andes, subsisting on barbecued monkey limbs and other local fare while living in rain-swept huts.[43] In November 1958, she wrote:

> Nearly three years have passed since that Sunday afternoon. Today I sit in a tiny leaf-thatched hut on the Tiwanu River, not many miles southwest of 'Palm Beach.' In another leaf house, just about ten feet away, sit two of the seven men who killed my husband. Gikita, one of the men, has just helped [my daughter] Valerie, who is now three-and-a-half years old, roast a plantain.[44]

Elliot later wrote,

> The growth of all living green things wonderfully represents the
> process of receiving and relinquishing, gaining and losing, living
> and dying... The truth is that it is ours to thank Him for and ours
> to offer back to Him, ours to relinquish, ours to lose, ours to let
> go of—if we want to find our true selves, if we want real life, if our
> hearts are set on glory.[45]

Through their testimony of love and forgiveness, most of the village,
including six in the murder party, turned to Christ. Dyowe, one of the mur-
derers, approached Rachel Saint and said,

> I want you to know... that I was one of the men... who killed your
> brother Nate when he was on the beach with the others. I know
> that God wants to forgive me. But I want to [ask] you too to forgive
> me for the things that I have done. I didn't understand anything
> back then, and I didn't know who they were. But I will say that I
> truly know God has forgiven me today. I want to give myself to
> Him. It was not only your brother who died. Many, many people
> died besides him at the point of my spear. But today is the last
> of my own spear for me. I have found a new spear to pierce the
> hearts of many people.[46]

The story of the Ecuador Five has been retold numerous times, most
recently in the 2005 motion picture *End of the Spear*. It has inspired Christians worldwide to consider a missionary calling and has sparked dozens of
books, movies, radio programs, and articles. More importantly, the violent,
short lives of the Huaorani (formerly called Auca or "savages") were transformed.[47]

According to Gordon-Conwell Theological Seminary's World Christian
Database, some eighty-percent of the Huaorani (population 1,900) have
heard the Gospel message, with forty-percent professing Christian faith.
(The Mission Aviation Fellowship, however, estimates that only a quarter of
the group is Christian.)[48] Whatever the precise figures, the initial growth
of the Huaorani transformation commenced by the scattering of five missionary seeds in 1956. These were later watered by the first friendly contact
by Elisabeth Elliot and Rachel Saint in 1958.

Steve Saint, Nate's son, was five-years-old when his father was martyred. He, too, experienced forgiveness through the supernatural power of the Holy Spirit. "When I was a little boy and my dad flew off and was killed," Steve said, "I thought, *How can life ever be good again?* But God gave me the man who killed my father to be like a father to me and a grandfather to my children."

The compassion of Jesus compelled the Ecuador Five to self-sacrifice. They submitted themselves wholly to the purposes of God. They were convinced of their identity in Christ. They sensed their Savior's heartbeat, and in this they found altruistic motivation.

Elisabeth Elliot clearly states the intentions of the five missionaries:

> Was it the thrill of adventure that drew our husbands on? No. Their letters and journals make it abundantly clear that these men did not go out as some men go out to shoot a lion or climb a mountain. Their compulsion was from a different source. Each had made a personal transaction with God, recognizing that he belonged to God, first of all by creation, and secondly by redemption through the death of His Son, Jesus Christ. This double claim on his life settled once and for all the question of allegiance. It was not a matter of striving to follow the example of a great Teacher. To conform to the perfect life of Jesus was impossible for a human being. To these men, Jesus Christ was God, and had actually taken upon Himself human form, in order that He might die, and, by His death, provide not only escape from the punishment which their sin merited, but also a new kind of life, eternal both in length and in quality. This meant simply that Christ was to be obeyed, and more than that, that He would provide the power to obey. The point of decision had been reached. God's command 'Go ye, and preach the gospel to every creature' was the categorical imperative. The question of personal safety was wholly irrelevant.[49]

What is the underlying motivation of your Christian life? Are you intrinsically driven to publicize the name of Jesus because you encountered God's scandalous grace or are you seeking recognition through your missional efforts? Only when you recognize that your identity is found in Christ can you operate in the supernatural Kingdom power promised to you.

It is evident that God's ways are altogether different than ours. Oftentimes, we shield ourselves from risk, concerned more for our temporal well-being than for those waiting at the other end of our obedience. The five missionaries compel us to an unconventional lifestyle—one in which compassion for the lost and obedience to the commands of Christ is primary. The tragic murder of the Ecuador Five opened the door to the Gospel message in a manner unforeseen. Their lives were seeds sown deep into the heart of the jungle. Salvation grew from the very soil where their lives laid down. Their compassion for God's lost children produced a mighty harvest as the bloom of salvation came to the Huaorani people at last.

Chapter Two

OBEDIENCE TO THE COMMANDS OF CHRIST

A Prayer from Shanxi, China

In the summer of 1883, a lone figure knelt to pray in his small study in the inner courtyard of a Chinese residence in Shanxi, China. Thirty-one-year-old Dr. Harold Schofield, a member of the China Inland Mission pioneered by Hudson Taylor, was the first Protestant missionary allowed to penetrate the interior of China. He had been a brilliant, young doctor at Oxford who gave his life to Jesus nearly three years earlier.

For months, his heart ached under the weight of lost souls in China. He felt God's passion for them, and was convinced that a mighty, spiritual revival would one day take place in the very spot where he bowed in prayer. He understood that there must be out there—perhaps on far off distant shores—men and women who would respond with radical obedience to the commands of Christ. Day after day, he knelt in prayer, often fasting from food, and beseeched God to send more workers into His harvest field to proclaim the Gospel among the Chinese. With hands clasped tightly and eyes squeezed shut, Dr. Schofield's prayer was explicit. He asked God to send a certain kind of person: "men of culture, education, and distinguished gifts, intellectual as well as spiritual."[1]

Why did Dr. Schofield pray such a specific prayer? Would God truly answer his request for the upper crust, the cream of the crop, and the *haut monde*?

He knew that there was nothing glamorous about nineteenth-century missionary life in China's interior. The stench of dung mingled with the stench of unwashed bodies everywhere. Disease was common, especially among the poor, peasant class; and in fact, Dr. Schofield would later die from typhus, contracted during his time on the field.[2]

Hawkers called to their customers in Shanxi's streets; the droning murmur of the town resounded through the alleys. Inside his little study, Dr. Schofield tuned out the world as he sought God in prayer. The Holy Spirit began to move in ways that the man could have never imagined. Prayer, the mighty engine that is to move the missionary work,[3] set the cogs of God's master plan into motion. For, as Arthur T. Pierson of the Student Volunteer Movement later said, "Every step in the progress of missions is directly traceable to prayer. It has been the preparation for every new triumph and the secret of all success."[4] The Chinese town was unaware of the impending move of God.

Whether God calls you to cross geographical boundaries to become a missionary or remain at home as a witness of His Kingdom, your prayers are powerful. Your heartfelt pleas pass beyond the dimensions of time and space; geography cannot contain your conversations with the Living God. Prayer directly affects the momentum of God's global plan on the earth.

The Bible teaches us in 2 Chronicles 16:9 that "The eyes of the Lord move to and fro throughout the earth that He may strongly support those whose heart is completely His." The angels paused to watch the Divine connection between God and man. The lone prayer warrior beseeched His Heavenly Father for workers in China's ready terrain. Pleasure filled the heart of God; His answer was already on the way.

Mere months after the plea for harvest hands, God responded to Dr. Schofield's prayer. Head of a well-known Cambridge University rowing team, Stanley Peregrine Smith began to sense the missionary call. "About the end of 1883," Smith said, "I wrote to Mr. [Hudson] Taylor telling him I wanted to come out to China."[5] God stirred Smith's heart and the hearts of his companions—young men who would go abroad as missionaries to the Orient. But before leaving England, their zealous appeals would spark a missional zeal among their countrymen, transforming the social landscape of twentieth-century Great Britain.

The subtle beginnings of a spiritual awakening commenced in England—in part, because of Dr. Schofield's distant prayers for revival. Young men and women from every walk of life dedicated their lives anew to God's service. This awakening touched both the common man and influential persons alike.

Had Dr. Schofield but seen the direct results of his prayer, he would have surely recalled Gabriel's words to the prophet Daniel: "The moment you began praying, a command was given."[6] After only three years in China, Dr. Harold Schofield left his earthly service on August 1, 1883, his last words spoken: "Tell Mr. Taylor and the [China Inland Mission] Council... that these three years in China have been by far the happiest of my life."[7] Now all was silent in the little study in Shanxi; the baton of his missionary service was passed on to more capable harvest hands. The commandment went forth at the very moment when Dr. Schofield pled with God; his request for "men of culture, education, and distinguished gifts" sparked what history would soon remember as the Cambridge Seven and the birth of the Student Volunteer Movement.

Such Noble and Influential Men

I contend that altruistic love for the lost and radical obedience to the commands of Christ are often preceded by an intense passion for prayer. Compassion for those outside one's concentric cultural, religious, and linguistic circles does not come naturally. If it does, it is too shallow to be considered unconditional love and might be better stated as mere intrigue, curiosity, or fascination.

But the missionary heart and mind are transformed through prayer. How can it not be so? When you spend time with your Heavenly Father, His values imprint your life. He loves lavishly, gives endlessly, and goes to great measures to rescue His creation. His presence propels your passion for people; prayer links your spirit to the Spirit of God.

Like threads divinely woven through space and time, the prayers of Dr. Schofield connected an earthly need with the heavenly will of God. For a humble tug on earth creates a simultaneous response from Heaven. Here, then, is the effect of prayer: When we utter our requests in faith according to the will of God, we know that we have the thing asked for.

The mind of a missionary understands that God hears his requests and thus craves a covering of prayer. "I believe it will only be known on the Last

Day," wrote James Fraser, an early twentieth-century missionary to China, "how much has been accomplished in missionary work by the prayers of earnest believers at home. I do earnestly covet a volume of prayer for my work—but oh! for a volume of faith too. Will you give this?"[8] History may not remember the infinitesimal part that Dr. Schofield played in the forthcoming revival and spiritual awakening; but beyond the thin veil where the natural and the supernatural meet, his prayers cast a spiritual net that caught the hearts of men.

The letter from Stanley Smith to Hudson Taylor was received in the final months of 1883. Smith, now captain of the Cambridge University rowing team, was joined by his best friend, Montague Beauchamp, whose family had been original sponsors of Hudson Taylor's China Inland Mission. Dixon Hoste made up the third member of the Cambridge Band. He had recently received a booklet written by Hudson Taylor called *China's Spiritual Need and Claims*. The contents were simple: There were 385,000,000 Chinese in the interior of China who were living in complete darkness. Hoste, overwhelmed by the spiritual need of the Chinese people, resolved to become a missionary. These three were joined by Charles Thomas Studd, who hailed from a wealthy family and lived in complete luxury. C. T. Studd, the captain of the Cambridge cricket team and one of the greatest players to have ever played the popular sport, became a household name throughout Great Britain. Friends of the Studd and Smith families—William Cassels, Cecil Polhill-Turner, and Arthur Polhill-Turner—encountered Christ and also became compelled to missionary service.

This band of brothers—Smith, Hoste, Beauchamp, Studd, Cassels, and the Polhill-Turner brothers—comprised the Cambridge Seven, all of whom were recognized either for their athletic prowess, educational genius, military valor, or spiritual stature. After their acceptance into the China Inland Mission, these seven young men toured the campuses of England and Scotland for one month in early 1885. They preached and appealed to their listeners to follow Christ's vision for the nations. Reluctantly, the students came at first to hear the messages of seven influential young men who were

> renouncing the careers in which they had already gained no small
> distinction, putting aside the splendid prizes of earthly ambition
> which they might reasonably expect to win, taking leave of the social

circles in which they shone with no mean brilliance, and plunging into that warfare whose splendours are seen by faith alone.[9]

The men of the Cambridge Seven deviated from the cultural norms of their day, unwilling to be swept up by the currents of social influence. Many people considered their missionary aims a sad waste of youth; they wondered why influential men with promising futures willingly cast aside their earthly ambitions for the foreign field. But the righteous deviants did not succumb to the sway of the masses. God's plans far eclipsed human aspiration; willing obedience to Christ's wishes became their only valid response. Though many naysayers discouraged their missionary zeal, the Cambridge Seven's submission to God's will quickly disarmed a dubious view toward the missionary enterprise.

Recalling one of the revival meetings, a certain Dr. Moxey wrote,

> Students, like other young men, are apt to regard professedly religious men of their own age as wanting in manliness, unfit for the river or cricket-field, and only good for psalm-singing and pulling a long face. But the big, muscular hands and long arms of the ex-captain of the Cambridge [rowing team], stretched out in entreaty, while he eloquently told the old story of Redeeming love, capsized their theory. And when Mr. C. T. Studd, whose name is to them familiar as a household word as perhaps the greatest gentleman bowler in England, supplemented his brother athlete's words by quiet but intense and burning utterances of personal testimony to the love and power of a personal Saviour, opposition and criticism were alike disarmed, and professors and students together were seen in tears.[10]

The simple testimonies spoken by the Cambridge Seven stirred those in attendance. Everywhere they went, the meeting rooms packed with students, hundreds being converted each night. Christ's commands were to be obeyed, they reasoned. Obedience to the will of God was not an option. "If Jesus Christ be God and died for me," said C. T. Studd, "then no sacrifice can be too great for me to make for Him."[11]

A revival is nothing else than a new beginning of obedience to God.[12] Indeed, it is the supernatural result of consistent deposits of prayer. So prophesied Andrew Murray:

> The coming revival must begin with a great revival of prayer. It is in the closet, with the door shut, that the sound of abundance of rain will first be heard. An increase of secret prayer with ministers will be the sure harbinger of blessing... The evangelization of the world depends first of all upon a revival of prayer.[13]

Riding swiftly on the coat tails of a private prayer from Shanxi, China, God used the traveling Cambridge Seven missionary band to bring revival throughout Great Britain. Throngs of people flocked to the meetings; lives changed and ambitions altered. As the spiritual awakening gained momentum, the Queen of England herself was pleased to receive a booklet containing the Cambridge Seven testimonies. Their influence impacted an entire nation. The foundations of a sleeping Church in England began to shake, and she was awakened to the need for global missions. But the scope of this spiritual awakening would travel far beyond the borders of Europe.

The influence of the Cambridge Seven surged across the Atlantic to the United States and led to the formation of the Student Volunteer Movement, an organization which toured college campuses, encouraging students to volunteer as missionaries. To this movement, we will return shortly.

At the last farewell meeting before their China-bound ship set sail, C. T. Studd challenged those in attendance with this query:

> Are you living for the day or are you living for life eternal? Are you going to care for the opinion of men here, or for the opinion of God? The opinion of men won't avail us much when we get before the judgment throne. But the opinion of God will. Had we not, then, better take His word and implicitly obey it?[14]

Studd's words gripped the hearts of his listeners; many dedicated their lives to the cause of Christ. His impassioned remarks also sank deep into the hearts and minds of the Cambridge Seven. The Great Commission command had been given. How could they disobey the Lord of Heaven and earth? Leaving behind all that was familiar, they set sail as missionaries to China where a new normalcy awaited them.

A Succession of Small, Willful Steps

Over one hundred years after the Cambridge Seven gave themselves to the missionary enterprise, their influence continued to impact global Kingdom workers. In 1997, alongside my missionary counterparts on a mission we called *HK Project*, I made my new home in Hong Kong as a Bible smuggler.

Every week we hosted visiting short-term teams from around the world who had heard about China's great need for Christian literature. A palpable hunger for the Word of God permeated the country. The underground Church saw tremendous growth from 1949 to present through the tumultuous seasons of persecution they underwent. In response to this overwhelming need for Bibles and Christian resources, our missionary band led teams from Hong Kong to China where the deliveries would then be distributed throughout the populous country.

On one particular morning in April 1997, when visiting teams had departed, our HK Project missionaries loaded bags full of Bibles and made our way by train to the border of China. The KCR train swerved northbound along a curving track through New Territories. The Hong Kong landscape was shifting, less studded with lofty skyscrapers, now a blur of rural countryside, ripe with verdant valleys.[15] I had taken this route over one hundred times before, my backpack and roller bags loaded with contraband Christian material. The entire trip—from our residence in Shatin, Hong Kong to the booming city of Shenzhen, China—took roughly three hours round trip. Seven KCR train stations to Lowu brought us to the labyrinthine corridors of immigration control. There, we queued in impossibly long lines, jostling for position with thousands of daily Chinese travelers.

We followed the crowd up the stairs, through the long hallway, and over the bridge, exiting Hong Kong. Across the bridge, on the China side, a certain stoic impassiveness emerged within the sterile, time-worn hallway, a sobering coldness contrasting the humid summer heat. The sensation lasted but a moment as the shuffling feet of the crowd forced us on, up more stairs, around a curving hallway, back down another staircase and into the wide customs hall.[16]

The long lines slowly inched toward passport control, and after thirty minutes in my queue, the customs officer waved me forward. He sat with hand outstretched inside a plexiglass encasement, and I slid my travel documents to him through a small opening along the countertop. Passport stamped with legal entry into China, I made my way toward a large x-ray machine for final inspection. Knowing that my bags filled with Bibles, tracts, and Christian literature, I furtively tried to skirt around a group of travelers without passing my luggage through the x-ray machine.

But I was quickly apprehended by a staunch Chinese official who blocked my passage into the country. Seizing my bags, the customs officer queried me vexedly: "Why do you want to take these books into China? Bibles are banned in my country!"

I had no choice but to hand over my Bibles. The officer confiscated my bags and replaced them with a red pickup slip. I was allowed to proceed into China but must collect my Bible-laden luggage upon my return to Hong Kong.

I had not entered China's border city of Shenzhen on a sightseeing tour, so with nothing to do, I decided to return immediately back to immigration control to retrieve my Bibles. Over three hours later, once back in Hong Kong, I stopped for a plate of Yangzhou fried rice. During the pitstop, I sensed the Holy Spirit tell me, *I want you to take these Bibles back into China.* I quickly consumed my meal and boarded the KCR train back to Lowu station and immigration control.

Nearly two hours later, I found myself subtly crouching behind Chinese travelers so as not to be detected by the officials at the x-ray machine. But to no avail. The same cross officer who had caught me red handed with Bibles less than two hours earlier espied me again endeavoring to sidestep the x-ray machine. Piqued by my audacity, his face flushed in displeasure and he ordered me to open my bag once again. The contents inside were no secret, and he immediately confiscated the Bibles, issued a new pickup slip, and instructed me to discontinue transporting contraband literature into The People's Republic of China.

The temperature soared to over one hundred degrees Fahrenheit, and back on the Hong Kong side of the border, my shirt was soaked with perspiration. I had spent nearly six hours of travel that day and had little success. My only job was to carry Bibles into China, and I had failed. Exhausted, I decided it was best to return home to Shatin. But again, I sensed the voice of the Holy Spirit beckoning me to return to the motherland with my loaded luggage.

I remembered the words of Brother Andrew in his book, *God's Smuggler*: "It's better to obey God rather than men." His Kingdom called for obedience and, in this instance, countercultural Christian fortitude. I was worn out and frustrated, and nearly unwilling to return to China after two failed attempts. But Brother Andrew's words rung in my mind: "That's the excitement in obedience, finding out later what God had in mind."

For the third time, I gathered my belongings and, physically exhausted, made my way by train back to immigration control. Hours passed, and upon final arrival at passport inspection, the same officer who had apprehended me twice already rushed toward me with rage in his eyes and slapped me on the right cheek. I was stunned. It was not the typical treatment that Americans receive from Chinese officials. I dazedly followed the officer to the small room where he had already emptied my Bibles onto the floor. "I told you not to bring these books into my country!" he shouted. Incensed by my return, he furiously scratched another red pickup slip for me to retrieve my Bibles upon my exit from China. "I don't want to see you again!" he said. I left stunned and overwhelmed.

After nine hours of laborious toil, I was ready to call it quits. But true to His nature, the Holy Spirit was not finished with me yet. *I want you to take these Bibles back into China*, I sensed Him say again. As the sting on my cheek from the officer's blow lingered, I reluctantly dragged my luggage back toward the train station. Had I been compelled by some external motivator—a dramatic newsletter update, recognition, congratulations, or perhaps Christian acclaim—I would have surely not returned to the People's Republic of China with my load of Bibles. Instead, I was compelled by the intrinsic motivation for God's glory to be established where it was little known.

On my fourth attempt to smuggle the load of Bibles into China, the narrative was much the same. I crossed the bridge overlooking the Ping Yuen River, elbowed my way upstairs, passed through the labyrinthine walkways, and arrived once again in the wide customs hall. At the far end of the room, I saw the officer who had thrice curtailed my smuggler's attempts. He spotted me from a distance and sauntered to the edge of passport control where I once again handed over my travel documents for processing. He waited with a stoic solemnity. I gestured respectfully to him by nodding my head, and he returned the nod. We were both fatigued by the day's numerous unwitting encounters. I forced a smile in silent observance of our intrepid duel, collected my passport, rolled my Bible-laden bags past the impassive man, and entered China without opposition.

I was dumbfounded. Something had shifted in the Heavenlies. I stood in the humid Shenzhen heat, soaked and perspiration-stained, as the evening lights flickered, backdropped by the sunsetting sky. It was an altogether curious and glorious moment.

But let me be clear: Obedience is less of an aggrandizing accomplishment than it is a series of decisions to walk in the will of the Lord. Obedience is a succession of small, willful steps in pursuit of the Master's footprints. It is often a seemingly inglorious excursion; yet submission and compliance to God's Divine plan produce many an opportunity for the advancement of His global glory.

I often wonder about the significance of that particular load of Bibles. It seemed that nothing should hinder them from entering the country and finding their way to an underground Church. I imagine the books delivered to an undisclosed location where spiritually hungry Chinese Christians met in secret, curtains drawn in secrecy. I envisioned my persecuted brothers and sisters weeping with joy as they kissed the Word of God with tender appreciation. Perhaps the books helped aid in a grassroots revival where the power of the Holy Spirit took the city by storm. It could be that the Bibles I smuggled into China that day in 1997, like Dr. Schofield's private prayer over one-hundred years earlier, caused a ripple effect in the Heavenly realms, and thus elicited salvation and revival.

But this is mere rumination and hopeful guesswork. Unfortunately, I did not witness the reality of the divine spiritual awakening that may have occurred. This is the way of the Spirit; He flows here and there to regions of His own bidding. He is the One Who brings life transformation. Our response must simply be willing obedience to the Master's harvest task.

If We Do Not Obey Him, Then He is Not Our Lord

I have an American-born, Laotian friend who, for security purposes, is known by his online alias, Tobias Issara, or simply the Asian Rough Rider. Beyond the comprehension of his parents who fled Laos as refugees, he gave up the American dream to become a missionary in the Asian communist state. He is a present-day evangelist and church planter who downplays personal glory, seeking only to establish God's Kingdom in Southeast Asia through radical obedience.

> We live in a globalized world where Christians in the West are more resourced and informed than ever but care less and less about God's global mission to establish His reign among every people, tongue, tribe, and nation. In the post-missional West,

secularism has invaded our faith, and Christian churches have lost their missional edge. We've become cultural Christians and are more concerned with national interests like Super Bowls, Sunday services, personal security, freedom of expression, and status quo spirituality. We don't actually want to change the world for Jesus because we are comfortable with just being in it.[17]

Pausing, the Asian Rough Rider shook his head. I sensed his frustration at the present state of our missions zeal. He went on:

At one point in history, Christians in the West led the way in missional living by sending our best and most influential as cross-cultural workers to advance God's Kingdom through pioneer mission in unreached nations. But now, churches in the West have reduced mission to our personal spheres, forgetting God's global agenda. We've privatized our faith to our 'Jerusalems' and can't even identify our 'Judeas' and 'Samarias,' let alone the ends of the earth.[18]

As I listened to the Asian Rough Rider, I recalled the words of Scottish missionary to Mongolia, James Gilmour: "I thought it reasonable that I should seek the work where the work was the most abundant and the workers fewest."[19] Indeed, countless millions still exist without a Christian witness. Why, then, have we not prioritized the expansion of God's Kingdom to the communities who have never heard of Jesus before? In more poignant fashion, Ion Keith-Falconer, a missionary to Yemen said, "I have but one candle of life to burn, and I would rather burn it in a land filled with darkness than in a land flooded with lights."[20] Jesus did not call us only to be recipients of His salvation. He instructed His disciples to give witness of His grace and glory among the nations.

Pastor and missiologist John Piper succinctly states our options by allowing us only three distinct courses of action: "Go, send, or disobey." This is not an oversimplification of our Christian task; it is a charge to play an active role in God's global plan. For is He not worthy? Should we not be expected to obey His orders? This is the God Who beckons storm clouds and they come. He tells the wind and the rain where to blow and fall, and they do it immediately. At His command, the sky bursts forth and storms ensue. The mountains comply with His every purpose and the seas submit to His every wish. Everything in all creation complies to God's orders until you get to men and women. We have the audacity to look Him in the face and say "no."

How might Jim Elliot, who was martyred for his faith on the banks of the Curaray River in Ecuador, feel about our present-day response to the commands of Christ? Do we enter the presence of God on our knees, crying out for the nations as Dr. Schofield did? Might we, like C. T. Studd, give up a life of luxury and creature comforts by saying, "No sacrifice can be too great for me to make for Him?" Would we, like the Asian Rough Rider, against all conjecture, dispose of the thought of worldly success and go forth in joyful obedience to the mission fields of the world?

The mind of every missionary must consider these contemplations. "It is simply a matter of obedience," says Nik Ripken, a veteran missionary of thirty years and the author of *The Insanity of God: A True Story of Faith Resurrected*. "If He is our Lord, then we will obey Him. If we do not obey Him, then He is not our Lord.[21]

Common sense states that we ought to stay put; that we dare not venture into the insanity of obedience. But this kind of "common sense" might be better described as a widely held misunderstanding by the ignoble and ordinary. When we are truly enamored by the goodness of God, willing obedience naturally follows. The true Christian finds deep joy in telling others about what God has done in her life. The missions-minded radical does not blindly follow the flow of culture. He publicizes the glory of God and gladdens the hearts of those around him. "I go out as a missionary not that I may follow the dictates of common sense," said James Gilmour, Scottish Protestant missionary to China and Mongolia, "but that I may obey that command of Christ."[22]

Do you desire to thrive on mission as you make known the glory of God to those around you? Radical obedience to the commands of Christ calls for countercultural nonconformity. Do you want to see God's Kingdom established on the earth? Dive head first into the deep end of an uncharted adventure with your Heavenly Father. He will guide the water's current and lead you to places you never thought possible. Make no mistake, this manner of unreserved compliance to the King's commission is not the common course of action. Your friends may call you crazy; even your family members might turn their lip and question your motivations. Common sense compels you to conform to the generally accepted, highly-overrated *modus operandi.* Don't give in. Status quo is not all it's cracked up to be. God values joyful acquiescence and willful obedience. He desires to journey with you and to show you the path of life. Only in His presence will you find fullness of joy and pleasures forevermore.[23]

The Evangelization of the World in This Generation

The record of the Cambridge Seven's departure to China was recorded in the 1885 book, *The Evangelisation of the World: A Missionary Band.* It became a national bestseller, and the influence of Smith, Hoste, Beauchamp, Studd, Cassels, and the Polhill-Turner brothers sparked a newfound missionary zeal. Stanley Smith wrote,

> We are all under obligation to spread the knowledge of a good thing... We want to come to the Chinaman, buried in theories and prejudices, and bound by chains of lust, and say to him, 'Brother, I bring you an almighty Saviour!' And it is our earnest hope and desire that the outcome of this meeting will be that scores and scores of those whom we now see before us will ere long go forth not to China only, but to every part of the world, to spread the glorious Gospel.[24]

These words had a powerful effect on the students who attended the revival meetings in England in February 1885. Just before their departure to China, the influence of the Cambridge Seven extended across the Atlantic to America at a time when the social and religious landscape was poised for transformation. The unsettled and expectant mindset of the people served as the perfect backdrop for the birth and growth of a missionary movement.

It began improbably when Dwight L. Moody, one of the greatest evangelists of the era, returned from England. Inspired by the examples of the Cambridge Seven men, he believed that North American students would follow suit. Praying for a newfound missionary zeal, he held a student conference at Mount Hermon, Massachusetts. In July 1886, 251 students from 87 colleges congregated there, and a compelling message was given by well-known mission enthusiast Arthur T. Pierson entitled, "Christ means that all shall go, and shall go to all."

Student Robert P. Wilder drew up and signed a declaration of purpose which read, "We, the undersigned, declare ourselves willing and desirous,

God permitting, to go to the unevangelized portions of the world."[25] By the end of the conference, one hundred students had pledged themselves to become foreign missionaries.

The next school year, Wilder traveled to 167 different schools to share the vision of world evangelization. As a result, more than 2,100 students volunteered for missions work. This led to the formation of the Movement with its watchword, "The Evangelization of the World in this Generation."

Between 1886 and 1920, the Student Volunteer Movement recruited 8,742 missionaries in the United States. Around twice that number went out as missionaries in this period. By 1945, about 20,500 volunteers had reached the mission field, but the Student Volunteer Movement had already arrived at its nadir.

Following the end of World War I in 1918, Protestant Christianity found itself in a new world. The missions optimism that was so common before the war was now passé. In its place, the 1920s witnessed the rise of cynicism and secularism and, with the Great Depression, the Student Volunteer Movement was moribund. Protestant churches began to feel that "The Evangelization of the World in This Generation" was not a realistic goal.

The Christian mindset shifted from its previous approach to global evangelism. Young people grew disenchanted and skeptical about Western civilization. American students began to view foreign missions and outreach at home as equally important parts of the same task. In fact, the cultural milieu of the 1930s and 1940s largely affected present-day Protestant Christianity, and ultimately pivoted our outlook on global missions. Recent missional movements stress an active participation in evangelism with a strong focus on discipleship. These are praiseworthy aspects of Kingdom work. But by unwittingly domesticating missional outreach, unreached nations and communities are left without opportunity to hear the Gospel message.

In 1945, the leadership of the Student Volunteer Movement announced that "the artificial separation of home and foreign missions is now passé, since the work of the Church, even as the world itself, is one."[26] The original declaration card of the Student Volunteer Movement (which formerly had offered only one option: commitment to foreign missions) reflected three new alternatives:

1. It is my purpose to become a Christian missionary at home or abroad.
2. I propose to seek further guidance regarding the missionary vocation.
3. I propose to support the world mission of the Church through my prayers, gifts, and daily work.[27]

Denny Spitters and Matthew Ellison, authors of *When Everything is Missions*, claim that this transmutation of the central plot of God's mandate, His Church, and her role in God's mission have led to severe missions drift. By prioritizing our "Jerusalems," we have largely overlooked the ends of the earth. Thriving on mission in our own contexts is commendable, but we cannot neglect the ends of the earth.

Between the years 1946-1960, an enthusiasm for evangelism drove young Christians into missions. Contrary to the nebulous cultural milieu of secularism, pluralism, public skepticism for Christian missions, and Protestant misunderstanding of God's overarching plan for the nations, two organizations emerged: Youth with a Mission (YWAM) and Operation Mobilisation (OM). Both developed new paradigms of missions around the potential of young people bringing their enthusiasm to the task of world evangelization.

YWAM began in 1956 under the leadership of Loren Cunningham. He pioneered short-term missions and introduced the idea that young people could be short-term missionaries. In 1957, OM founder, George Verwer, began mobilizing young people for summer missions. These organizations developed a term-limited approach to missions work with the intention to harness the passion of young people. This innovation was reminiscent of the Student Volunteer Movement. But with the advancements in modern travel, evangelistic opportunities focused on the short-term experience. They hoped to generate a broader worldview and, in turn, long-term missionaries. The notion of spending a specific term "on the field" stuck in the missions community; and in the 1980s and 1990s, missiologically-progressive churches began to take a project approach to missions. They capitalized on directing present energy into short-term missions trips, vacations with a purpose, designated projects and offerings, and ministry teams, thus unwittingly giving birth to a redefinition of "missions." We will explore this more in the next chapter.

A Rendezvous with Destiny

An indifference to the stories of those who have preceded us in past generations leaves Christians handicapped by a lack of knowledge of how to thrive on mission today. The scriptures continually call us to remember what God has done through men and women in ages past. This must now include the history of Christian mission through the centuries, continuing from the book of Acts to present.

We are too easily captivated by the contemporary and so steeped in a myopic perspective of current events that we tend to overlook the overarching theme of God's global vision. The present moment seduces us into a short-term narrative that separates our experience from the broader plot. We fail to see ourselves as an integral character in God's grand drama.

An understanding of Christian history empowers us in many ways. Looking back to the "great cloud of witnesses" who have gone before us, we uncover precedents of how God chooses to use His Church in the world. This perspective sheds light on our current circumstances; we develop a sense of continuity and understand that this point in time is interconnected with times past. An understanding of God's timeless missions mandate helps us flourish in the power of God's promises for His people today. It is, therefore, healthy to recall the past, recognize history's seasonal quality, and consider the cyclical nature of life. For we connect our life cycle with the seasons of nature, not only to link our personal past to our personal future, but also to locate our own life within a larger social drama.[28]

"There is a mysterious cycle in human events," President Franklin Roosevelt observed in the depths of the Great Depression. "To some generations much is given. Of other generations much is expected. This generation has a rendezvous with destiny."[29] Using Roosevelt's words as a backdrop, I want to demonstrate how young people today are returning to the missionary mindset of their predecessors. Have we, in fact, wrongly stereotyped this generation? We must remember that God does not require perfection; He requires obedience. The passion and capabilities of this generation may, perhaps, surpass those who have gone before them. Could it be that we are on the cusp of a new missionary awakening? To explore the potential of a forthcoming worldwide revival, we must return to 1860, when the first babies of the "Missionary Generation" were born.

In *The Fourth Turning: An American Prophecy - What the Cycles of History Tell Us About America's Next Rendezvous with Destiny*, authors William Strauss and Neil Howe trace America's history from 1433 to present, and describe a theorized recurring generation cycle in American history. In fact, this cyclical turning in history relates in many ways to generations from every race and country. The authors describe each turning as lasting about twenty to twenty-two years. Four turnings make up a full cycle of about eighty to ninety years,[30] which the authors term a saeculum, after the Latin word meaning both "a long human life" and "a natural century."[31]

The influence of the Cambridge Seven, beginning in 1883, and the subsequent Student Volunteer Movement of 1886, ushered in the Third Great Awakening and the worldwide missionary movement. This group of men were a few of the numerous Christians who felt God's leading to foreign missions fields. Thus the "Missionary Generation" is the name given by sociologists to describe the generation of people born from 1860 to 1882. The birth years of the Cambridge Seven men fall within this era:

- C. T. Studd: December 2, 1860
- Stanley Peregrine Smith: March 19, 1861
- Dixon Hoste: July 23, 1861
- Montague Beauchamp: April 19, 1860
- William Cassels: March 11, 1858
- Cecil Polhill-Turner: February 23, 1860
- Arthur Polhill-Turner: February 7, 1862

You might ask, *How do the lives of these Missionary Generation men affect the present-day missions endeavor? Do global Kingdom workers of the past have any bearing on our modern-day missional efforts?* This is a legitimate query.

Allow me to bring this conversation forward into the 21st-century. To uncover the divine calling and potential of today's youth, let's trace the generation year spans and defining historical events from the Missionary Generation to present.

- 1860-1882: Missionary Generation; entered childhood during the Reconstruction/Gilded Age.
- 1883-1900: Lost Generation; entered childhood during the Third Great Awakening/Missionary Awakening.
- 1901-1924: G.I. Generation; entered childhood during World War I/Prohibition.

- 1925-1942: Silent Generation; entered childhood during the Great Depression/World War II.
- 1943-1960: Baby Boom Generation; entered childhood during Superpower America.
- 1961-1981: Generation X; entered childhood during the Consciousness Revolution.
- 1982-2004: Millennial Generation; entered childhood during the Culture Wars and Postmodernism.
- 2005-present: Homeland Generation;[32] entered childhood during the Great Recession/War on Terror.

Seven generations have elapsed since the birth of the influential "men of culture, education, and distinguished gifts." The Cambridge Seven inspired tens of thousands of people to follow their examples of radical obedience to the commands of Christ. They make up a small part of the great cloud of missionary witnesses of the past, and the baton has been bequeathed to succeeding generations. The future of missions now rides on the obedience of today's young people.

In his book, *The Cambridge Seven: The True Story of Ordinary Men Used in No Ordinary Way*, author John Pollock reminds us that "Theirs is the story of ordinary men, and thus may be repeated."[33] Indeed, there are those who think today's generation has a divine rendezvous with destiny. Sociologist Naomi Riley is one of them. She believes that a new "Missionary Generation" is forming in the children of the 2010s.[34]

Referring to a rising generation of missionaries, Riley says,

> For Missionary Generation students, religion is central... [They] think of their lives in terms of calling and vocation, with a strong desire, indeed a sense of obligation, to use their God-given gifts and talents to make a difference in the world.[35]

What if we could harness the gifts and passion of this generation for God's global mission? "If we can join these two things," wrote Jill Richardson, "—a generation of people thirsting for empowering work and a world mission field that is suffering from support fatigue and disconnectedness—we could ignite an atomic force for good."[36] I believe this generation is called by God for such a time as this. The cyclical rhythms of history have led us to a pivotal moment: a rendezvous with destiny. The passion of the Missionary Generation can now be seen in the Millennial Generation. A recent Barna study shows Millennials are sharing their faith more than any other generation at present. In fact, Millennials are the only generation among whom evangelism is significantly on the rise.[37] Christian leaders across the board must recognize this trend. Our task is to empower today's young people to thrive on mission both locally and globally.

Sarita Hartz, a missionary coach and an advocate for holistic health on the field, feels that our misconceptions toward this generation negatively impact the future of our missional endeavors. "It saddens me to see how we are failing this generation of global workers," she said. She argued that if something doesn't change, we will continue to view this generation as nothing more than "missionary fodder."[38] Her recent *Millennials on a Mission Survey* found that young people today crave personal growth through mentoring; they recognize that health on the mission field directly affects their Christian impact. Over 120 Millennial missionaries took her survey. "What came through these voices was not laziness, but passionate commitment," Sarita said; "not arrogance, but a desire to be learners; not colonialist pretention, but globally-minded servanthood."[39]

Today's generation of young people are poised to finish the Great Commission task, but they need our help. We must encourage them to thrive in their gifts and become the vessels through whom the Spirit of God flows. Pray for today's young missionaries! God hears your passionate pleas and is poised to stir hearts to action.

Throughout the cyclical turnings and generational rhythms of history, the missionary baton has been passed to this generation. Today, people are waiting at the other end of your obedience. You may be a Boomer born into the Baby Boom Generation. I am a Gen Xer born into the Thirteenth Generation. The Asian Rough Rider, a Millennial, has this to say:

> In twenty to thirty years' time, the world's leadership positions will be filled by people from my generation. But the best years of our lives are not in the future; they are now. Now is the time to go all in for the sake of God's Kingdom. We have been conditioned by a post-missional Church culture to play it safe, to give the best years of our lives to our educations, careers, and personal security. But Jesus said that 'If anyone would come after Me he must deny himself, take up his cross, and follow Me.'[40] We

> need to take advantage of the time we have left and start living
> on mission, sacrificing the 'good life' for the future hope and
> Kingdom we will one day receive.[41]

Let's face it: a lot of people undervalue the potential of Millennials. We see their selfishness or unwillingness to sacrifice. Their "entitlement" comes through in John Crist's Christian comedy spoofs.[42] We readily recognize the "Barbie savior mentality"[43] as the downsides of overseas "volunteerism." Jamie the Very Worst Missionary openly admits her shortcomings on the field through her coarse anecdotes.[44] We focus on their "feelings" and their desire to be "heard" and "understood." Fairly or unfairly, Millennials have gotten a bad rap.

We need to realize that this generation does not fit the "missionary mold" set by past generations. In fact, many of these "righteous deviants" have an uncanny calling and ability to propel the Gospel message far beyond our abilities. Sarita Hartz agrees. She said, "I'm convinced we are in danger of missing out on the most powerful force for good in the world of missions and social justice if we do not learn how to empower Millennials."[45]

"The farther backward you look, the farther forward you are likely to see,"[46] Winston Churchill once said. The challenge is to look at the future not along a straight line, but around the inevitable corners. To know how to do that, you have to practice looking at how the past has turned corners.[47] We are now turning a corner in the missions endeavor. New times call for new wineskins. I believe God is pouring His Spirit into this generation, preparing them to carry His message to the ends of the earth.

You stand on the edge of eternity. The world is waiting to witness the power of Jesus manifested in their midst. You cannot elicit a supernatural breakthrough on your own; you need the body of Christ and the indwelling power of the Holy Spirit. He will enlighten your mind to His movements and purposes. And as you attune yourself to His voice, you may just sense Him speaking to you about your role in His global mission.

A Glorious Tapestry

On March 18, 1885, the Cambridge Seven landed in Shanghai, China. The young men were met by China Inland Mission founder, Hudson Taylor, who had landed in China before their arrival to arrange for their immediate travel inland.

In May, the seven men reached Taiyuan, the capital of Shanxi Province, and found themselves in the home of Dr. Harold Schofield. Nearly two years earlier, he had been called away from earthly service, and now they stood where his work had been laid down. They were the living answer to his many solitary prayers.

In the small study in Shanxi where Dr. Schofield prayed for men of influence to give themselves to the missionary cause, the Cambridge Seven now stood with Hudson Taylor. God's providence was evident in this monumental moment. Elicited by the single thread of prayer, the initial weaves of a glorious tapestry had now commenced.

In *The Story of the China Inland Mission*, author M. Geraldine Guinness depicts the scope of the missionary task:

> Vast, needy, populous Shanxi, the sphere of their labours, was everywhere wonderfully open to the Gospel. The people, won by the kindness of the foreigners during the awful famine, were on all hands accessible, and favourably disposed. Dr. Schofield's medical skill had done much to deepen friendly feeling, and in many places Christian teachers had only to go, to be welcome.[48]

Guinness describes the field to which the men were called by saying,

> Larger than the whole of England, or the American States of New York and Massachusetts put together, and with a population of nine million, Shanxi boasted as of yet only three mission stations. Small churches gathered in the capital and surrounding counties, but that was all. Still there were more than a hundred cities, with towns and villages innumerable; still, there were thousands and thousands of homesteads, millions upon millions of souls, untouched by the Light of Life.[49]

Shanxi province was a great field, ripe for harvest, and the young missionaries filled with anticipation at the task of serving the Chinese population.

Time fails to follow every detail of their endeavors, but the scope of their efforts proved successful. In the four years from 1886 to 1890, they baptized over six-hundred people. During that same period, their presence assisted in the opening of eight new mission stations in various parts of the province.

At the time of Dr. Schofield's death, two little bands of workers, with fifty or sixty converts, in two widely separated stations, had been the only Christians among a population of nine-million Chinese. Seven years later, in 1890, there were more than forty missionaries of the China Inland Mission working in the same sphere, at ten stations, with thirty native helpers, and between 700-800 native Christians. The work grew, until in 1893, more than seventy missionaries labored in seventeen stations in Shanxi Province.

Though their time in Shanxi was brief (some of the men made their way to new inland fields as far as Tibet and beyond China to India and Africa), the Cambridge Seven helped catapult the China Inland Mission from obscurity to "almost embarrassing prominence." Through their influence, many new missionary recruits joined the China Inland Mission and other mission societies. In 1885, when the seven men first arrived in China, the entire missionary task force of the China Inland Mission had 163 missionaries. By 1890, the number of missionaries had doubled; and by 1900, roughly 800 Kingdom workers made their way to mission fields around the world. This count represented one-third of the entire Protestant missionary force at the time.

One cannot underestimate the integral value of each member of the body of Christ. Some men and women played a visible role while others were seemingly tiny cogs in the missionary machine. Each one helped transform China's landscape through their prayers and willing obedience to the commands of Christ.

It is amazing what can be accomplished when no one cares who receives credit. In this manner and with this mindset, the Cambridge Seven simply acted as conduits through whom the glory of God was displayed.

CHAPTER THREE

PASSION FOR THE GLORY OF GOD

What Will You Do For Me?

In a sermon delivered by Charles H. Spurgeon on September 25, 1870, we find a compelling argument for the centrality of God's glory:

> The motive is this, 'Oh! that God could be glorified, that Jesus might see the reward of His sufferings! Oh! that sinners might be saved, so that God might have new tongues to praise Him, new hearts to love Him! Oh! that sin were put an end to, that the holiness, righteousness, mercy, and power of God might be magnified!' This is the way to pray; when thy prayers seek God's glory, it is God's glory to answer thy prayers.[1]

Spurgeon's impassioned words encapsulate the missionary fervor you are about to experience. We have learned that compassion for the lost coupled with obedience to the commands of Christ are powerful motivating forces in the missions endeavor. Still another aspect bonds a third strand to fashion the strong cord of altruistic motivation into the missionary mind.

The emphasis of God's glory must be the core of missionary work. Without it, missionary labor gradually turns into drudgery. This, then, leads to exhaustion and often to the abandonment of the missions call. Love for the lost is not enough. Even the act of obedience devoid of God's glory can sour the hearts and minds of global Kingdom workers. Everything is a hard toil without God's sustaining supernatural empowerment of glory.

The prophet Isaiah confirmed this by saying, "All that we have accomplished, You have done for us."² A focus on the glory of God acts as a powerful ingredient in the mind of a missionary. It creates a supernatural headway through the hands of the global Kingdom worker and also relieves unnecessary stress from his mind.

This emphasis on God's glory throughout history transformed the missions world as we know it today. A particularly apt example of this is a young German heir to one of Europe's leading families of the 18th century. The young Nikolaus Ludwig von Zinzendorf grew up in a pious atmosphere of Christian values. In childlike sincerity, the six-year-old count penned love letters to Jesus. He would then climb to the castle tower and toss them out of the window. They scattered around the courtyard like innocent prayers.

During the Great Northern War, Swedish soldiers overran Saxony in 1706. When they entered the castle where young Zinzendorf resided, they burst "into the room where the six-year-old count happened to be at his customary devotions." In *Count Zinzendorf*, author John Weinlick describes the scene: "They were awed as they heard the boy speak and pray... The incident was prophetic of the way the count was to move others with the depths of his religious experience the rest of his sixty years."³

His zeal for Jesus grew over the years and, as was the custom of the day, when Zinzendorf completed his studies, he embarked on a "grand tour" of centers of learning on the continent. During this time, the course of his life altered once he encountered the Savior in an art museum. For the rest of his life, Zinzendorf pointed to this one experience that influenced him the most, confirming his call to Christian service.

The boy riveted as he stood before Domenico Feti's *Ecce Homo* ("Behold, the man"), a portrait of Jesus bearing a crown of thorns. He read the Latin inscription below it: "Ego pro te haec passus sum Tu vero quid fecisti pro me," which when translated is, "This have I suffered for you; now what will you do for Me?" Young Zinzendorf was profoundly moved. The great conviction that fell over him led to an intensely personal faith in Christ. There and then, Zinzendorf pledged, "I have loved Him for a long time, but I have never actually done anything for Him. From now on I will do whatever He leads me to do."⁴

Missionaries who minister around the world often point to a similar experience that catapulted them into their missions work. On a scorching summer day in China, Coretta Christy heard the audible voice of God while on a short-term missions trip. "Chills went down my spine, and my body turned involuntarily," she told me. Her gaze fell upon a young man, and she told him about Jesus. His heart was opened to the Gospel, and he immediately gave his life to the Lord. "My eyes were opened to the supernatural working of the Kingdom of Heaven on earth," she said.[5] Indian-born Coretta returned to her adopted home in New Zealand, quit her job, and took active steps to return to the mission field. Now she has been serving as a missionary in Cambodia for the past three years and has never felt more alive.

Mike Falkenstine was already on staff with The Navigators when he went on a five-day vision trip to China. "I was sitting at an outdoor market eating noodles with one of The Navigators staff when a fly suddenly flew into my bowl," Mike told me. "Without batting an eye, I grabbed the fly with my chopsticks, flung it to the ground, and continued eating my noodles. The Navigators staff looked at me wide-eyed and said, 'You were made for this place!'"[6]

When I heard this story, I realized that some callings are less grandiose than others. That seemingly silly incident catapulted Mike into a lifetime of service for the Chinese people. Today, he is the president of One Eight Catalyst, and is presently focused on Bible translation for an unreached community in China.

My wife, Lorna, was twelve-years-old when the Holy Spirit spoke to her about the spiritual need of the Chinese. It was a Sunday morning in Manila, Philippines when her pastor gave an impassioned call to serve God on mission. She closed her eyes and sensed the Holy Spirit whisper the word "China." After getting married in 2003, Lorna joined me in reaching unreached people groups in Southwest China.

After attending an Acquire the Fire youth conference in 1994, my world was turned upside down. I joined short-term missions trips to Russia, Hong Kong, China, and India, and my missionary calling was confirmed in 1997 while smuggling Bibles into China.

"I have always been a fan of Keith Green's music," said Bevin Ginder. "After he died, I went to his memorial concert at Hershey Park. That's where God got ahold of my heart." Loren Cunningham, founder of Youth With A Mission, gave a passionate appeal from Keith's last message, "Jesus commands us to go!"

"Suddenly I got a picture of Revelation 7:9," Bevin said, "—every nation, tribe, people, and language gathered around the throne of God in worship. I thought to myself, 'What a privilege it would be to have a small role in bringing some of those people groups into the throne room.'"[7] As a result of that powerful encounter, Bevin moved to Southeast Asia. He has served for over twenty years as a missions trainer, mentor, and coach with Youth With A Mission.

While traveling in the Bahamas in 1956 as part of a Gospel quartet, Loren Cunningham saw a vision while laying in his room:

> Suddenly, I was looking up at a map of the world. Only the map was alive, moving! I sat up. I shook my head, rubbed my eyes. It was a mental movie. I could see all the continents. Waves were crashing onto the shores. Each went onto a continent, then receded, then came up further until it covered the continent completely. I caught my breath. Then, as I watched, the scene changed. The waves became young people—kids my age and even younger—covering the continents... going out as missionaries! What an idea![8]

Four years later, Loren and his wife Darlene Cunningham founded Youth With A Mission (YWAM), an evangelical interdenominational, Christian missionary organization that provides opportunities for young people to serve on the mission field. Today, YWAM has an estimated 18,000 staff serving in more than 1,100 ministry locations in over 180 countries.[9] They train upwards of 25,000 short-term missions volunteers annually.

But despite the supernatural callings and confirmations that Zinzendorf, Christy, Falkenstine, Ginder, Cunningham, and my wife and I experienced, To Every Tribe founder, David Sitton reminds us that dramatic calls to ministry are the exception. "I was never called to be a missionary, nor was I drafted," Sitton says. "I volunteered. No special call was needed. I chose to go; I wanted to go; I was compelled to go. And where I go is always determined by an open Bible and a stretched-out map of the regions where Christ is still unknown and un-praised!"

With the typical snarky wit that Sitton is known for, he continued by saying,

> I chuckle when I hear missionaries and pastors talk about 'surrendering to the call' of ministry. I always want to ask, 'After you

surrendered, were you water-boarded, or just hauled off in hand-cuffs and leg irons?' Was it really necessary for you to be abducted by a Heavenly vision before you would go into the work of the Gospel? The missionary call is not like a prison dog that tracks us down, sniffs us out, and hog-ties us for the nations. That is silly-talk and really bad theology. Nowhere in Scripture is a mysterious (supernatural) call a prerequisite before we can respond to the Great Commission.[10]

A Heavenly vision is not always a "call" to mission. It is more often a specific guidance for Christians who are already living on mission and are intent about God's glory being revealed in the nations.

I Have but One Passion

The mind of a missionary is interlaced with vertical and horizontal circuitry. One cannot keep to himself the gift that is received from God. A mission-ally-minded individual must pass on the goodness that God has both for himself and for others. Thus, the holy vision of Jesus' query to Zinzendorf was relayed from Heaven to earth and subsequently to those within his vicinity.

Upon reaching maturity in May 1721, Zinzendorf purchased from his grandmother the estate at Berthelsdorf, Germany. Soon after, learning that the large-hearted Zinzendorf might allow refuge on his land, exiles who fled Moravia (today the Czech Republic) to escape religious persecution arrived at the rich young ruler's door.

The first group of ten Moravian refugees arrived in December 1722. The name for the settlement, it was decided, was to be "Herrnhut" meaning "under the Lord's watch" or "on the watch for the Lord." By May 1725, ninety Moravians had settled at Herrnhut. Initially, the small settlement served as a refuge for persecuted believers; but by late 1726, the population swelled to 300 persons. The three initial houses established for the religious exiles grew into a small city.

During its first five years, the Herrnhut settlement was completely devoid of spiritual power. Former Catholics, Separatists, Reformed, and Anabaptists joined the new community. With so mixed a group, serious clashes and disputes arose, not to mention economic pressures and language difficulties. By 1727, dissension and conflict inundated the community. It was an improbable site for revival.

Determined that the little community would not destroy itself, Zinzendorf, in the manner of a pastor, visited house to house, counseling each family with the Scriptures. The vision that filled his mind was to form a vibrant Christian community, so he dedicated himself to prayer and revival. In time, a spirit of cooperation and love revealed itself. He laid down a set of manorial rules for life at Herrnhut, and the people wholeheartedly entered into the "Brotherly Agreement" with him and the Lord.

May 12, 1727 marked the first day of a spiritual revival. A new Spirit-led life and power manifested in the community. The incessant bickering receded, and unbelievers were converted. Recollecting on the advent of this revival, Zinzendorf later said, "The whole place represented truly a visible habitation of God among men."

As generally occurs amidst revival, a spirit of prayer was birthed, and the fellowship experienced God's divine outpouring. On August 27 of the same year, nearly fifty people in the community covenanted to spend one hour each day in scheduled prayer. This seemingly menial moment acted as a catalyst for the next one-hundred years.

The prayer watch was unlike any other in Christian history. It continued, unbroken for over a century. Historian A. J. Lewis said of the prayer meeting: "For over a hundred years the members of the Moravian Church all shared in the 'hourly intercession.' At home and abroad, on land and sea, this prayer watch ascended unceasingly to the Lord."[11] If we long for a glorious, spiritual breakthrough to come, prayer must precede compassion for the lost. A holy communion with God undergirds willful obedience to the commands of Christ. When God's glory is at the epicenter of our mindset, the advent of spiritual revival is inevitable.

"God's glory is the goal of all things," says pastor and author, John Piper. It is "the unifying goal of history." The mind of a missionary thinks on these things, knowing that he was created to display God's glory in the earth. The Shorter Catechism states, "Man's chief end is to glorify God, and to enjoy him forever." Piper, tailoring the text ever so slightly, says, "the chief end of man is to glorify God *by* enjoying Him forever."[12] This is not drudgery; it is the lifeline of every Christian. When we glorify God, we are attuned to His heart. It is inevitable, then, that when we worship the Living God, we feel a deep sense of satisfaction. God delights to share His joy with His children.

The prayer vigil by Zinzendorf and the Moravians awakened in the small community a fervency to reach others for Christ. Six months after the beginning of the prayer watch, Zinzendorf challenged the community toward a bold outreach aimed at the West Indies, Greenland, Turkey, and Lapland. His challenge was met with initial skepticism, but Zinzendorf stood his ground. His Savior's words compelled him: "What will you do for Me?" The following day, twenty-six Moravians volunteered for world missions wherever the Lord might lead.

Nothing daunted Zinzendorf or his fellow heralds of Jesus Christ— prison, shipwreck, persecution, ridicule, plague, abject poverty, and threats of death. His hymn reflected his conviction:

> *Ambassadors of Christ,*
> *Know ye the way you go?*
> *It is a path not strewed with flowers,*
> *But yielding thorns and woe.*[13]

When God makes His habitation among men, a missions fervor is inevitable. Prayer is the breeding ground for a thriving missional lifestyle. When believers step out of the limelight and allow God's glory to take center stage, missionary service is the natural outcome.

Church historians look back to the eighteenth-century, astonished at the impact of the Great Awakening in England and America, which swept countless thousands into God's Kingdom. Yet, is it possible that we have overlooked the driving force that the round-the-clock prayer vigil had in altering the course of history? We rarely speak of the Moravians' century-long prayer watch that thrust a wave of missionaries around the world. Nothing garners a missions zeal and evangelistic fervor like time spent in the presence of the Almighty God. The Moravians lingered in the company of God. Their focus was not on the outcome of their prayers but rather in the act of prayer itself.

"I have but one passion," Zinzendorf said, "it is He, it is He alone. The world is the field, and the field is the world; and henceforth that country shall be my home where I can be most used in winning souls for Christ."[14] Do you recognize the man's central focus? When once Christ became his all in all, he inevitably felt compassion for the lost. He stepped out in faithful obedience to the commands of Christ. God's glory was the hub of all his activity. It mattered not where he went as long as God's glorious presence went with him.

By 1791, sixty-five years after commencement of that prayer vigil, the small Moravian community sent three-hundred missionaries to the ends of the earth.

Our God is a Global God

The Moravian missionary movement was one of the most remarkable Christian movements in history. Within thirty years, the church sent hundreds of missionaries to many parts of the world. Their reach went far and wide, from the Caribbean to North and South America, the Arctic, Africa, and to the Far East.

They held firmly to the belief that every member was a minister and every disciple a disciple-maker. The Great Commission was not for the chosen few but a command to be obeyed by all. There were to be no spectators in the Church. Each individual was convinced that they were invited to be involved in God's grand global mission.

We would do well today to emulate the godly zeal of the Moravians. Indeed, many Christian churches encourage their members to be active in Christian outreach. Yet in this zealous approach to missional living, a subtle shift took place in recent decades. An "every Christian is a missionary" mindset permeated the Church and had a substantial impact on our understanding of the unique role of global Kingdom workers.

Toward the end of the 1960s, Short-Terms Abroad (STA) was a missions agency that emerged specifically to harness the enthusiasm for the recently conceptualized notion of short-term missionary work. STA defined its purpose as being for the "assistance to Christian missions in the United States and in other countries by recruiting and selecting personnel for special short-term service."[15] In practice, this meant encouraging their evangelical audience to reconsider the definition of the word "missionary" itself.

Missions agencies and the evangelicals of the 1970s generally defined a missionary as a long-term, career worker in cross-cultural Christian ministry. But a shift was on the horizon. STA contacted InterCristo to assist them in promoting the idea of short-term missionary service. Part of the strategy was to redefine the image of the missionary in the Christian imagination. What began as a good idea soon turned into a diluted understanding of the classic missionary definition.

The following is a radio spot that was proposed by ABC News producer, Phill Butler, to Short-Terms Abroad on in a letter dated May 30, 1973. Scripted as a conversation between two friends (with a few lines of voiceover), it is entitled "Pictures."

A. I'd like to show ya some pictures.

B. Of what?

A. Missionaries!

B. Oh! All right!

A. Here! This is the first one.

B. That's no missionary!

A. What?

B. That's no missionary, that's a mechanic! Anyone can see that!

A. They can?

B. Sure. He's got grease on his hands!

A. Well, that's because he is a mechanic.

B. But you said he's a missionary.

A. Well, he is! But he's also a mechanic—you might call him a "missionary mechanic."

B. Wait a minute. How can someone be a mechanic and a missionary?

A. The same way a person becomes a nurse and a missionary.

B. Howzat?

A. By writing a letter.

B. By writing a letter?!

C. 5,600 openings for short-term Christian service. Openings for professionally-trained people as well as those with general aptitudes. To find out how you can be part of the short-term service, simply write to Intercristo, Box 9343, Seattle.

B. Here, let me see another one of those pictures.

A. Ok, here's one of another missionary.

B. But this one shows a lady takin' care of some little kids. You tryin' to tell me that she's a missionary too?

A. (Despairingly) I'll tell you what. Why don't you drop a note to
Intercristo. They'll explain "short-term" service to you.

C. Intercristo, Box 9343, Seattle, 98109.[16]

This was not the first occurrence of blurred terms and definitions. In 1873, Charles H. Spurgeon unwittingly popularized the belief that "Every Christian is either a missionary or an imposter."[17] Zinzendorf himself said, "Missions, after all, is simply this: Every heart with Christ is a missionary; every heart without Christ is a mission field."[18]

Today, believers regularly hear messages that every Christian is a missionary—that is, that every Christian ought to be a missionary. The little chorus that says, "Be a missionary every day!" sounds good, but this kind of fuzzy thinking only clouds the issue. Some believers believe that every Christian is a missionary. Others don't want to be missionaries at all. Still others have no idea what the definition actually describes.

Today, it is not uncommon to see a sign posted over a church exit that reads, "You are now entering the mission field." Is this kind of thinking true or helpful? Matthew Ellison and Denny Spitters share their apprehensions in *When Everything is Missions*: "We are concerned that an uncritical use of words, and in particular a lack of shared definition for the words mission, missions, missionary, and missional, has led to a distortion of Jesus' biblical mandate [and] ushered in an everything-is-mission paradigm."[19]

In a *Christianity Today* article entitled "Involving All of God's People in All of God's Mission," Ed Stetzer explains the importance of God's people defining His mission:

> It will help all of God's people to be involved in all of God's mission if we will do the work of both defining the mission and choosing an appropriate cultural articulation of the mission. As Stephen Neill has said, 'When everything is mission, nothing is mission.' The mission of God cannot be the catch-all that includes everything from folding bulletins, to picking up trash on the highway, to coaching a ball team, to the Gospel infiltrating a previously unreached people.[20]

In other words, every Christian cannot be a missionary, nor should be. We need to abandon the aggrandized portrait of the missionary as one who is superior to other distinct callings in the body of Christ. Every citizen in

God's Kingdom is significant. We must realize that though we all have an integral part to play in God's glorious story, we cannot all be considered missionaries just as we are not all apostles, prophets, pastors, teachers, or evangelists.

"What difference does it make after all?" Gordon Olson questioned.

> Are we merely nitpicking in our definition of a missionary? Look at it this way. If every Christian is already considered a missionary, then all can stay put where they are, and nobody needs to get up and go anywhere to preach the Gospel. But if our only concern is to witness where we are, how will people in unevangelized areas ever hear the Gospel? The present uneven distribution of Christians and opportunities to hear the Gospel of Christ will continue on unchanged.[21]

Considering the reality of the yet unreached people groups of the world, Olson's words charge us to rethink our stance about whether every Christian is actually a missionary.

While "everybody is a missionary" thinking has been intended to level the playing field for greater participation in making disciples, has this inclusivism had another unintended result, at times? Has it led to a serious decline in interest in and support for apostolic, pioneering missions activity?[22] Today, over fifty percent of professing Christians do not know what the Great Commission is.[23] One must simply consider the unfinished task to which Jesus called us to recognize that the "everybody is a missionary" mindset is flawed.

A quick Google search provides an immediate, albeit, poor definition of a missionary: "a person sent on a religious mission, especially one sent to promote Christianity in a foreign country." But before we can talk intelligently about missionaries, we must dispel the myths that surround even the basic connotations of the term. Is a missionary a man with a pith helmet and shorts who is frequently in danger of being eaten by cannibals? This is the stereotype found in secular humor. Is it a person who goes from a civilized country to an uncivilized country to bring the blessings of civilization to the "natives?" Or is it somebody who can't make it in the business world, and tries to find himself by "seeing the world" or losing himself in another culture?[24]

David Platt articulates the International Mission Board's definition of a missionary by saying, "A missionary is a disciple of Jesus set apart by the Holy Spirit, sent out from the church, to cross geographic, cultural, and/or linguistic barriers as part of a missionary team focused on making disciples and multiplying churches among unreached peoples and places."[25] Missions agencies across the board may swap a word or two here and there, but share this general position.

Missiologist and veteran missionary to China, Herbert Kane, author of *Christian Missions in Biblical Perspective*, suggested that although it is not possible to give a flawless, scientific definition of a missionary, the following one should suffice:

> In the traditional sense the term missionary has been reserved for those who have been called by God to a full-time ministry of the Word and prayer (Acts 6:4), and who have crossed geographical and/or cultural boundaries (Acts 22:21) to preach the Gospel in those areas of the world where Jesus Christ is largely, if not entirely, unknown (Romans 15:20).[26]

At this point, some Christians might grow antsy about such semantics. But let me be clear. The goal of exploring a biblical portrait of the definition "missionary" is not to elevate one role above another, but that Christians from all walks of life can find their unique part in God's global mission. Thinking like a missionary is helpful, but we must remember that "missionary" is not a rank; it's a role.

Jesus' parting instructions to His disciples make plain the missionary heart of God: "But you will receive power when the Holy Spirit comes on you; and you will be My witnesses in Jerusalem, and in all Judea and Samaria, and to the ends of the earth."[27] It is clear that every Christian is a "sent one" who is "on mission" and is called to "live missionally." But does that mean that every Christian is actually a "missionary" in the proper definition of the word?

Acts 1:8 is suggestive of degrees in ministry. Missiologists use the terms M1, M2, and M3 to describe these degrees.

- M1: Mission within a local context where a common language is used.
- M2: Mission within a local context where a different language is used or where crossing cultural boundaries is required.

- M3: Mission outside a local context with a different language, culture, and/or geographical location.

The point is this: Many people in the world today are still unreached by the Gospel despite an overabundance of resources to fulfill the Great Commission. If only M1 is adopted, many will perish without knowing Christ. As believers in the Lord, therefore, we ought to prioritize reaching the remaining unreached people groups. The unreached people are those tribes and communities who, as of now, have not had an opportunity to receive the Gospel and respond to it because of geographical, linguistic, or cultural barriers, or a combination of these.[28]

When it comes to the Great Commission, there's great confusion. The priority of engaging cross-culturally—which is the mandate Jesus gave us to make disciples of all nations—has become obscured. A closer look at Acts 1:8 causes us to recognize this importance: "...you will be My witnesses in Jerusalem, *and* in all Judea *and* Samaria, *and* to the ends of the earth." Notice Jesus did not state, "...in Jerusalem *or* Judea *or* Samaria *or* to the ends of the earth." The mandate is one of simultaneous outreach, both locally and globally.

In Matthew 28:18-20, we again see Jesus' command to "go and make disciples of all nations." Matthew Ellison says,

> Sadly, so many churches have domesticated the Great Commission by divorcing 'making disciples' from the object of 'all nations.' As a result, we have 7,000 unreached people groups living in the shadow of darkness today. And they're unreached, not because they're unreachable, but because we've made the decision not to reach them.[29]

This begs the question: Is the Christian Church unconcerned about God's Kingdom expansion to every corner of the earth? Many big-hearted Christian leaders would disagree with this assessment. However, the truth is unavoidable: our evangelistic efforts do not prioritize regions that are still unreached by the Gospel. If the context of our disciple-making endeavors remains within our own zip codes, countless millions will perish without a chance to meet their Savior.

The recent missional movement has had wonderful success with its emphasis on making disciples, not simply converts. In this context, committed Christians understand that as believers, they are followers of Christ, and are living out their faith day to day. "However," adds Denny Spitters,

> the Gospel has been truncated significantly, relegated to the context of the local church. It's all about being on mission in your own context, and I think that's pretty narrow. If all it took to make missions happen [around the world] was for everybody to take a title—to act like a missionary and think like a missionary, then everything will happen—I think it's absurd.[30]

Many Christians can often be heard saying, "I'm a missionary in my hometown," or "I'm a missionary to my family." Today, we have barista missionaries, hiking missionaries, and gap-year missionaries. The list goes on. But why do we feel so compelled to use the term missionary? What purpose does this accomplish besides blurring the lines between a normal Christian witness at home and a witness in foreign lands to advance the Gospel where it is not yet known? I say this not to dismiss altruistic Christian ministry. God wants us to thrive on mission wherever we are—that is a given. The point is that our subtle misuse of definitions blurs the mandate to take the Gospel where it is not. Certainly, we are all called to operate to some degree in the fivefold ministry gifts. But again, it is silly to believe that every Christian should be a missionary (in the true sense of the term) just as it is ludicrous to think we should all be apostles, prophets, pastors, teachers, or evangelists.

If we truly have a passion for the glory of God and know that He will one day receive praise from every tribe and language and people and nation, should we not set our sights beyond our small borders? "We must be global Christians with a global vision," John Stott said, "because our God is a global God."[31]

Our Heart Is Restless Until It Finds Its Rest in You

Is passion for the glory of God one of the main motivating forces in the mind of missional Christians? If so, how is God glorified in our lives? "When I look back on the beginnings of my missionary journey, I wonder what I was thinking!" Scott Fletcher, a missionary in Southeast Asia told me about his first steps toward the mission field:

My wife and I moved to Taiwan when our son was not even a year old. We arrived in Asia without a budget, without a dollar in the bank, and with little foresight or planning. But through prayer, we caught a glimpse of the world through the mind of God, and it touched us so greatly that it moved us beyond ourselves.[32]

Scott said that God's glory was so big in their hearts that it caused him and his wife to neglect practical steps and trust God to come through for them. God's glory as the focal point of their missionary zeal brought them to a level of supernatural mindset that compelled them to believe God for the impossible. "But that original passion is not enough," he says. "We need a continual boost of God's glory so we can run with the vision God defined in our lives—especially when we feel that original passion wane."[33]

The missionary must always remember this: Missions was never intended to be your life. Christ was. Missions is the overflow of a life in love with Christ.[34] In the first paragraph of *Confessions*, Augustine penned his now famous line, "You stir man to take pleasure in praising You, because You have made us for Yourself, and our heart is restless until it finds its rest in You."[35] Does this ring true in your heart? Do you, like me, tend to overwhelm yourself with the work of God, forgetting that the ultimate goal of the Christian walk is simply to know Him more? We are busy with religious activity for Christ, devoid of relational intimacy with Him. Like Martha, we forget to join Mary at the feet of Jesus. After all, this is the one thing that Jesus desires above all else—that we love the Lord our God with all our heart, soul, mind, and strength and, in turn, love our neighbor as ourselves. When our primary goal is to glorify God, it follows that we make Him known in the earth.

One of the most famous quotes attributed to St. Irenaeus is, "The glory of God is man fully alive." Here we have the original context of that quote in Irenaeus' discussion of the vision of God which gives life:

> The glory of God gives life; those who see God receive life. For this reason, God, Who cannot be grasped, comprehended, or seen, allows Himself to be seen, comprehended, and grasped by men, that He may give life to those who see and receive Him. It is impossible to live without life, and the actualization of life comes from participation in God, while participation in God is

to see God and enjoy His goodness...[Jesus] revealed God to men and made Him visible in many ways to prevent man from being totally separated from God and so cease to be. Life in man is the glory of God.[36]

He desires that we experience the abundant life Jesus alluded to in John chapter ten. This is God's promise to His children. Not only does God desire the adulation of man; He delights to satisfy us as we glorify Him. Our lives should be marked by a sacrificial, selfless, and satisfying devotion to His will. John Piper states it more succinctly for the modern reader: "God is most glorified in us when we are most satisfied in Him."[37] God's glory is central to the overarching narrative of His global redemption plan. Beyond belief, He delights to share His glory with us, His ministers on the earth. Through us, He displays the riches of His glory for all humankind to see. Paul writes to the Colossian Church: "The mystery in a nutshell is just this: Christ is in you, so therefore you can look forward to sharing in God's glory."[38] To the Corinthians he says, "So all of us... can see and reflect the glory of the Lord. And the Lord—who is the Spirit—makes us more and more like Him as we are changed into His glorious image."[39]

The culmination of the ages is backdropped by the glory of God. The image that Revelation depicts is of the Lamb who was slain for the sins of the world; to whom the hosts of Heaven declare: "With Your blood, You purchased for God persons from every tribe and language and people and nation. You have made them to be a kingdom and priests to serve our God, and they will reign on the earth."[40] John in Revelation continues to paint the picture of God's glory:

> Then I looked and heard the voice of many angels, numbering thousands upon thousands, and ten thousand times ten thousand. They encircled the throne and the living creatures and the elders. In a loud voice they were saying: 'Worthy is the Lamb, who was slain, to receive power and wealth and wisdom and strength and honor and glory and praise!' Then I heard every creature in Heaven and on earth and under the earth and on the sea, and all that is in them, saying: 'To Him who sits on the throne and to the Lamb be praise and honor and glory and power, for ever and ever!' The four living creatures said, 'Amen,' and the elders fell down and worshiped.[41]

At the culmination of the ages, people from every corner of the globe will be present before God's throne. What part will you play in ushering the nations into His throne room? Recognizing that praise from all nations is, in fact, the reward of Jesus' suffering, are you prepared to do everything in your power to make Him known in the world?

The Reward of His Suffering

At nightfall on Saint Thomas, a warm breeze of ocean air drafted across the coastline. The scorching heat waned in increments; the sky threatened rain. The breathtaking beauty of the West Indies in the Caribbean was broken only by the reality of injustice that took place in the archipelago.

Conquered by Denmark-Norway, the land divided into plantations and sugarcane production was the primary commercial activity. The economy of the entire island highly depended on slave labor and the slave trade, and for some time the largest slave auctions in the world were held on Saint Thomas.

It was here, after a long day's toil, that a black slave frequently sat on the seashore and earnestly sighed for a knowledge of the Gospel. Of this, he had caught some imperfect notions from European colonizers, but the man longed for the truth for which he and thousands of his fellow sufferers perished from lack of knowledge.

It was not long after he had fallen into this train of feeling that his master took him away from the island and brought him to Copenhagen. There, he heard the good news of the Gospel. He believed, was baptized, and was given the Christian name of Anthony Ulrich. Having come to the saving knowledge of Christ, his soul immediately yearned with affection and sympathy towards his sister who was left behind as a slave in the plantations.

In 1731, a divine appointment took place. While attending the coronation of Christian VI in Copenhagen, Zinzendorf met Anthony Ulrich, who had come from Saint Thomas with his master to the coronation. He shared with Zinzendorf the conditions in the Islands, of the hardships which the slaves suffered, and of their need for the Gospel. Bursting with emotion, Anthony cried, "Oh, that someone would go to preach the Gospel to my sister in Saint Thomas!" Anthony's accounts of his people's plight so moved Zinzendorf that he asked him to come to Herrnhut to speak about the state of slavery in the West Indies.

On July 23, 1731, the day after Zinzendorf returned to Herrnhut, he reported to the church the wretched state of the slaves and their need of a missionary. His words produced such an effect on a young man named Johann Leonhard Dober that he, there and then, resolved to offer himself to these poor, enslaved races.

Then on July 29, Anthony arrived from Copenhagen to give his own account of the deplorable condition of the black slaves in the West Indies. But he deemed it impossible for a missionary to reach these poor creatures in any way other than becoming a slave himself, for their toils were so incessant and exhausting that there was no opportunity of instructing them, except when they were at work.[42]

The Moravians were motivated to see the Gospel take root among the slaves in the islands. They understood that the posture of their mindset must be that of the Apostle Paul's:

> Though I am free and belong to no one, I have made myself a slave to everyone, to win as many as possible... I have become all things to all people so that by all possible means I might save some. I do all this for the sake of the Gospel, that I may share in its blessings.[43]

Zinzendorf himself said, "I am destined by the Lord to proclaim the message of the death and blood of Jesus, not with human ingenuity, but with divine power, unmindful of personal consequences to myself."[44] The missions call was one of sacrifice: to preach the Gospel, die, and be forgotten.

The picture of God including us in His global redemption narrative is paradoxical. Ultimately, He does not need us, yet He exults to include us in making His glory known to all peoples. "The grace of God," says David Platt, director of the International Mission Board, "evokes the surrender of man." Platt continues, "We have an incomprehensibly great God who has looked upon a sinfully depraved people and sent a scandalously merciful Savior, and as a result, we have an indescribably urgent mission."[45] A. W. Tozer expounds on God's self-sufficiency with these challenging remarks:

> Almighty God, just because He is almighty, needs no support. The picture of a nervous, ingratiating God fawning over men to win their favor is not a pleasant one; yet if we look at the

popular conception of God, that is precisely what we see. Twentieth-century Christianity has put God on charity. So lofty is our opinion of ourselves that we find it quite easy, not to say enjoyable, to believe that we are necessary to God... Probably the hardest thought of all for our natural egotism to entertain is that God does not need our help. We commonly represent Him as a busy, eager, somewhat frustrated Father hurrying about seeking help to carry out His benevolent plan to bring peace and salvation to the world... Too many missionary appeals are based upon this fancied frustration of Almighty God. An effective speaker can easily excite pity in his hearers, not only for the heathen but for the God who has tried so hard and so long to save them and has failed for want of support. I fear that thousands of young persons enter Christian service from no higher motive than to help deliver God from the embarrassing situation His love has gotten Him into and His limited abilities seem unable to get Him out of. Add to this a certain degree of commendable idealism and a fair amount of compassion for the underprivileged, and you have the true drive behind much Christian activity today.[46]

Here is the reality: God does not involve us in ministry and mission because He needs us. He involves us in ministry and mission because He loves us. Compelled by this love and against terrible odds, two young Moravians resolved to give themselves as missionaries to the enslaved races in the West Indies.

Ocean blue and the sapphire sky met on the line of the distant horizon as the ship was readied to set sail from Copenhagen. On October 8, 1732, Johann Leonhard Dober and David Nitschmann, the first Moravian missionaries, commenced their two-month voyage to the West Indies. They stood on deck as the families were there weeping. Many questioned the wisdom of their missionary task. The two young men might never return; still they were willing to sell themselves into slavery if it was the only way to reach the slaves.[47]

As the ship set sail, the gap widened between land and sea. The hawsers curled around the posts on the pier, and the young men linked arms. They gazed back at their well-wishers, lifted their hands as if in a sacred pledge, and called out to their friends on shore: "May the Lamb that was slain receive the reward of His suffering!"[48]

This clarion call was to become the cry of Moravian missions. Their zeal was unquenchable. Nothing was more important than representing and declaring God's glory to the ends of the earth. His authority on earth allows us to dare to go to all nations. His authority in Heaven gives us our only hope of success. And His presence with us leaves us no other choice.[49]

As Dober and Nitschmann stepped ashore in the West Indies, they opened a new chapter in the history of modern Christianity. They were the founders of Christian work among the slaves. For fifty years, the Moravian Brethren labored in the West Indies without any aid from any other religious denomination. They established churches in St. Thomas, in St. Croix, in St. John's, in Jamaica, in Antigua, in Barbados, and in St. Kitts. They had 13,000 baptized converts before a missionary from any other church arrived on the scene.

God's glory compels us to Himself. As we sit at His feet in wonder and worship, He then reminds us of His lost children. Is it not pure joy to share God's glory with the world? Is it possible to keep this saving message to ourselves? The true Christian, motivated to display God's honor in the earth, delights in this Divine enterprise, for selfless love for others springs from supreme love for Christ.

EXPECTATIONS

God set eternity in your heart. He created you to display His glory on the earth. As a child of the Living God, you have the privilege of demonstrating the values of His Kingdom to people around you. But in the framework of a fallen world, living for eternity is no small task. Your negative internal monologue questions every aspect of your Christian walk. The strong currents of popular culture seek to derail your missional zeal. To thrive on mission today, you must examine the root of your expectations and the world's expectations of you. Only an expectant posture rooted in the values of God's Kingdom brings mental freedom amidst life's uncertainties.

In section two of *The Mind of a Missionary*, the lives of Robert Moffat, Jackie Pullinger, and David Eubank help us evaluate the foundation of our expectations. Humanly speaking, the missions venture is an impossible task. God's Kingdom is established, not by might nor by power but by His Spirit. The more missionary you become, the more you sense your need for His supernatural empowerment. Your human deficiencies are the perfect means through which God's glory manifests. When you take captive every thought and make it obedient to Christ, you thrive in the gifts God granted you; when you swim against the influence of social norms, heavenly opportunities open to you.

The missionary examples in section two, *Expectations*, remind you that you are sent into the world to transform it with God's Kingdom values. You will learn about Solomon Asch's conformity experiment, which sought to understand the strength of social pressure upon the human mind. Robert Moffat overcame his negative internal monologue; Jackie Pullinger strayed from the cultural mores of her day; and David Eubank allowed God to reshape his paradigm of the "normal Christian life." As you break away from the world's prevailing cultural mindset, you become the "righteous deviant" God willed you to be, thus changing the world for eternity.

CHAPTER FOUR

THE INTERNAL MONOLOGUE

Conscious of His Deficiencies

The first blush of sun rose slowly and deliberately over the verdant landscape in Kuruman, South Africa. The crisp air wafted through the garden, gently grazing against daffodil and periwinkle petals. Robert Moffat rose, like any good man devoid of electricity might, to the sound of a rooster's crowing and the clucking of chickens, to the pitter-patter of fowls' feet strutting upon the African earth.

It was an early morning in 1837, and warped floorboards creaked as Moffat shuffled across the porch. He found his favorite outdoor chair and slumped his stiff body into the seat. Sleep still encrusted in the corners of his eyes, he surveyed the valley, yawned, and stretched his legs forward along the deck.

Hues on the horizon gradually shifted, revealing gold, sapphire, and faint traces of pastel pinks and baby blues. A layer of thin, white mist spread over the agrarian countryside, floaty and delicate. The panorama, a subtle mnemonic of the expansive Scottish homeland Moffat hailed from, stirred nostalgia. He remembered the heathery glens of the Lowlands, the towering mountains, glittering lochs, thick woodland, and miles upon miles of golden beaches. Moffat's hometown shared similarities with his adopted home; although here, patchwork lean-tos of poverty-stricken tribal families replaced the quaint Scottish cottages.

The sight might have been resplendent—magical or romantic even—were it not for the looming reality of the underlying darkness. Creation in all its grandeur was veritably innocent enough, serene and steady, but smeared with a tinge of decay left from the fall of mankind. The misty milieu, though superficially charming, suddenly left an indelible mark on the man watching from his porch.

The floorboards creaked sullenly as Moffat leaned forward in his chair. He squinted his deep, doleful eyes, his sight converging upon the scattered ramshackle homes bejeweled in the distant valley. Leisure sunlight warmed the terrain, and the man fixated on the thin wisps of smoke rising slowly then vanishing above foreign homes.

With a sudden burst of compassionate sentiment, tears streaked down Moffat's cheekbones, pooling in his white, timeworn beard. He recognized it again; he caught another glimpse of the spiritual reality that he long understood but had so grown accustomed to, even overlooked. *Villages without Christ, without God, and without hope in the world,* he pondered, weeping at such thought.

This moment—this quiet valley layered with mist and slow sunrise and the smoke of a thousand villages—would become the catalyst of his missionary campaigns. Uncharted regions remained untouched by the presence of the Gospel, and he could not stand by idly. From his adopted home in South Africa to the North and East, Robert Moffat would champion the cause of Christ. He would pioneer new territory and trailblaze new routes for numerous succeeding missionaries. His simple yet profound platitudes would have an immense effect on those who heard him speak about the unreached peoples among whom he served.

The following year in 1838, Robert, his wife, Mary, and their children boarded a ship to England for their first furlough after twenty years of missionary service. The voyage took three months. But as is the case with most career missionaries, the home they once knew was now a distant memory; and Robert, according to his son's recollections in his book, *The Lives of Robert and Mary Moffat,* "was in no hurry to land, and remained on board to attend to the baggage and write letters."[1] No doubt a flurry of contemplations made the man anxious. Had he been forgotten after so many years of service? Would anyone be waiting on deck to welcome him back home? And if so, what might be expected of him and how might he articulate the difficulties of the frontier mission field, the feeling of uselessness, and the small seeds of hope he had witnessed along the way?

That age-old inner critic, the haunting voice that every missionary hears, babbled like a cacophony of self-doubt and anxiety. For though Robert Moffat had plowed the hard ground and sown seeds where no missionary had ever stepped, he was far more conscious than anyone else could be of his deficiencies.[2]

We Lived with a Menace in Our Ears

A common feature of the missionary mind is a strong sense of belief. The Gallup CliftonStrengths assessment[3] (formerly Clifton StrengthsFinder) describes the "Belief" strength in the following manner:

> If you possess a strong Belief theme, you have certain core values that are enduring. These values vary from one person to another, but ordinarily your Belief theme causes you to be family-oriented, altruistic, even spiritual, and to value responsibility and high ethics—both in yourself and others. These core values affect your behavior in many ways. They give your life meaning and satisfaction; in your view, success is more than money and prestige. They provide you with direction, guiding you through the temptations and distractions of life toward a consistent set of priorities.[4]

Faith was a prominent feature of first-century Christian teaching. Jesus charged His followers to fix their eyes not on the temporal but on the eternal. They, in turn, stressed the importance of trusting in the God who dwells beyond our sight. It follows that global Kingdom workers live in the space between the known and the unknown. In the "now" and "not yet" of the Kingdom, they walk by faith, not by sight. Without this sense of belief, it is impossible to please God.

"The Belief strength is prominent in the missionary community," explains strengths coach, Luke Gilbert.

> The overarching goal of the cross-cultural missions endeavor is to reveal God's glory to the nations, but the journey is laden with the inevitable setbacks and disappointments. A person with a strong sense of Belief understands their core values and is not

easily deterred when they encounter the occasional hiccups. Without this hallmark value in place, the temptation to concede to the negative inner monologue would be unbearable. It's not surprising, then, that an overly large percentile of the missionary community shares this elemental characteristic. Missionaries tend to be those most fervently decided about their core beliefs.[5]

Missionaries have left home and country for strange lands and new frontiers. They work tirelessly to help the poor, trafficked, uneducated, unreached, and spiritually lost. They sensed the call of duty and have responded by going where many Christians dare not. But this does not make them superhuman. In fact, the global panorama of human suffering that they witness makes missionaries increasingly aware of their own inabilities in the face of such an overwhelming need.

This striking conflict between an altruistic drive to make a difference in the world and the negative internal monologue of the carnal man circuit the thoughts of every cross-cultural missionary. Their minds are ever a battlefield between good and evil. The voice they believe determines the future they will experience.[6] This is as true of our missionary heroes as it is for every missionally-minded Christian. "All through those years of beginnings," said legendary missionary to India, Amy Carmichael, "we had lived with a menace in our ears. It was like living within sound of the growls and rumblings of an approaching storm."[7] This statement comes from a missionary woman whose impact lasted for decades, and continues to inspire Christians to follow her missional example.

Faith Hassett, an American missionary who cares for abandoned babies in South Africa, hears the rustling murmurs in the back of her mind as well: "You're not naturally suited to being a missionary," they say. "Your introverted nature isn't needed here. You will never make a significant difference in Johannesburg!"[8] Faith tries her best to shake off these lies.

To Chase McNorton, who creates contextualized media for unreached people groups in Thailand, the voices say, "You're in over your head, buddy! You're going to fail. What are you even doing here?" The voices are relentless. "Your supporters would pull out in a minute if they really knew who you were. You're worthless in the Kingdom. You have nothing to offer."[9]

For Hannah Lim, a missionary in Southwest China, the power of speech that plays most upon her mind is of homesickness. "You're missing out on everyone's life,"[10] they tell her, then she thinks about her family in Singapore.

The deception that Steve Jennings hears is blunt, haunting him in his home in the Arab Peninsula where he is a church planter: "You might see something happen if you prayed harder!"[11]

The voices speak not only of the personal expectations they have of themselves and of their ministries, but they also tell of identity. *Who are you, really?* they query. *You are defined by your responsibilities and duties, callings and tendencies. Are you really a son or daughter of the King before you are a missionary?* These are their challenging thoughts. "Many times, I buckle under the weight of this constant chatter," says Katie Cavanaugh, a missionary in South Africa.

> I know full well that I'm not alone, yet I tend to convince myself otherwise. It is easy to let the chatter rage within, feeling the weight of discouragement and anxiety. When I face adversity on the mission field, it is easy to question if this is where God wants me to be. *Maybe I didn't hear His voice?* I wonder. As another birthday approaches I, a single woman on the mission field, again question, *God, are You sure this is where I am supposed to be? What about getting married and having kids?* I often ponder my life outside of the mission field. However, God continually brings me back to the question He first posed to me when I gave my life to Him: 'Is what you're living for worth Christ dying for?' Yes, missionary service is a sacrifice. Certain things I desire may not pan out the way I planned, but the sacrifice is minimal compared to all He has done for me.[12]

Paul provides a proper response to the negative internal monologue. Writing to the Church in Corinth, he said, "We demolish arguments and every pretension that sets itself up against the knowledge of God, and we take captive every thought to make it obedient to Christ."[13] To the Church in Philippi, he wrote, "And the peace of God, which transcends all understanding, will guard your hearts and your minds in Christ Jesus."[14]

Describing the malleability of the brain, Dr. Caroline Leaf expounds on the following verse:

Our genetic makeup fluctuates by the minute based on what we are thinking and choosing. Clearly, then, following the advice of Philippians 4:8 will have a profound healing and regenerative impact on our bodies and minds by affecting our genetic expression: 'Finally, brothers and sisters, whatever is true, whatever is noble, whatever is right, whatever is pure, whatever is lovely, whatever is admirable—if anything is excellent or praiseworthy—think about such things.' Make this truth your life choice.[15]

No amount of Christian activity compensates for an authentic relationship with Jesus Christ. Still, it is natural and healthy for the missionary to ponder the validity of his or her work. This is God's work and the ministry He calls us to is true, noble, right, pure, lovely, admirable, excellent, and praiseworthy. The inner critic, however, seeks to derail positive assessments of a ministry's value, skew the whole plot, and create frustration and doubt.

As we explore the motivations and expectations in the mind of a missionary, we are essentially recalling the mind's power to redesign the landscape of the human brain. In her book, *Switch On Your Brain*, Leaf says,

Our thoughts, imagination, and choices can change the structure and function of our brains on every level: molecular, genetic, epigenetic, cellular, structural, neurochemical, electromagnetic, and even subatomic.[16] Our brain is changing moment by moment as we are thinking. By our thinking and choosing, we are redesigning the landscape of our brain. Our mind is designed to control the body, of which the brain is a part, not the other way around. Matter does not control us; we control matter through our thinking and choosing. We cannot control the events and circumstances of life, but we can control our reactions.[17]

It is easy to lock into a loop of negative thoughts. The mind is, after all, a serious battlefield. Every success or failure emerges from this staging point; every triumph or defeat finds its genesis in the mind. Global Kingdom workers around the world struggle with this reality just as Christians do at home. But God in His goodness grants us the tools to negate half-truths and deception. With the power of the Holy Spirit's guidance, we can refashion the landscape of our brain. Our thoughts collectively form our attitude, which is our state of mind. Our DNA does not dictate the future; our attitude and outlook determine much of the quality of our lives.

The thoughts we think become a physical reality in our brain and body. This state of mind is not imaginary and immaterial; it is a physical, electromagnetic, quantum, and chemical flow in the brain that switches groups of genes on or off in a positive or negative direction based on our choices and subsequent reactions. Scientists call this *epigenetics*;[18] it is the ordinance of Deuteronomy 30:19: "I have set before you life and death, blessing and cursing; therefore choose life, that both you and your descendants may live." We are not victims of our biology; we are overcomers through Jesus Christ!

Romans 12:2 admonishes us by saying, "Do not conform to the pattern of this world, but be transformed by the renewing of your mind. Then you will be able to test and approve what God's will is—His good, pleasing, and perfect will." Your mind (soul) exists between the duel dimensions of body and spirit. With one foot in each of these spheres, God gives us choice and free will. Popular culture cannot command our compliance; the world's manmade patterns cannot impose our subservience. The chatter of the inner critic is quelled when we set our minds on Christ.

He Wondered What Effect His Words Might Have

When Robert Moffat finally stepped off the ship onto his native land, the people greeted him with great enthusiasm. The reception in London was a surprise for which he was hardly prepared. He found himself at once plunged into a whirlpool of public meetings even before he could get his luggage through the custom-house.[19] Pressing in from all sides—perhaps reminiscent of the throngs of humanity that often encircled Jesus—clergymen and Christian leaders, parishioners and friends came to greet the missionary family.

Moffat had not expected a welcome like this. A "shy and diffident man" by nature (his son's later description of his father), Moffat typically sought to elude the crowds. He shrank from landing on what had come to be like a strange country to him. But the brotherly warmth that welcomed him on the dock that day in 1838 flooded his heart with joy and comfort.

Moffat didn't linger long among his own people. The popular demand for his services of the missionary deputation could not be withstood. He arrived in London at the perfect time, for the missionary heart of England stirred to the depths by the recent visits of many good and earnest workers in various parts of the world. The public mind readied with expectation. Moffat, sensing the receptivity of his countrymen, obliged to the hectic agenda. The effects of his obedience would profoundly transform the spiritual landscape. The public hurried him from town to town with scant opportunity for a moment's rest.[20] At that time, an enthusiasm for foreign missions permeated the Christian mind. People were eager to hear stories of God's handiwork in foreign lands.[21] The missions enthusiasm of 1838 was unlike any other in history.

Today, people are fatigued by a wide array of divisive social issues. Unlike generations past, we are constantly bombarded with topics like education, civil rights, poverty, terrorism, pollution, ineffective government, immigration, racism, and climate change. With the advent of the internet, Christians are left with little energy to think about the state of global missions. In fact, thoughts about the Kingdom of God are often not even forefront in our minds.

Jeremy Blakley, a former American missionary to Chiang Mai, Thailand agrees with this assessment of the present-day missions enthusiasm of the Church in general. He is from a small town, south of Oklahoma City, and has served overseas for more than a decade. But he often feels out of sight and out of mind, questioning how to respond to the expectations of his sending church and supporters. When I asked him about his returning discouragements, he was quick to answer: "Sometimes it feels like we're just a name on a piece of paper or a face on the missionary board in the foyer of our church." An artistic creative whose passion is to produce culturally-relevant media resources for unreached people groups, Jeremy wishes he had a deeper connection with the people back home. "I wonder if anyone really reads our missionary newsletters," he pondered. "When people give to our mission, it often feels forced. It's rare to receive an email asking how we are really doing."[22] What Jeremy prays for is, in effect, that God would again stir the Church from its sleep and restore a zeal for the missions venture.

A Filipino missionary to Southwest China, who wishes to remain anonymous, shares this sentiment: "I know it's just a lie, but still I wonder if anyone back home actually cares about what I am doing." He left Cavite, Philippines over ten years ago to reach Chinese college students and has now ministered to thousands of spiritually-hungry young people. He has witnessed hundreds of salvations, baptized new believers, and is discipling them in their newfound faith. Some might consider this a stunning missions breakthrough. He inspires impressionable hearts and minds across China; but the ordinarily jovial Filipino, like Robert Moffat, understands his own inadequacies. He folded his hands beneath his chin and continued: "I admit it, I often feel a sense of self-pity, like I've been forgotten by the very people who sent me."[23]

I resonate with missionary struggles like these. I feel compassion for overseas workers who have gone to the mission fields of the earth with a strong sense of belief, only to be greeted with apathy by the very ones who sent them. I served on the mission field in Southeast Asia for the past twenty years and returned home numerous times to give testimony about what God is doing through our ministry, Within Reach Global. I have spoken to thousands of people about what God is doing among unreached people groups. There have been those beautifully rare occasions when I received standing ovations from church congregations. After such services, people lined up for hours and asked me to pray for them. They longed to play their part in global missions, and their hearts broke for the Gospel-deprived peoples of the world. These were awe-inspiring moments.

But I have also experienced nonchalance—even cold indifference—toward the missionary endeavor. This, of course, stems from ignorance about God's overarching mission. When the Church struggles to define the basic aspects of the Great Commission (to go and make disciples of all nations), missions fervor wanes in the pews. I have witnessed compassion fatigue and an utter lack of concern for those beyond the church's local outreach endeavors. Many times, I flew around the globe, armed with prayer cards, brochures, and compelling promotional videos. I prepared riveting testimonies of breakthrough and salvation, only to find ninety percent of the church seats unoccupied. This sort of response is terribly discouraging for a missionary.

In an atmosphere of overwhelming compassion fatigue, it is easy to fall under the spell of the negative inner monologue. A missionary's consciousness of God's voice is often obscured by the mental static in and around them. This is the perfect segue for the inner critic who snickers with the "woulda, coulda, shoulda" and "I told you so." But amidst the marked passivity for global missions that too often permeates the body of Christ, God has given us the ability to choose the dialogue we believe and respond to.

The 1838 Church's response to and enthusiasm for missions was something special. Moffat was called upon to meet the imperious demands of the churches. He never could say no to any call to what seemed to him like an opportunity of serving the missionary cause; and for some months, he was almost swept away by a torrent of engagements, which scarcely gave him a moment's breathing time, day or night. It was a time of great anxiety to his faithful partner, who, naturally anxious in disposition, viewed with fear, almost with resentment, the demands that were made on her husband's powers both of mind and body.[24]

Inwardly, Moffat longed to be at the work which had brought him home: preaching to the heathen, raising up African disciples, planting churches where there were none. But he plodded on from church to church, giving witness of God's missionary heart and Divine sovereignty. In between each engagement, his inner critic spoke often. He wondered what effect his words might have upon those who came to hear him speak. Nor did the outer chatter cease its droning murmur. An article in the *Times* stated rather aptly the cynical mindset of many missionary observers: "It is the fashion in some quarters to scoff at missionaries, to receive their reports with incredulity, to look at them at the best as no more than harmless enthusiasts, proper subjects for pity, if not for ridicule."[25]

But after all that he had seen on the frontline of the mission field, Robert Moffat could not remain silent. Though he may not have realized it at the time, his words did not fall on deaf ears.

Take Captive Every Thought

Life is essentially a journey of discovering our true selves in relation to God. It is an odyssey of understanding our new identity in Christ and thus finding the purpose for which we were created. *The Passion Translation* beautifully describes this self-realization in light of God's sovereignty in Ephesians 1:22-23:

> And everything now finds its essence in Him, and He alone is
> the Leader and Source of everything needed in the Church. God
> has put everything beneath the authority of Jesus Christ and has

given Him the highest rank above all others. And now we, His
Church, are His body on the earth and the completion of Him
that fills all things with His presence flowing through us!

Our lives orbit the centrality of God. He is the focal point of all creation.
The living God is a missionary God, and our essence and purpose is found
in Him. But discovering who we are in Christ is not a one-time event. It is
an ongoing, life-giving, often paradoxical, and sometimes brain-bending
experience.[26]

Because Christians have one foot in the door of the spirit and one foot in
the door of the body, numerous conundrums arise within this juxtaposed
experience. All the Heavenly resources to overcome the inner critic are at
our disposal, yet the ongoing chatter remains incessant. How, then, can
those who serve on the mission fields of the earth experience victory in the
battlefield of the mind? In his letter to the church in Colossae, Paul's focus
returns to his theme of our identity in Christ: "Since, then, you have been
raised with Christ, set your hearts on things above, where Christ is, seated
at the right hand of God. Set your minds on things above, not on earthly
things. For you died, and your life is now hidden with Christ in God."[27] Paul
firmly subscribed to the reality and revelation of our fastening and inter-
connection with Christ. Yes, Christians are still *in* the world, but we are not
of it. Rather, we are *sent into* the world and we possess the mind of Christ.
As our mindset conforms to His perspective, an infallible victory is ours to
be claimed.

Global missionaries are confronted with a vast array of expectations.
The exterior expectations from family, friends, sending churches, missions
agencies, or even from locals in the host country can be difficult to manage.
These outward social expectations can be overwhelming enough. Add to
the mix the internal expectations in the missionary mind, and the battle
becomes amplified.

Missionaries have big expectations. They are most often motivated by
altruism. Yet, prompted by compassion for the lost, zeal to obey the commands of Christ, and desire for God's glory, they often fail to remember
the fierce spiritual battle they are in. They anticipate learning the language quickly, planting churches without drawback, sharing the Gospel
unhindered, and witnessing new salvations effortlessly. All this will be

accomplished, they presume, with uninterrupted physical, emotional, and spiritual health. These misplaced expectations do more damage than good.

In the past, missionaries arrived with a long-term perspective. They believed they were there for a career, and understood they could do little until they learned the language, culture, and worldview of the people. Today, workers often feel pressure from within themselves or from their churches to do something in ministry. Such expectations may stem from the focus of their Bible and missions training, from the pace of their lives before they arrived, or from Western success standards.[28] Pressured to preform by producing numbers (salvations, baptisms, or disciples), the missionary lives in a fishbowl. Whether these expectations arise from his sending church or originate from within her mind, severe effects often appear in a life under such scrutiny. (We will see real-life examples of this in chapters eight and nine.)

When these expectations are not met, there are massive, negative ramifications. Outwardly, the ministry suffers, relationships may be severed, and the missional impact weakened. Internally, the missionary often feels like a failure, begins to recite the negative internal monologue, and may end up leaving the mission field.

Equipping Servants International trainer, David Frazier, ministered in the Middle East for twenty years before writing *Mission Smart: 15 Critical Questions to Ask Before Launching Overseas*. Expounding on the missionary's unmet expectations, he says:

> Statistics tell us that many people—particularly Americans—who board a plane and head overseas for long-term, cross-cultural ministry end up struggling on the field. Often, they return home after a few years quite beat up spiritually and emotionally. They fail to learn the language well. They fail to acculturate to the new environment. They fail to connect with and impact the target people. Others have such bitter conflicts with fellow Christian workers that they leave the field in discouragement and disillusionment. The result? Mission failure, broken dreams, and great loss of resources.[29]

Amy Carmichael understood her identity in Christ. Missionaries Faith Hassett, Chase McNorton, Hannah Lim, Steve Jennings, Katie Cavanaugh, Jeremy Blakley, and my Filipino friend are convinced that they are called of

God. Their callings are irrevocable. God desires to display His glory through them. But while they are on the front lines of the battle field, the enemy continues to whisper lies of discouragement in hopes of hindering the advancement of God's Kingdom. Throughout history to the present time, the kingdom of darkness ever seeks to disrupt the purposes of God on the earth.

It is remarkable to note that the inner critic is evident in every global Kingdom worker, regardless of their perceived strength of character. Even the most renowned and "successful" missionaries pass through the dark night of the soul. For some, this pilgrimage lasts for years.

"Put your hand in [Jesus'] hand, and walk alone with Him. Walk ahead, because if you look back you will go back." These parting words from her mother were imprinted on the heart of eighteen-year-old Gonxha Agnes Bojaxhiu as she left her home in Skopje to commence her life as a missionary. The young Albanian woman's decision was not a whim of her youthful years but rather the fruit of her profound relationship with Jesus. Even as a child, Gonxha felt a missionary call. "From the age of 5 and a half years, when first I received [Jesus], the love for souls has been within. It grew with the years, until I came to India with the hope of saving many souls."[30]

Departing her homeland, the zealous young missionary wrote to her loved ones at home: "Pray for your missionary, that Jesus may help her to save as many immortal souls as possible from the darkness of unbelief."[31] Little did the future Mother Teresa realize the "interior darkness" that would come to mark the secret life of her missionary service.

"Come be My light," Jesus had requested, and Mother Teresa strove to be that light of God's love in the lives of those who were experiencing darkness. For her, however, the paradoxical and totally unsuspected cost of her mission was that she herself would live in "terrible darkness."[32] In a letter to one of her spiritual directors, she wrote:

> Now Father—since 49 or 50 this terrible sense of loss—this untold darkness—this loneliness, this continual longing for God— which gives me that pain deep down in my heart—Darkness is such that I really do not see—neither with my mind nor with my reason—the place of God in my soul is blank—There is no God in me—when the pain of longing is so great—I just long and long for God—and then it is that I feel—He does not want me—He is not there—God does not want me—Sometimes—I just hear

my own heart cry out—'My God' and nothing else comes—The torture and pain I can't explain.[33]

A household name around the world, Mother Teresa was a Roman Catholic nun and missionary to India. She founded the Missionaries of Charity, a religious congregation which had over 4,500 sisters and was active in 133 countries in 2012. But though people all over the world have been inspired by Mother Teresa's servant-hearted ministry to the poor, few realize the inner darkness she experienced throughout her life.

This inner turmoil was an integral aspect of her vocation, the most challenging demand of her mission, and the supreme expression of her love for God and for His poor. Beyond providing care for the downtrodden and outcasts, she was willing to embrace their material and spiritual suffering, their state of being "unwanted, unloved, uncared for," of having no one. Although this intense and ongoing spiritual agony could have made her despondent, she instead radiated with remarkable joy and love. She was truly a witness to hope and an apostle of love and joy, because she built the edifice of her life on pure faith. She glowed with a kind of "luminosity," as Malcolm Muggeridge described it,[34] which flowed from her relationship with God.[35]

The decisions you make today become part of the thought networks in your brain. That's why you need to stop rehearsing the negative internal script. When you attune your ears to the voice of God, something shifts in your perception. When you objectively observe your own thinking by capturing rogue thoughts, you stop the negative impact and rewire healthy new circuits into your brain.[36]

Your inner critic will be your lifelong foe. Your decision to take captive every thought to make it obedient to Christ is your enduring objective. The key is training your mind to know the difference between the enemy's threats and God's whispers—and conditioning your heart to respond accordingly.[37]

The Smoke of a Thousand Villages

The sun set over London and a chilled breeze blew through the city. But despite the winter flurry, a sizable crowd of people hurried down the street, pressing their way through the chapel entrance, courteously competing for seats nearest the dais.

Scottish missionary, Robert Moffat, was scheduled to preach in the evening service. He had now been twenty years in Africa and had endured to the full the privations and hardships that fall to the lot of the pioneer. Though still in early middle life, he was a veteran in the service, and his work had impressed the imagination of the home churches to a degree he had little idea of. As happens in such a case with a popular missionary, Moffat immediately found himself overwhelmed with engagements. The clamorous public demanded its hero on every possible occasion, and his own ardent spirit made him only too willing to respond.[38]

Though he was exhausted from the previous week of meetings, he took to the stage and silently surveyed the congregation. In attendance that night was a young man named David Livingstone, whose life goals were about to be rearranged by the Spirit of God. With hushed timbre, Moffat opened his message with a portrait of his life in South Africa. "Many a morning have I stood on the porch of my house, surveying the landscape," he began. "In the vast plain to the north, I have seen, at different times, the smoke of a thousand villages—villages whose people are without Christ, without God, and without hope in the world."[39] These opening words depicting the great imbalance of global missions pricked the heart of twenty-five-year-old David Livingstone. He felt as if Moffat spoke directly to him, his poignant words resounding in his mind: "The smoke of a thousand villages... The smoke of a thousand villages."

Born in 1813 and raised in a humble Scottish home, Livingstone set out to change the course of his future. His heart set on achieving success by becoming a medical doctor. He was accepted to medical school in London, but God had other plans. After the service ended, Livingstone could not sleep. The lure of Africa caught him, and he knew he must lay down his small ambitions for the cause of Christ. He imagined Africa's millions waiting in the shadow of darkness, and pictured the smoke rising from their hutted homes—"The smoke of a thousand villages." He tossed and turned in bed all night as Moffat's words rang on in his ears. Feeling compelled, he abandoned his self-established portrait of personal success and joined Moffat as a missionary in Africa.

For a missionary who was far more conscious than anyone else could be of his deficiencies, Moffat could never imagine the impact his words would have. The enthusiastic response gave striking proof of how Moffat had been privileged to rouse the hearts of thousands to a deeper missionary interest and purpose. On November 3, 1842, Moffat received this message:

> Your visit to us we never can forget... We feel ourselves your debtors. We have reaped a real and pure pleasure from the pictures you have given us of missionary life—your romantic adventures, your hairbreadth escapes, your bold exertions, your surprising successes. You have opened before us a new page of human society and character, and have confirmed our attachment to the missionary cause by showing that there is no tribe too degraded for the Gospel to elevate, no heart too polluted for Christianity to purify.[40]

Moffat's testimony ignited in Great Britain a newfound missions zeal. The most notable event of this visit was the willful obedience to the missions call by the young man, David Livingstone. Moffat's pioneer spirit impacted Livingstone in a remarkable way, rousing the missionary explorer to unlock much of the African continent to the Gospel of Jesus Christ.

"I feel persuaded," Moffat wrote in 1840 after his return to South Africa,

> that the period has arrived when we must abandon the idea of long, expensive, tiresome, and in some instances dangerous journeys... to remote distances in the interior. It is now quite time to look to the eastern and western coasts of the continent, and form a chain of [mission] stations.[41]

From these words, it is evident that Livingstone followed no hasty and impulsive scheme of his own. Longing to witness the advancement of the Gospel in Africa's interior, Moffat naturally took a deep interest in Livingstone's subsequent explorations.

Over the next thirty years, Livingstone traveled over 29,000 miles, preaching the Gospel, providing medical services, building churches, and mapping the vast African continent. Of his work he would later pen this journal entry:

> People talk of the sacrifice I have made in spending so much time in Africa. Can that be called a sacrifice which is simply paying back a small part of a great debt owing to our God which we can never repay? Away with the word in such a view and with

such a thought. It is emphatically no sacrifice. Say rather it is a privilege.[42]

Livingstone was convinced that if a commission by an earthly king is considered an honor, a commission by a Heavenly King should not be considered a sacrifice.

The African continent forever transformed through the willing service of David Livingstone, "the prince of missionaries, the pioneer, the modern pathfinder in the Dark Continent, a philanthropist living beyond the limits of the little island soil on which he was born."[43] On March 19, 1913, marking the hundredth-year anniversary of David Livingstone's birth, a small delegate of ministers and leaders gathered in Westminster Abbey to honor the memory of the pioneer missionary. As the rays of sunlight filtered through stained-glass windows and glimmered on the flowers placed before them, an awe-inspiring silence befell the assembly. The hearts of those in attendance swelled as they issued the following solemn consecration:

> We will see to it that the door he has opened to the heart of Africa shall not be closed. We will see to it that the message he carried to the Children of the Shadows shall be taken further until all have heard. We will see to it that the outstretched hands of [Africa] shall be linked with the outstretched hands of the Son of God.[44]

The menacing murmur of the inner monologue can be overcome. Unwarranted expectations inundate the missionary mind. Moffat was no stranger to this conundrum. He recognized his inadequacies and hurled himself upon the strength of God. His willing obedience led to Livingstone's call to Africa, which opened the continent to the Gospel of Jesus Christ. I find it remarkable how seemingly menial moments in history lead to mighty spiritual breakthroughs. I believe triumphs such as Moffat's are still possible today. We are no less weak than the Scottish missionary; our strength comes from an Almighty God as well. As we listen intently to the voice of the Holy Spirit and follow His leading, the negative inner monologue loses its grip on our minds. Our perspective changes and the horizon widens before us. And who knows what great global advances will come from a mindset established on God's promises.

Chapter Five

SOCIAL INFLUENCE

Do Not Conform to the Pattern of This World

Christians often hear the challenge to "change the world" and "make a difference" in the earth. Unfortunately, a significant number of believers seldom take these words to heart. We mean well; it's just that we don't always mean what we say. Mouthing the words is easy when, in fact, the willingness to follow through is far from our hearts. Why do so few professing Christians live the victorious lives that inevitably transform the world? One reason is that in the Christian context, altering the course of the world means explicit nonconformity to many widely accepted cultural norms.

Jesus called His followers to radical, cross-bearing self-denial[1]—not the first choice on most peoples' bucket list. His poignant call to uninhibited obedience caused many to turn away.[2] Jesus was not interested in lukewarm compliance or half-hearted acquiescence. To follow Christ meant that everything else became secondary to the godly pursuit of Him and His Kingdom.

Following Jesus leads not only to difficult choices but to crucifixion. He said, "Whoever does not take up their cross and follow Me is not worthy of Me."[3] Paul mirrored the words of Jesus when he wrote, "I have been crucified with Christ. It is no longer I who live, but Christ who lives in me."[4]

Jackie Pullinger understands a bit about the cross. For more than fifty years, she dedicated her life to the drug addicts, street sleepers, prostitutes, and gang members in Hong Kong's Kowloon Walled City. Pullinger says,

The principle of the Gospel is this: the Gospel always brings life to the receiver and death to the giver. If the Gospel brought death to Jesus Christ, why would we think that in preaching the Gospel it would be any less for us? If you've known the love of God, if you've tasted of His sweetness at all, there's no other way to serve Him except giving up your life. And this is voluntary. This is not a sentence at all! We're not sentenced to death; we're just privileged to answer His call.[5]

Only by a cross does the world truly change, and the only way to the cross is by nonconformity. In just a moment, we will learn about Jackie Pullinger's transformative ministry in the Walled City of Hong Kong. We will join her deviant journey through the blood-stained, needle-strewn corridors where even the most courageous missionary dared not plod. In the end, we will witness the cracks that emerged on the walls enclosing roughly 33,000 inhabitants.[6] The light of the Gospel bled through the darkened alleys, casting radiant beams to unsuspecting souls; the dragon's grip weakened in the Walled City. Thousands of captives fled from the shadows; drugged eyes dilated as they squinted in a sunlit glow they had long since forgotten. All this because of one young British woman. But before the telling of that story, we turn first to the psychological whys and wherefores of normative social influence, conformity, and groupthink.

Let's begin with a few definitions:

- *Normative social influence* is the idea that we comply in order to fuel our need to be liked or belong.[7]
- *Conformity* describes how we adjust our behaviors or thinking to follow the behavior or rules of the group we belong to.[8]
- *Groupthink* is the mode of thinking that occurs when the desire for harmony in a decision-making group overrides a realistic appraisal of alternatives.[9]

In 1955, Solomon Asch conducted an experiment to investigate the extent to which social pressure from a majority group could affect a person to conform. Fifty male students at Swarthmore College in the United States participated in the "vision test." Using accomplices to the plot (also known as confederates), Asch created the illusion that an entire group of participants believed something that was clearly false (i.e., that dissimilar lines were actually similar).

Participants were shown two large white cards. The first card displayed a single vertical black line—the standard to be matched. The other card showed three vertical lines of various lengths. One of the three lines corresponded exactly to the line on the first card; the other two substantially different lines ranged from three-quarters of an inch to an inch and three quarters higher than their companion line. Asch asked the participants to judge the similarity between one of three corresponding lines on the second card. Each person in the room stated aloud which comparison line (A, B, or C) was most like the target line.

Asch conducted eighteen trials in total, and the confederates gave blatantly false answers on twelve tests (called the critical trials). The unsuspecting participant sat at the end of the row and gave his answer last. Although the correct answer was always apparent, the startling results surfaced.

Asch measured that on average, about one third (thirty-two percent) of the participants placed in the social situation went along with the clearly incorrect majority on the critical trials. When asked to make the judgments in private, participants gave the correct answer more than ninety-eight percent of the time.

Why did the participants conform so readily? When Asch interviewed the subjects after the experiment, most of them said they did not really believe their conforming answers, but they went along with the group for fear of being ridiculed or thought "peculiar."

"That social influences shape every person's practices, judgments, and beliefs is a truism to which anyone will readily assent," Asch wrote. A child yields to the nuances of his or her culture; young people succumb to "the deliberate manipulation of opinion;" and "a member of a tribe of cannibals accepts cannibalism as altogether fitting and proper." Normative social influence generates a profound effect on creative thinking, alternate courses of action, and individuality. "The tendency to conformity in our society... is a matter of concern," Asch said. "It is so strong that reasonably intelligent and well-meaning young people are willing to call white black."[10]

The Asch conformity experiment findings are also prevalent in the Christian landscape. The force of our present-day social milieu still influences conformity and often leads to groupthink. While the *vox populi* contains positive attributes, the subtleties of social influence tend to elicit lethargy rather than positive deviant behavior. In many ways, conformity impedes emphatic missional living—particularly those focused on the foreign mission fields of the earth, thus perpetuating the remaining state of unreached people groups. Simply stated, the global Christian Church has not prioritized the Great Commission task that Jesus gave us before He returned to Heaven for fear of being thought peculiar. We brush aside His charge to live out His Kingdom culture both at home and simultaneously abroad.

In Romans 12:2, Paul urged us not to "conform to the pattern of this world," but to be "transformed by the renewing of your mind."[11] He directed us to a Kingdom mindset. Nonconformity to the ways of the world does not infer that we oppose every aspect of our cultural context. Jesus did not arbitrarily push against the current of His culture like a resentful zealot. Instead, He swam against the cultural streams that did not align with God's Kingdom values.

Culture in and of itself glorifies God just as a painting glorifies its painter. Every culture is a masterpiece stamped with the unique features of its Creator. God affirms, strengthens, and perfects the parts of culture that are already in line with His, converting the elements that are not.[12]

Yet, so often, as it relates to culture, Christians are fond of using the familiar "in, but not of" the world slogan.[13] In this configuration, we often mistake the starting place as our unfortunate condition of being "in" this world. Our mission, it appears, is to not be "of" it. So, the direction is moving away from the world.[14]

On the eve of His crucifixion, Jesus prayed to His Father: "I have given them Your Word, and the world has hated them because they are not of the world, just as I am not of the world." His following words reverse our directional understanding of being "in, but not of" the world. "I do not ask that you take them out of the world," Jesus prayed, "but that You keep them from the evil one." His surprising prayer culminates with a commissioning "into" culture: "As You sent Me into the world, so I have sent them into the world."[15]

David Mathis, the executive editor for *Desiring God*, writes that it serves us better to "revise the popular phrase 'in, but not of' in this way: 'not of, but sent into.'" He says that the beginning place is being "not of the world," and the movement is toward being "sent into" the world. "The accent falls on being sent, with a mission, to the world—not being mainly on a mission to disassociate from this world."[16] Jesus called us to deviate from what culture generally accepts as normal. He commissioned us as His righteous deviants to declare the praises of a God who called us out of darkness into His marvelous light.[17]

Jackie Pullinger personified a righteous deviant. Despite being rejected by several missions agencies, she found the cheapest ship to the Orient, bought a ticket, and was all set. Skeptical friends sought to dissuade her from going. Even her father curled his lip at the thought of her missionary venture, insisting his daughter "think long and careful on [her] 'slow boat to China.'"[18]

In 1966, at the age of twenty-two, Jackie departed England for Hong Kong. A surreptitious city of anarchy[19]—a former military fort-turned-densely-populated structure controlled by vicious gangs—quickly drew her attention. The dragon of Hong Kong's notorious alleyways coiled at her arrival. The Kingdom Presence she conveyed produced not only rifts in the fence line of social conformity but also triggered a series of cracks and fissures in the fortified blocks of the Walled City.

The City of Darkness

The Kowloon Walled City in Hong Kong is one of history's great anomalies. It was, in fact, a world unto its own.[20] Two governments claimed jurisdiction, but neither actively administered it; anarchy reigned while secret societies presided over the no-man's land. High-rise apartments situated atop a labyrinth of dark, filthy corridors. A mere six acres sheltered the estimated 33,000 people who resided within the Walled City, swelling the population density to 3.25 million people per square mile.[21] It was the most densely populated spot in the world. (In contrast, Manhattan has the highest population density of any city in the United States at 27,000 people per square mile.)[22] Crazy-angled apartment blocks obstructed water pipes; without proper sanitation, excrement had to be emptied into the stinking alleys below. At street level, two toilets served all 33,000 residents. The "toilets" consisted of two overflowing cesspools—one for men and one for women. Damp, narrow alleyways with open drains harbored drug peddlers, addicts, pimps, and prostitutes. Triad gangs operated openly in the favored secret hideout; criminal activity ran rampant. Newcomers were immediately recognized and suspiciously monitored; few outsiders dared venture into the heart of the city of anarchy.

The history of the Walled City traced its roots back to the Song dynasty (960-1279) when the Chinese established an outpost to manage the salt trade. For hundreds of years afterward, little took place at the lonely fort, until 1842, when China ceded Hong Kong Island to Britain by the Treaty of Nanjing. As a result, the Qing Dynasty authorities felt it necessary to bolster the fort, check British influence, and maintain a stronghold opposite the harbor. In 1847, the construction of a formidable defensive wall finalized.

The Convention for the Extension of Hong Kong Territory of 1898 leased additional portions of Hong Kong (the New Territories) to Britain for nine-ty-nine years.[23] The lease excluded the Walled City, which at the time had a population of roughly seven-hundred people. The British government allowed Chinese officials to continue there, given they did not interfere with the defense of British Hong Kong. The Qing dynasty ended its rule in 1912, leaving the Walled City to the British.

In 1945, at the end of the Second World War, refugees fled mainland China, seeking protection in the Chinese territory surrounded by British land. By 1947, two-thousand squatters occupied the Walled City. After a failed attempt to drive them out in 1948, the British adopted a "hands-off" policy in most matters concerning the Walled City. The city was left to its own devices, and to develop, as Governor Sir Alexander Grantham described it, into "a cesspool of iniquity, with heroin divans, brothels, and everything unsavoury."[24] The Kowloon Walled City began its transformation into the squalid enclave of vice for which it later became notorious.

Locals called the place by its alternate name: the City of Darkness. "As I began to know it better," Jackie Pullinger said, "I learned how true this name was. The Walled City was a place of terrible darkness, both physical and spiritual."[25] Jackie's first visit brought her through a narrow gap between outside shops where she started down "a slime-covered passageway."

"I will never forget the darkness and the smell—a fetid smell of rotten foodstuffs, excrement, offal, and general rubbish. The darkness was star-tling after the glaring sunlight outside,"[26] she later reported.

In 1966, Jackie arrived in Hong Kong by boat. Her heart brimmed with great aspirations, for the British missionary had come to make a difference in the world. Jesus called her, and the young woman responded. Thus, she expected to witness great breakthrough, changed lives, and ministry "success." Little did she understand the extent of the pervading darkness of her new mission field; her naiveté would be challenged on every level.

She strode gingerly through the dank, labyrinthine corridors so as not to puncture her foot on the shattered glass or one of the many discarded needles. Splatters of blood lined the damp floor and mingled with human feces. She continued through the maze of walkways. She passed a plastic flower factory on her right; on her left, an old prostitute huddled at the threshold of a darkened doorway. Aged, ugly, and no longer able to turn tricks, she employed several child prostitutes, one of whom Jackie determined to be mentally handicapped. She walked on, head down, in case someone chose to empty their chamber pot from an overhead window. Her eyes grew wide at each appalling sight in the multi-storied slum: an illegal dog restaurant, pornographic film-show house, gambling dens, and dingy corners crowded with heroin addicts.

The Walled City filled with residents who lived to "chase the dragon." This Chinese method of drug-taking had a sort of magic ritual all its own. Addicts placed the small, sand-colored grains of heroin on a piece of silver tinfoil, heated the foil with a slow-burning spill of screwed up toilet paper, and melted the drug into a dark brown treacle. The addicts then placed the outer casing of a matchbox in their mouth to act as a funnel through which to inhale the fumes. They followed the pool of treacle with their mouth as it moved from one end of the silver foil to the other. This is called "chasing the dragon."[27]

How can such a place exist inside the British Crown Colony of Hong Kong? Jackie wondered.[28] Why did Christian outreach remain so scarce in one of the most desperate spots on the earth? The hopeless poor would not come searching for the truth of the Gospel; she must go to them.

The second time Jackie returned to the Walled City, her heart thrilled with joy, and the sensation continued over the next dozen years. "I hated what was happening," she said of the drug abuse, violence, and prostitution,

> but I wanted to be nowhere else. It was almost as if I could already
> see another city in its place and that city was ablaze with light.
> It was my dream. There was no more crying, no more death or
> pain... I had no idea how to bring this about but with 'visionary

zeal' imagined introducing the Walled City people to the One who could change it all: Jesus.[29]

Local churches in Hong Kong did not share Jackie's missional enthusiasm, thinking that the triad members, drug addicts, and prostitutes were beyond salvation. Decades of anarchy reinforced vice and violence in the City of Darkness, cementing Christian indifference. Mesmerized and caught up in the unique internal logic of their group dynamics, many believers did not believe for transformation. Pervasive groupthink permeated the Christian landscape, leaving the Walled City's lost in the dragon's clutches. But though group behavior is powerful, so too is individual choice.

Jackie did not fit the classic mold. She began passing out Gospel tracts and telling people about Jesus. Her early evangelistic efforts incited opposition both from triad members and disapproving Christians. The former threatened her life; the latter warned Jackie about "rice Christians"—a pejorative term used to describe someone who professes Christ for material benefits rather than altruistic reasons. Her good-intentioned service made little impact.

Jackie realized she needed to demonstrate Jesus rather than talk about Him. Young people understood nothing about the Kingdom of God. Their horizons limited to the brothel next door, the gambling dens down the road, and the opium dens beyond. "There was nowhere in the Walled City where you could go and do anything neutral," Jackie said, "let alone take part in constructive activity."[30]

She decided to start a youth club to reach out to the thousands of young men whose only future lay with the triads and young women fated to prostitution. The birth of a counter-cultural ministry formed in the heart of the Walled City.

The *Vox Populi* is Not the Voice of God

God fashioned you for eternity. You are a spiritual being having an earthly experience.[31] Thus, He desires that you set your mind, not on tangible things, but on His Kingdom.[32] This is no easy task when your spirit resides in your temporal frame. And the sway from an eternal perspective increases as you situate within the confines of your cultural context.

Day by day, the world seeks to usher you deeper along the currents of pop culture; it attempts to skew your perspective of Kingdom values and merge them with an earthly *modus operandi*. But the *vox populi* is not the voice of God; the opinions of the majority do not necessarily reflect the values of the Kingdom. As a Christian in the state of "not of, but sent into" the world, you confront this culture clash round-the-clock. Thankfully, God enables you to overcome the world's influence by the power of His Spirit. He gives you the mind of Christ and sends you into the earth to shine the light of His glory.

The enemy seeks to steal, kill, and destroy; and he often accomplishes his mission through social influence. Today, many fallen aspects of culture impact the Christian mindset and permeate the Church at large. Our practices, judgments, and beliefs sway to social pressures, often giving way to the world's breed of groupthink.

Could this be one of the reasons why over fifty-percent of professing Christians do not know what the Great Commission is,[33] why evangelism is going out of style,[34] or why so few believers thrive on mission today? Or more broadly, why so few answer the call of Christ to cross cultural, geographic, and/or linguistic boundaries to publicize the name of Jesus in foreign lands? After all, the collective social codes of behavior pay little respect to such radical expressions of love for Christ.

The effects of social influence, conformity, and groupthink in the Church often leave little wiggle room in understanding the decision to go abroad. Most believers are comfortable to remain on the home front. That is fine and well as long as every believer recognizes that Christ sent them into their cities and neighborhoods to display the glory of His Kingdom. But when we downplay God's mission, our sight grows myopic, and our worldview becomes ethnocentric. We no longer see the expansive fields that are ripe and ready for harvest—either at home or abroad.

Most of Jackie Pullinger's church friends and family discouraged her aspirations for missionary work. Her story is not uncommon. A while back, one of my relatives asked me why I don't "get a real job." Given the obscurity and negative connotations surrounding the "missionary" label, I gave them the benefit of the doubt. Perhaps they meant well or did not realize the toil that missionary work requires. Still, it hurt. I wondered why they thought that responding to Jesus' last commands to "go into all the earth" did not seem like "real job" status. "A family member recently said something similar to me," Todd Tillinghast, a missionary friend in Panama told me. "They asked why I left a great job to become a missionary. After years on the field, I was surprised how much statements like that still bothered me."[35]

Scores of present-day workers told me similar stories of friends and church members who questioned their choice to become missionaries. Many believers who do not grasp God's worldwide redemption plan perpetuate the social expectation to veer away from overseas work. Is missional service abroad so deviant from conventional social norms that even professing followers of Christ cannot comprehend this manner of obedience?

In 1922, at the height of his spiritual yield in Africa, renowned British cricketer, C. T. Studd, received great pressure to return home. "The apostle to that region" faced illness and summons back to Britain. Even after a lifetime of Kingdom service in China, India, and now Central Africa, looming social expectations from his country of origin weighed heavily on him. But by then, he was a well-known witness in Ibambi (a city in the present-day Democratic Republic of the Congo.) The sixty-one-year-old "gaunt figure with the thick beard, aquiline nose, burning words, and yet merry laugh" blazed new Gospel trails in the heart of the African continent toward the end of his missionary career. "How could I spend the best years of my life in living for the honors of this world, when thousands of souls are perishing every day?" he challenged. The missionary stood his ground against the supposed well-intentioned expectations of others. "Had I cared for the comments of people," he said, "I should never have been a missionary."[36]

A wide array of subtler expectations marks the stories of missionaries serving abroad. In *Mission Smart*, David Frazier says,

> Today, workers often feel pressure from within themselves or from their churches to do something in ministry. Such expectations may stem from the focus of their Bible and missions training, from the pace of their lives before they arrived, or from Western success standards.[37]

Jesus plainly called us to bear fruit that lasts; but He also stated that all fruitfulness flows from intimacy with Him.[38] God is not looking for mindless gears in the missionary machine, but passionate lovers who seek first His Kingdom and His righteousness.[39] He is not looking for "payback" from His people in the form of reluctant obedience. God is relational above all else; His love propels and sustains His followers. His mission does not hinge upon our begrudging compliance; He cares for the well-being of His sons and daughters. But such pressure to perform on the field often results in fatigue, broken relationships, or missionary attrition (which we will explore in chapter seven).

"In my years of missionary service, I have come across many pastors and church leaders who cared more about a return on investment than the missionaries themselves." Steve Schirmer is the president of Silk Road Catalyst and a former full-time missionary in China. He feels that many sending churches convey harmful expectations to their missionaries. "I personally experienced this phenomenon," he said.

> One of our supposed 'partner churches' communicated only in regards to numbers. They wanted to know our five-year plan, how many churches we planted, and how many converts we made. But their interactions were never relational; not once did they ask about the spiritual, emotional, or physical health of our family.[40]

Schirmer confirmed his appreciation for missional plans and strategies, but not at the expense of the Kingdom worker's health. "Without the latter in check," he said, "the ROI does not matter because the missionary will end up returning home broken and battered."[41]

"It is imperative that missionaries and churches protect the physical, emotional, and spiritual health of those going out," missionary coach Sarita Hartz confirmed; "that they don't unwittingly send the message that the missionary is worth less than the mission."[42]

The ultimate goal of missions is the glorification of God. A high value for His honor drives missional living both at home and abroad—in our "Jerusalems," "Judeas," "Samarias," and to "the ends of the earth." The extravagant grace of our great King includes His people in His glory; thus, every believer in the body of Christ matters. God gifted each of His children with their unique faculties to make a difference in the world. Our roles are different, but our goal is the same: love God and love others. "Let me give you a new command: Love one another," Jesus said. His words revealed His high regard for counter-cultural Kingdom living. "In the same way I loved you, you love one another. This is how everyone will recognize that you are My disciples—when they see the love you have for each other."[43] If Jesus' words seem too simple, you may be overcomplicating your missional calling.

The more you yield to the influence of God's Kingdom, the easier it is to deviate from the adverse currents of popular culture. The naysayers may remain, and your negative internal monologue will endure. But as you set your mind on Heavenly thoughts, the power of social influence wanes. Jackie Pullinger was about to prove this truth to the pimps, prostitutes, gang members, and drug addicts in the Kowloon Walled City. Her ministry of love ran counter to the expected social norms; the City of Darkness was no place for this young British woman, many thought. But Jackie was not deterred. Into the dragon's lair she went, shining the light of God's Kingdom in Hong Kong's darkened alleys.

The Battle with This Dragon Could Be Won

Jackie's youth center situated in the heart of mayhem. She led a handful of curious young people in games, singing, and Bible storytelling. Just outside, the alleys lined with heroin addicts. "Day after day, I walked past them and could not tell whether they were asleep or awake," Jackie said. "They nodded all day, showing the yellow of their eyes in a heroin haze."[44] Around the corner, outside the pornographic film theaters, mama-sans pulled men up the wooden steps into dilapidated brothels. Compared with the prices charged in other places by the more glamorous Suzie Wongs, five-Hong-Kong-dollar prostitutes in the Walled City were cheap. Child prostitutes could start their careers as early as nine years of age. The young girls saw only a small portion of the menial payment; triad gangs controlling the area kept the bulk of the cash.

Jackie paid little heed to the generally accepted social norms; the righteous deviant overstepped boundaries to be the light of the world in dismal surroundings. Instead of skirting around the unfortunate victims, she paused for people like a good Samaritan. One day, she squatted beside a young heroin-addicted prostitute, placed her hand on the girl's shoulder, and said, "Yeh sou ngoi nei" ("Jesus loves you" in Cantonese). The young woman cringed away from Jackie, feeling sorry for the "good Christian girl" who ought not to interact with people like herself. The young prostitute was embarrassed that a "clean girl" made an error and touched a "dirty one." Jackie Pullinger's Kingdom witness employed a personal touch. She did not distance herself from suffering but spent time with societal outcasts.

Nonconformist behavior raises eyebrows and curls lips. Popular culture cannot comprehend Christ's radical brand of love. Mother Teresa's words expose the social sentiment of our time: "Today it is very fashionable to talk about the poor," she said. "Unfortunately, it is not fashionable to talk with them."[45] But the missional Christian stops in her tracks to convey God's scandalous grace. She is not content to stand at arm's length or safeguard her life from sadness. She knows that light is made for the darkness. And even when the darkness cannot comprehend such Light, God's Kingdom manifests through sacrificial love. The Kingdom of Heaven is, indeed, like a tiny seed; and Gospel seeds sown generously eventually take root, bloom, and transform the environment.[46]

Despite setbacks, Jackie continued ministering to the young people who joined her youth club. It was a hard toil. Many who attended did not yet profess Christ but joined merely out of curiosity. Recognizing her commitment to her place of calling, triad gang leaders allowed Jackie to continue her outreach. Day in and day out, she walked the tortuous alleys, but no harm came to her. God seemed to open impossible doors for her. But after four years of missional service in the Walled City, Jackie was about to encounter her greatest opposition yet.

In 1970, she returned to her youth club only to find the room in shambles. The smashed and scattered remains of benches, books, ping-pong bats, and skateboards littered the room. Far worse, someone had deliberately heaped piles of sewage all over the floors and walls. Jackie was crushed. She thought she made headway in the lives of the young men of her group. Their true nature now seemed to tell otherwise. Her pride crushed and her "unstructured youth work" trivialized, Jackie dropped to her knees and cried. "Enough is enough!" she told God. "If they don't want me or You, I don't have to stay here. I can be a Christian in [England] and do normal things like normal people." Resentment burned inside her. "I'm willing to pour my life out for them, but if they don't want it, they need not have it. Let's close the room up."[47]

Suddenly, the Holy Spirit reminded her to "turn the other cheek" and "go the extra mile." This was not Jackie's natural response. She later recalled the difficulty of walking the extra mile: "There seemed to be a lot of Christians who did not mind walking one, not many who could be bothered to walk two, and no one who wanted to walk three. Those in need that I met seemed to need a marathon."[48]

She spent the day sweeping up the place and, through fits of sobbing, tearfully muttered, "Praise God, praise God." The next night, Jackie opened the club as usual. Outside the door stood a young man she had never seen before. He told her that a high-ranking triad boss sent him to guard the center. She was shocked, but soon found that the unsolicited triad protection came with high expectations. In order to bolster his grip in the City, the leader wanted Jackie to help his gang members get off drugs as it lessened their usefulness.

Two notorious triad gangs operated in the Kowloon Walled City: Sun Yee On, who controlled the heroin dens and east-side prostitution rings, and the far more feared 14K, who controlled all opium dens, gambling, pornographic theaters, illegal dog restaurants, and child brothels in the western territory of the City. The triad societies subsisted as a pyramid of relationships; a complicated hierarchy of ranks and duties made up each gang.

In 1945, anti-communist Kuomintang Lieutenant-General Kot Siu-wong founded the 14K in Guangzhou, China. He organized the group to support the Chinese Nationalistic cause. Following the Chinese Civil War in 1949, the group fled the communist uprising and relocated to Hong Kong. Up until the 1990s, the 14K Triad operated as the world's largest triad, reputedly claiming 100,000 members worldwide; 60,000 in Hong Kong alone. Today, the criminal activity of the 14K includes large-scale drug trafficking around the world, mostly of heroin and opium from China or Southeast Asia. They are also involved in illegal gambling, loan sharking, money laundering, murder, arms trafficking, prostitution, human trafficking, extortion, counterfeiting, and home invasion robberies.[49]

Following the looting of Jackie's club, Winson, the 14K protector, clocked in night after night to stand guard outside the door. Winson ranked number 426 in the 14K Triad—the exclusive ranking of fight-fixer. This meant that he chose the location, weapons, and strategy to unleash violence against rival triad members. Jackie began telling Winson about Jesus. Initially, he did not want to hear what she said. But under orders to guard the youth club, he could not escape the Gospel message.

Jackie soon learned about Winson's opium addiction and invited him to join her inside the youth club during worship. Finally, he obliged. He participated in song, belting out a solo tuneless sound: "Give me oil in my lamp!"

Jackie marveled as she watched Winson let down his guard. Suddenly, he began to pray in Chinese. "I have never since listened to such a joyous prayer," Jackie said. "I kept thinking, *Where did he get that from?* Although, of course, I knew."[50]

The Holy Spirit permeated the room and gave Winson the gift of tongues. Without any manmade help or encouragement, he spoke in a Heavenly language. After half an hour, the extraordinary session culminated with a miracle. Winson and Jackie both knew he was completely cured of his drug addiction; he had come through withdrawal as he prayed. "When Winson came into the youth club and was set free from his opium addiction," Jackie later recalled, "God showed me that the battle with this dragon could be won."[51]

In this way, the youth club grew in numbers as new believers brought their friends to hear about Jesus. The 14K crime boss recognized the supernatural power at work through Jackie's efforts. Incredibly, he renounced all claim on the boys who became Christians—a deed unheard of in triad societies.

A pattern of supernatural deliverance occurred. Jackie frequently witnessed long-term addicts surrender their lives to Jesus and kick their addiction without pain or trauma. She opened a home to help her young men assimilate into society outside the Walled City. Those who escaped the dragon's clutches found jobs, joined Christian churches, and some continued to serve alongside Jackie. By the year 2000, St. Stephen's Society, Jackie Pullinger's ministry center, housed three hundred men, women, teenagers, and children from all over Hong Kong.

Jackie did not know what the future might bring in a political sense or what would be permitted in terms of social structure. "I had always wished for such simplicity, no need for organization," she admitted. "One poor man reaching one poor man. 'Love your neighbor as yourself' seemed to sum it up."[52] Her disciples may have failed society, school, and parents, but the overwhelming love of God pursued them down the labyrinthine corridors of time. His vessel of choice to usher in His Kingdom: a tenacious young woman who did not conform to the influence of cultural mores. In so expressing God's counter-cultural love, Jackie raised up a group of unlikely dragon slayers to transform the social landscape of the Walled City.

Show Them What God is Like by the Way You Live

Jackie Pullinger spent years pursuing the unruly dragon in the City of Darkness. Her initial presence seemed laughable. *What can one young woman accomplish?* the dragon must have thought. But days turned to weeks and months to years, and the unassuming warrior would not cease her efforts. The dragon thrashed inside the Walled City, stunned and enraged by his pursuer. His body coiled; his claws loosened their clutches on his prized possessions. The fire-breathing monster's tail writhed and flailed, tearing against the walls of his lair. The cracks became fractures; a breach had been made. Rays of light streamed into the heart of the city, and the dragon's eyes dilated. His seething shrieks could be heard for miles. The dragon's kingdom was about to cave on itself.

Though crime rates had dropped, the Kowloon Walled City had become increasingly intolerable both to the British and Chinese governments. Sanitary conditions remained far behind the rest of Hong Kong. The crumbling six-acre city neared its end. On January 14, 1987, Great Britain and the People's Republic of China announced their joint decision to tear down the Walled City. After years of planning, demolition began on March 23, 1993, and continued until April 1994.[53]

The ghetto razed and the rubble now cleared, work quickly began on the construction of a new park. The Walled City's transformation from "slum" to "oasis of leisure" completed in August 1995,[54] during my first mission trip to Asia.[55] The award-winning Kowloon Walled City Park situated amid the surrounding urban sprawl and opened to the public on December 22, 1995. The park's design is modeled on Jiangnan gardens of the early Qing Dynasty and stands in stark contrast to its previous squalor and lawlessness.

The park features pavilions, winding galleries, rockeries, stone paving, and wood and bamboo carvings. In the heart of the Kowloon Walled City Park sits a large, vertical stone known as the "Jackie Pullinger Rock." A small plaque beside the monument acknowledges Jackie's work:

> Ms. Pullinger came from the UK to Hong Kong alone in 1966 to spread the Gospel. In the Walled City, she looked after teenagers who were led astray, and despite interference from the triad society, she fearlessly helped drug addicts overcome addiction

through the teachings from the Gospel. Her pastoral work subsequently developed into a number of Hang Fook Camps[56] in various parts of the territory, leading many drug addicts, prostitutes, and street sleepers to start their lives anew. Even some triad members have subsequently turned over a new leaf through believing in Jesus and dedicated themselves to missionary work.

In 1981, Jackie established St. Stephen's Society in Hong Kong, an international ministry providing rehabilitation homes for recovering drug addicts, prostitutes, and gang members. By December 2007, the ministry housed two-hundred people.[57] St. Stephen's Society does not treat people with medications and typical treatment methods. Instead, ex-addicts gather people in a room for ten days, praying over drug addicts until they experience breakthrough and recovery.

Jackie Pullinger's unwillingness to conform to societal norms left a lasting, tangible impact in her place of service. After over fifty years of ministry, she continues to focus on evangelism and drug rehabilitation. Today, her ministry brings hope to society's hopeless. St. Stephen's Society reaches around the world, with centers in India, Sri Lanka, the Philippines, Indonesia, Malaysia, and Europe.

"We love our people whether they turn out well or not," Jackie said. "The successes do not vindicate our ministry nor do the disappointments nullify it. What is important is whether we have loved in a real way—not preached in an impassioned way from a pulpit."[58] This brand of nonconformist devotion marks her missionary career.

On November 25, 2016, a three-day celebration of Jackie's jubilee year in Hong Kong commenced.[59] From Friday evening through Sunday evening, hundreds of people gathered under a large tent at the Kowloon Walled City Park where the City of Darkness once stood. Fifty hours of continual worship, prayer, and testimony made for an extraordinary mix of wonder, joy, and healing. Former drug addicts and triad members testified how God changed their lives through Jackie's sacrificial service. Tears streaked down her cheeks as she recalled the goodness of God. "My mission was to help the Walled City people to understand who Christ was," she said. "If they could not understand the words about Jesus, then we Christians were to show them what He was like by the way we lived."[60]

Her seemingly simple words revealed the counter-cultural mode of the Kingdom of God. This upside-down Kingdom approach meant that by going lower, we grow higher, and by becoming nothing, we become God's instruments of choice. The world's mindset opposes such deviant methodology; popular culture expects you to remain within the confines of the status quo. But that is not how the power of the Gospel manifests. Only the radical go forth to fight against the darkness, slay dragons, and return with the fortunes of war. Jackie Pullinger's example calls us to self-sacrificing service and altruistic missional fervor. So onward, missional warriors! Advance, noble maidens! There are other dragons to be slayed.

Chapter Six

A POSTURE OF EXPECTANCY

Without a Care in the World

David Eubank's jaw was chiseled for military service. Cut square and clean-shaven in the manner Hollywood depicts soldiers of war, symmetrical lines crease his cheeks when pulled back in half smile. His cunning grin reveals a youthful mirth; his hazel eyes glint with pleasure. His favorite army-green *Free Burma Rangers* cap covers his receding hairline, shading the wrinkles on his brow. He appears both pensive and playful. The God-fearing military man exudes optimism. His presence is commanding, but not in a conceited, militant manner. Eubank's personality is the perfect mix of masculinity and modesty.

Never short of breath, Eubank is a master storyteller. His words flow at a million miles per minute. His jaw-dropping tales of risk and adventure need no embellishment; he simply recounts the facts as he remembers them, and the stories speak for themselves. He peppers each narrative with his high opinion of Jesus. Happily postured in a position of expectancy, the man is always on call and ready to respond to the purposes of his Master.

On January 16, 2018, my family and I ran into Eubank at the United States consulate in Chiang Mai, Thailand. David's wife, Karen, and their three children, Sahale, Suuzanne, and Peter—ages sixteen, fourteen, and eleven, respectively—accompanied him to the consulate. They sat in the last row of chairs in the outdoor waiting space while their passports were being renewed. The Eubank family had just returned from Iraq, one of the many conflict areas where they care for families and provide medical aid to victims of war. David's left forearm was wrapped in a bandage, still recovering from a recent bullet wound in Mosul.

I approached Eubank and shook his hand. "David, thank you so much for your service," I said. "We're blessed by what you and your family are doing." He smiled humbly. "Thank you," he replied. "It's an honor to serve where God calls us."

I recently read articles from major news sources covering the family's daring feats. The headlines spoke for themselves: "Thousands of Iraqis Have Fled Mosul, But This American Family Moved In" on *The Washington Post*. "Ex-US Soldier Says 'God Opened a Way' to Save Girl Trapped by ISIS" on *CBN News*; "The Man Who Willingly Takes His Family to War" on *ABC Australia*. *BBC, CNN, CBS, Fox News*; a slew of other well-known news agencies covered the Eubanks' outreach.

For thirty minutes, I stood speechless as David relayed the details of their work in Iraq. His account filled with words like "AK-47s" and "RPGs," "enemy fire," "dead bodies," and "near-death escapes." He told me about his rescue of a five-year-old girl with pink pigtails. "I saw about seventy dead bodies strewn all over the ground," he said, "women, children, guys in wheelchairs—all shot dead." In the center of the horrific scene, he saw movement. A little girl peeked out from underneath a black burqa. "'Jesus, help me,' I whispered under my breath," he told me, and he ran headfirst into ISIS gunfire. Smoke dropped by Allied Forces and firepower from Iraqi soldiers gave him the cover he needed. Buried in rubble, the little girl hid under her dead mother's burqa for two days until her rescue on June 2, 2017. "As I began to run, I thought, 'If I die today trying to save this child, my wife and kids will understand.'" He said he did it simply for love. "I remembered the scripture that says, 'Greater love...'" David closed his eyes, paused, and choked back his tears. "'...has no man than this, that he lay down his life for his friends.'"

Our conversation came to a close as my family and I were called inside for our scheduled appointment. Apologetic, I shook David's hand and entered the main office. Our passports did not take long to process, and in ten minutes, we returned to the outdoor seating area where the Eubank family awaited their appointment. Sahale, Suuzanne, and Peter still sat in the last row of seats. David reclined on three chairs on their left, his head nestled in Karen's lap. He was fast asleep, without a care in the world.

Unlimited Possibility

The previous two chapters were all about inner and outer expectations, and how global Kingdom workers respond to them. We continue to inspect the missionary mind by exploring the neighboring (yet, vastly different) word, *expectancy*.

The definitions[1] of the two neighboring words are as follows:
- *Expectation* is "a strong belief that something will happen or be the case in the future."
- *Expectancy* is "the state of thinking or hoping that something, especially something pleasant, will happen or be the case."

At first glance, there seems to be little difference between the two. The practical application, however, reveals that these two words are in direct opposition to one another. Expectation assumes a certain outcome, or that the outcome will occur a certain way. There is nothing wrong with having an expectation. The downfall, however, is that our expectations (or the expectations of others) can imprison us in a box of presuppositions. This can hinder the work of the Holy Spirit by blinding us to anything outside the box of our expectation. In contrast, expectancy does not limit outcomes. Expectancy is full of hope. It trusts the results to God. It requires an open mind and gives room for the Holy Spirit to accomplish His purposes as He sees fit. When we posture ourselves in expectancy rather than cling to expectations, we set ourselves up for unlimited possibility.

I would go out on a limb and say that David Eubank undoubtedly deals with inner and outer expectations. He is no stranger to the voice of the negative inner monologue. He has his own set of expectations, and frustration exerts itself when things don't go as planned. He needs the help of the Holy Spirit to take captive every thought to make it obedient to Christ.

Because he lives in the public limelight, people have their own expectations of him. But noble as they may be, he is not meant to bend to their every wish. He requires an ample dose of grace to follow God's unique leading in his life. And as he does, the peace of God that passes all understanding will guard his heart and mind.

Eugene Peterson, the translator of *The Message*, encourages a posture of peaceful surrender to God's will by writing:

> Hoping does not mean doing nothing. It is not fatalistic res-ignation. It means going about our assigned tasks, confident that God will provide the meaning and the conclusions. It is not compelled to work away at keeping up appearances with a bogus spirituality. It is the opposite of desperate and panicky manipu-lations or scurrying and worrying. And hoping is not dreaming. It is not spinning an illusion or fantasy to protect us from our boredom or our pain. It means a confident, alert expectation that God will do what He said He will do. It is imagination put in the harness of faith. It is a willingness to let God do it His way and in His time.[2]

The missionary mind brims with ambition, is built on belief, and resides in the realm of reliance. It hopes to make headway among the bruised and broken and witness God's rule and reign in the earth. The catch is that Kingdom workers must cast aside conjecture and relinquish assumed notions of success. Our vision is finite; God's perspective is eternal. We per-ceive a small part of the puzzle; God fits each piece into perfect harmony. We are bound by space and time; God sees the entire panorama from beginning to end. It is impossible to thrive on mission when our opinions or conclu-sions are formed on the basis of incomplete information. God's global plan *will* be accomplished. Every knee *will* one day bow before His breathtaking might, but most likely not in the manner we presently imagine.

"Expectancy is absolutely critical to the missionary," says Bradley Bell, a former missionary in East Africa and the author of *The Sending Church Defined*. "God delights to fill the open hands of expectant missionaries— to infuse them with the mystery of Christ Himself, in whom is hidden all treasure."[3]

The expectant Christian does not only seek an end product or an outcome; his prize is the very Person of Christ Himself. Naturally, he desires to be of use to his Master—to hear Him say, "Well done, My good and faithful servant." Above all else, his greatest reward is the pleasure of intimacy with God. He need not strive to meet unwarranted expectations; sonship permits a calm and peaceful spirit.

Scripture points us toward a posture of expectancy; it prompts us to action while residing in a calm state of trust. "I wait expectantly for your salvation," wrote the author of Psalm 119. "God, I do what You tell me."[4] In great distress and amid Saul's persecution, David wrote, "I wait expectantly, trusting God to help, for He has promised."[5] Notice how the posture of expectancy combines with a forward progression and obedient behavior. "Hope does not involve what we already have or see," Paul wrote. "For who goes around hoping for what he already has? But if we wait expectantly for things we have never seen, then we hope with true perseverance and eager anticipation."[6]

Are you a Christian who seeks to reach your city with the Gospel? God wants you to know that He is continually moving in the hearts of people around you. With eager anticipation, make His glory known in word and by deed, and trust the results to Him. Are you an overseas missionary who desires to see God's Kingdom established in a foreign culture? Continue to shine the light of Jesus wherever you go, knowing that the Holy Spirit is in full control.

If you want to thrive on mission, you must cast your expectations at the foot of the cross. God desires to establish His Kingdom on earth more than you could ever wish. He delights to include you in His redemptive narrative. Undoubtedly, you are an integral part of God's global plan, but it's better to be a small part of a big thing than a big part of a small thing.

This Is Our Place in God's Kingdom Work

I first met David Eubank on June 21, 2003. My friend, Andrew Marshall, a British journalist who then worked as a foreign correspondent for *TIME Asia*, heard about the former U.S. Special Forces operative-turned aid worker. He had to meet Eubank, and he invited me to tag along.

Less than two years earlier, Marshall was on a fact-finding mission for his forthcoming book, *The Trouser People*, which chronicled Burma's tumultuous history as a British colony to its then junta-ran narco nation. He needed a Mandarin-speaking interpreter to accompany him across the border but came up empty-handed. Perhaps it had something to do with his pitch: "Do you want to come and look for a semi-mythical mountain lake not seen by white man since 1937, and now protected by one of Southeast Asia's largest drug-trafficking organizations?" Marshall asked.[7] Apparently, I was foolhardy and audacious enough to concede. For one week, we hiked over mountain and valley in the rain, hoping to dodge ethnic insurgents. Our hair-raising trip culminated in our capture and interrogation by the United Wa State Army, who was armed to the hilt with assault rifles and M-22s. You can read about our adventure in the in the Pulitzer Prize-winning journalist's book, *The Trouser People: Burma in the Shadows of the Empire.*

With our shared interest in Burma, Marshall and I showed up at Eubank's home in Chiang Mai, Thailand. We were excited to meet the legendary missionary. The moment we disembarked our taxi, Eubank sprinted toward us, tossed us two pairs of shorts, and slapped us on the backs. "Put these on quick!" he panted. "We're in the middle of a serious soccer game, and we need you on the field now!" Andrew and I hurriedly suited up and ran out to the makeshift field. The rough-and-tumble pickup game revealed the weak links on the field. We gasped and wheezed as we ran back and forth across the field. Eubank's superhuman Free Burma Rangers easily outmatched us. The game culminated with Eubank's impressive goal from midfield. "Good game, guys!" he laughed, breathing normally. Drenched in perspiration, Andrew and I panted toward the sideline for a cup of water. "You were a huge help today, Marshall!" I quipped. He smirked. "Yea, you were amazing, too!"

We spent the rest of the afternoon learning about the Free Burma Rangers, Eubank's multi-ethnic humanitarian service movement. He described in detail the suffering and injustice he saw. "Little girls raped, villages burned," he reminisced, "I wanted to help in any way I could. I said, 'Lord, should I do something? Can I do something?' And I just felt God say, 'Go!'" The Free Burma Rangers conducted humanitarian missions in Burma's war zones, pushed past enemy fire, treated the wounded, and shared the love of God to internally displaced peoples. "This is our place in God's Kingdom work," David said. "It's not more or less important than anyone else's place. It's just our place. And we love it!"

Peculiarly, Eubank's story finds its origins way back on April 2, 1948, at the end of World War II. Even before David's birth, God arranged the pieces of the puzzle to fit perfectly into His timeline. God uses subtle and seemingly menial moments in history to cast considerable ripples along the landscape of time.

The conflict between the Burma (now Myanmar) government and ethnic minority militia commenced after the conclusion of the second world war and at the end of British colonial rule. The fighting has ebbed and flowed across the country for more than sixty years and is labeled the world's longest-running civil war.[8] It is called the "Internal Conflict in Myanmar," otherwise known as "The Burma Conflict."

For more than six decades, a series of dictators controlled Burma ever since it gained independence in 1948. The army attacked the ethnic peoples who comprise almost half the population of the country. Fighting was largely fueled by feuds, competition over natural resources, and demands for more autonomy.[9] There are no less than fifteen different armed rebel groups active in Myanmar. Some of them, like the Kachin Independence Army and the United Wa State Army, have controlled and administered large swaths of territory for years.[10] The complicated conflict pits ethnic guerrilla fighters toting a hodgepodge of weapons—from rusty carbines to M-16s—against Burmese army battalions. Land mines litter jungle paths, driving more than 150,000 ethnic people into refugee camps along neighboring country borders.[11] To date, more than a million people have been internally displaced.

In August 1961, when David Eubank was an infant, his parents, Allan and Joan, moved from America to Thailand, just East of Burma. After language study, Allan and Joan spent eight years planting churches and conducting rural development among the Thai and Lao Song people in Central Thailand. Unwilling to shield their son from real-world poverty and suffering, David joined his parents on village trips by bus, river excursions by canoe, and jungle expeditions by elephant. He grew up a missionary kid on the forefront of adventure and Christian service.

At the age of eighteen, following in his father's footsteps, David returned to America and enlisted in the U.S. armed forces. He commanded units in the Infantry, Rangers, and Special Forces, and ran missions in Central and South America. In 1992, after nearly ten years in the military, he left the Army and enrolled at Fuller Theological Seminary. At Fuller, David met his wife-to-be, Karen, who was studying to become a teacher. They married the following year.

In 1996, Christian members of the Wa tribe—one of the many ethnic peoples in Burma—approached the United States government asking for military help. They said the Burmese government was attacking them and they had no way of protecting themselves. The U.S. government denied help, and so they turned to the missionary community. Well-known among the ethnic peoples in the region, Allan and Joan hosted a meeting of Wa leaders in their home. At that time, one of the Wa leaders saw a photo of the Eubanks' son, David, outfitted in Green Beret fatigues.

"Is he a follower of Jesus?" the Wa man asked.

"Yes, he is in seminary in America," Allan replied.

"We are a warrior people," the man said. "Most of the Wa do not believe in Jesus. They are animists. We need a Christian man with warrior skills who can help us."[12] The Wa leader requested the Eubanks' son to come and teach them survival and military skills.

Allan immediately called his son in America and explained the situation. David felt the Holy Spirit's leading in the matter and promised to help where possible. In 1996, David and Karen flew to Thailand, "extra-legally" (without government-issued visas) crossed the border into Burma and began providing aid to the local resistance.

The same year, Eubank flew to Rangoon to hear Aung San Suu Kyi speak during a brief period of freedom between house arrests. As the youngest daughter of Aung San, Father of the Nation of modern-day Myanmar, Suu Kyi was the General Secretary of the National League for Democracy (NLD). The Nobel Peace Prize laureate publicly criticized the ruling military junta, and spent almost fifteen years under house arrest, becoming one of the world's most prominent political prisoners.

Eubank secured a chance meeting with Suu Kyi and spoke with her for thirty minutes. "We need unity," she said. "We will never have peace without unity. And we need prayer. Please pray for us."[13] Impressed by the spirited, Buddhist woman, Eubank gave Suu Kyi his Special Forces crest. She took the insignia with its two silver arrows crossed with a dagger, and inscription, "De Oppresso Liber," which translated from Latin means, "To Free the Oppressed."

Suu Kyi said, "Aren't the things of war often very beautiful?"

Eubank then gave her his Bible. "This is the most valuable thing I own," he told her.

"I read the Bible every day," she replied. She quoted her favorite scripture: "'And ye shall know the truth, and the truth shall make you free.'"[14]

Stirred by the providential meeting, in 1996, Eubank initiated the *Global Day of Prayer for Burma*, a publication and annual prayer event that now takes place on the second Sunday of March each year. During the Burma Army offensives of 1997, Eubank formed the Free Burma Rangers, a humanitarian service movement that conducts relief, advocacy, leadership development, and unity missions among the people of Burma.

Eubank's *modus operandi* ran counter to typical Christian missionary work. His grassroots movement accepted volunteers from multi-faith backgrounds. Some Free Burma Rangers carried guns into the jungle to protect staff and volunteers from hostile attacks. Dangerous territory called for extreme measures. But Eubank made his intentions clear: "We exist to free the oppressed," he said. "We stand for human dignity, justice, and reconciliation. We bring help, hope, and love to people of all faiths and ethnicities in the conflict areas.[15] I'd rather do something than just talk about it."[16]

To date, the Free Burma Rangers have trained 300 ethnic relief teams, conducted over 1,000 relief missions, treated over 550,000 patients, and helped more than 1,200,000 people.[17]

"I want to be where I'm most needed," Eubank said, "and I feel that's where people are being attacked or where they're in trouble." When asked if the former U.S.-Special-Forces-soldier-turned-combat-missionary second guesses his walk on the wild side, Eubank said,

> I sometimes wonder what I'm doing out here. Is it worth the risk?
> Am I making any difference at all? Do I have the wrong motives?
> But when I think of the people who have suffered great injustice
> and pain, I know our place is to stand with them.[18]

For Me, This is Normal

David Eubank blows up our paradigms of what the normative Christian life should be. Most of us will never experience dodging bullets in a fast-paced sprint through the jungles of Burma. The rough-and-tumble, raw reality of war zone outreach is a foreign concept to us. But to Eubank, a keyed up, high-octane mission *is* the normal Christian life. I say this not to glorify one man's calling over another, but in hopes to unlock the secret behind a radical commitment to Christ and a dedicated service to mankind. Too often, the average disciple finds it difficult to minister to his next-door neighbor, let alone believe that God can use him in conflict areas around the world. Perhaps Eubank's example will reset our portrait of "normalcy."

In 2014, word of the Free Burma Rangers spread around the world, and they were invited to Sudan's Nuba mountains to help displaced people. The next year, friends who worked in Kurdistan asked them to come and assist there. They also spent time in Syria and Iraq, delivering food and medical supplies to people on the frontline of war.[19]

There's something else you need to understand about David Eubank: he rarely ventures into war zones alone. His wife, Karen, often accompanies him to conflict areas. He also takes his three young children to the frontlines of battle. "Our kids have all experienced gunfire, mortars, and machine guns," Eubank said.

> We don't want our kids to die—we try to protect them. But we don't want to protect them from other peoples' needs. We don't want to insulate them from the real situation of the world or inhibit what God can do through their lives to help other people.[20]

Who willingly takes their family into a war zone? It seems preposterous until you realize that the Eubank children aren't exactly your typical kids. They have been sneaking back and forth across the Burma border since they were in diapers. Picture Bear Grylls hunting, fishing, and handling knives as a kid, and you start to get the picture. The Eubank kids shot caribou when they were shorter than the rifles they were shooting. Peter, the youngest child, ran a five-kilometer fun run in the United States when he was three-years-old. "For me, this is normal," sixteen-year-old Sahale said. "There are people in Burma who live in a war zone all the time, and for them, that is normal. Who's to say what a normal childhood looks like?"[21]

Many Christians tend to shield their children from the world's brokenness. If your missional calling does not include taking your kids into war zones, you should find a way to expose their minds to God's global plan. Do you want your children to grow into faithful Christian disciples? Read the *Trailblazers Series*[22] missionary biographies to them. Pin up a map on their bedroom wall and pray for missionaries serving in foreign countries. Gather world events from the news and discuss them around the dinner table. Let them see the world's needs and permit them to experience the Kingdom of God in action.

My career missionary journey began in 1998 when I moved to Southwest China. I joined an apostolic group of families who regularly took their young children on trips to the rural countryside. They interacted with kids in stilted bamboo homes. They handed out balloons to impoverished children. They saw pigs slaughtered for Chinese New Year, and chickens sacrificed to local ancestors. Their parents did not cover their eyes every time they encountered suffering. They allowed their children to witness God at work among the nations, even when it was uncomfortable. Today, many of those missionary kids are involved in global ministries. They witnessed the wonders of God in a fallen world and were better for it.

The teachings of Jesus were straightforward and in your face: "Anyone who loves their father or mother more than Me is not worthy of Me," He said. "Anyone who loves their son or daughter more than Me is not worthy of Me."[23] You can try to soften His radical statements, but you will be left with a feeble faith and impotent religion. David Platt, director of the International Mission Board, expounded on Matthew 10:37 by saying, "In our culture today, we idolize our children and our marriages... to the point where Jesus Christ gets the leftovers from our affections. This stance is completely un-Christian."[24]

A posture of expectancy is not only for adults. Your kids need to see what it looks like to thrive on mission, too. The Holy Spirit speaks to the impressionable minds of children because He wants to build them into passionate disciples, even from a young age. Think of the Chinese children in *Visions Beyond the Veil* by H. A. Baker. In the 1930s, during an outpouring of the Holy Spirit at an orphanage in Southwest China, young children saw divine revelations of Heaven. Impassioned, the kids began to share the Gospel with young people and adults alike. Their innocent faith sparked a supernatural revival in the city and surrounding areas.

Or think of three-year-old Colton Burpo's near-death experience on March 5, 2003. During the months after the surgery, Colton told his parents about his experiences in Heaven. He also described events and people that seemed impossible for him to have known. The New York Times best-selling book, *Heaven Is For Real*, recounts his Heavenly visions. Many Christian critics claimed the book, and subsequent movie, were "extra-biblical," but that is beside the point at hand. The fact remains: children are often more sensitive than adults to things in the supernatural realm. When we create an atmosphere for our children to experience the world's pain and the Holy Spirit's healing balm, the results are immeasurable.

"We found these human bones—backbone, ribcage, and pelvis of a small child—that ISIS murdered. They're just here on the street. We found the clothes and blood stains on the other side." Sahale Eubank kneeled on the dusty Kurdistan road. Her auburn-blond hair tossed in the breeze and a tear streaked down her cheek. Her YouTube channel[25] fills with videos about her life as a missionary kid in Burma, Sudan, Kurdistan, and Iraq. She hopes to shine a light on the current conflicts in war-torn countries. In this particular video, the camera pans across an open graveyard of rubble and human bones. "It makes me sad because this could have been my family." She pointed to a decayed cranium on the ground. "That could have been me," she said.[26]

Sahale has witnessed her fair share of atrocities, but her outlook on life is far from gloomy. Her Instagram account[27] reveals a completely different picture. In one photo, a monkey perches on her shoulder. In another, she glides through the air on horseback. She rides dirt bikes in Burma and drives an armored vehicle in Iraq. A group of smiling Rohingya children gathers around her in Bangladesh, and she administers novocaine to a military general in Syria. A broad smile stretches across her face as she shoots a machine gun. She summits a snowy Alaskan peak and lounges in a jungle hammock.

Fourteen-year-old Suuzanne is named after the Burmese Nobel laureate, Aung San Suu Kyi. Though she realizes her life is atypical of her peers, she does not consider her family's lifestyle abnormal. "Some of my friends think our life is pretty crazy," she admitted with a smile. "I dunno. It feels pretty normal to me." Her life is a series of exciting snapshots. When she was eight-years-old, she caught and killed a five-foot python. She posts adventurous photos on her Instagram account[28] for her friends to see. She smiles atop a camel in the Syrian Desert and rafts down a river on the Thailand-Burma border. In one post, the text reads: "I live with fear and danger, but sometimes I leave them behind and go skydiving." The image shows her jumping headfirst out of a prop plane in the Czech Republic. Another photo shows a young Syrian girl covering her mouth in mid-laughter. Her eyes glint with joy as she gazes at the camera. "Just a laugh can change a day," Suuzanne wrote, "and just a day can change the world for someone."

I am riveted by all the beautiful images. The Eubanks' normalcy is strikingly different from the normalcy of the general population. Suuzanne shrugs it off as she poses horseback beside a military Humvee that is backdropped by a bombed-out Iraqi building. The text of another post reads,

> Happy birthday to the best dad in the whole world! Thank you for always pushing me through the hard stuff, even when I want to quit... I'm blessed to have a father that follows God with all his heart and trusts Him no matter what. I love you so much, and I can't imagine life without you! Happy birthday, daddy![29]

The photo shows David Eubank pushing an Iraqi child in a wheelchair. The boy laughs hysterically as David pops a wheelie and takes him on the ride of his life.

Dressed in a camouflage sweatshirt and army pants, Peter Eubank stood at the threshold of a bombed-out house in Kurdistan. His somber demeanor concealed the carefree mannerisms of a typical eleven-year-old boy. "You can still smell the scent of dead, decaying bodies under the rubble," he said, pointing past the darkened doorway. "It makes me sad. We should do more to help." The Eubank family is fond of asking, "Whose life is more valuable?" Peter knows the answer to the rhetorical question. In the midst of such evil and sadness, his voice rang out with the rest of the relief team: "I love you! You are my friend!" He sang songs about God's love, performed skits for the children, and taught about basic health care. That day, the dusty plains of Kurdistan resounded with children's laughter.

The children's programs Karen and the kids run are usually held out of harm's way, but that definition is a little loose in conflict areas. One day, while working with children in a local school in Mosul, they came under attack. They huddled inside as bullets battered the outside of the building. The Eubanks were shaken, but not ready to call it quits. Karen said, "When the Iraqis saw that, they said, 'You really do think that we are as valuable as you are.'"[30] Their testimony changed paradigms and opened hearts to the God's love.

The Eubanks understand that they are a small part of the puzzle. They realize the world is broken and in need of repair, and the complicated issues in conflict areas must be mended in increments. "Our team barely scratched the surface of such a large and dynamic problem," Sahale said. "But we believe that God has called us to stand with the oppressed; to bring help, hope, and love to the children and families. We want to let them know that they're not forgotten, and to remind them that in the midst of their suffering, God has a special plan for their lives."[31]

People around the world hail the Eubanks as heroes—a label they themselves do not necessarily subscribe to. Such lofty definitions do not fit within their family framework. They live by the Golden Rule: "Do to others what you would have them do to you."[32] These global Kingdom workers challenge us to consider our response to the commands of Christ. Are we truly sold out and radically committed to God's global plan? Do we actively seek first the Kingdom of God and His righteousness? Are we willing to allow God access to every part of our hearts and minds? If we really want to thrive on mission, we must allow God to redefine our definition of the normal Christian life.

There Will Be Perfect Harmony

The Eubank family has earnest expectations. They pray for peace to overcome conflict. They hope for love to conquer war. They long to see God's Kingdom established wherever they go. They eagerly anticipate the fulfillment of God's complete rule and reign on earth. However, these outcomes will not be accomplished effortlessly and often not in the way we might imagine. Just as a single pebble dropped in water casts far-reaching ripples, God uses the actions of His people to create widespread transformation.

The Christian postured in faith fills with expectancy. She hopes in the Lord and fixes her eyes on His promises. She remembers that the storms of life silent themselves at the command of Jesus. This truth calms her soul and pacifies her anxious mind. God promises perfect peace to those whose minds are set on Him.[33] He says, "Be still, and know that I am God; I will be exalted among the nations, I will be exalted in the earth."[34]

Global Kingdom workers around the world are in a similar spot. They cross cultural, linguistic, and geographical boundaries to build God's Kingdom in the earth. There are a lot of things worth doing in the world, and missionary life is their expression of devotion to God. Will they encounter speed bumps and hiccups along the way? Absolutely. And when they do, they are left with a choice: tackle the problems in their own strength or trust in God's capacity to overcome all odds.

The dilemmas that overseas missionaries meet are analogous to the struggles of every Christian believer. Regardless of your place or position in the body of Christ, you too will face physical challenges, emotional struggles, and spiritual hurdles. Your circumstances may look different on the exterior, but the crux of the matter remains the same: when you are weak, then you are strong. This notion runs counter to human comprehension. Nevertheless, God rigged the world in such a way that His might manifests through human deficiency.

Apostle Paul explained this reality to the Corinthian church: "But [God] said to me, 'My grace is sufficient for you, for My power is made perfect in weakness.'" Paul's response challenges our concept of competence:

> Therefore I will boast all the more gladly about my weaknesses, so that Christ's power may rest on me. That is why, for Christ's sake, I delight in weaknesses, in insults, in hardships, in persecutions, [and] in difficulties. For when I am weak, then I am strong.[35]

Peace of mind comes in the acceptance of God's sovereignty. We do what little we can; the Holy Spirit then does the real work of altering circumstances and transforming hearts. I have a hunch that David Eubank understands this truth. When I saw him at the U.S. Consulate in Chiang Mai, Thailand, he still had shrapnel in his leg from Iraq; his left forearm bandaged from a bullet wound. Instead of a man battered by the battles of life, I saw an enthusiastic agent of peace.

The Eubank family lives in a paradigm unlike any others I know. Yet, there is a commonality between their lives and ours. God meets all of us in our particular circumstances. He calls us to obedience to His commands, sensitivity to His voice, and clarity to know what matters and what doesn't. He beckons us to display sacrificial love, and to lay our lives on the line for the sake of others. This is the commonality that links us together as the body of Christ.

Their narrative is an incredible expression of God's faithfulness working in and through mankind. In a world where many people see pacifism as the only way of life, the Eubanks' story calls into question what we value most. I am both moved and terrified by such stories of sacrificial service for the Kingdom of God. Their extraordinary generosity in such violent settings confuses my perception of what missional living ought to look like. The Eubanks set before us a vivid example of risk-takers who lay their lives on the line for Jesus Christ and for people.

"I didn't choose these battles," Eubank said. "God opened the doors, and I simply walked through them. That's what God had for me and what the people involved needed most." He then told me about his rescue of an Iraqi woman buried amongst the dead in Mosul. For three days, she hid in the heat under ISIS gunfire, pretending to be dead. He threw her a severed electric wire and she tied it around her arm. Eubank dragged her blood-drenched body across the rubble to safety. She looked him in the eye, and cried, "Thank you for not leaving me behind."

"I have often found that evil is so great and humans so weak that we cannot accomplish the mission," David said. "But when we ask for God's help, He overcomes our weakness to defeat evil, and empowers us to carry the wounded to safety. To me, that is the essence of the Gospel. In dire circumstances, I often feel overwhelmed. But I believe that is good for my heart."[36]

As I listened, the truth of Eubank's words struck me deeply. Come hell or high water, God's sovereignty is ever relevant to our daily lives. His power overshadows our inabilities and His dominion exceeds our deficiencies. He does not question His authority. God knows what He is doing. He provides perfect peace for those whose minds are centered on Him.

"God is bigger than all these issues," Eubank said.

> He will give each of us—from the plumber to the president—the answers we need for today. The answer He gives you will be different than the answer He has for me. And if we follow His answers, there will be perfect harmony—like an orchestra of instruments that play in sync.[37]

Perhaps that was the key to David's untroubled rest at the U.S. Consulate that day. The world raged, but his mind fixed on the promises of God. Sprawled out on three waiting room chairs, his head nestled in Karen's lap. Fast asleep, without a care in the world, I imagined his dreams filled with the resonance of a Heavenly symphony.

RISKS

The Christian journey is rarely smooth sailing. The thought of dying to self that the life of Jesus might shine through you stands in stark contrast to human comprehension. Inevitable trials permeate the passage of life. Missional believers roam over trails laced with thorns and woe. Jesus promised you abundant life, but in a fallen world, this reality is not always evident. God's glory undergirds your earthly existence; His joy propels you to give witness of His Kingdom. But the physical challenges, emotional struggles, and spiritual hurdles often throw a wrench into your most altruistic endeavors.

In section three of *The Mind of a Missionary*, the lives of Nik and Ruth Ripken, William Carey, and Hudson Taylor inspire us to take calculated risks to display the power of God. This seemingly unstable and precarious stance leaves you wondering if you are, after all, on the right path. Unable to remedy the risk that the mission field entails, scores of global Kingdom workers threw in the towel and abandoned their ministry posts. This is called missionary attrition. The stress of cross-cultural life often led to ill health, broken relationships, wounded spirits, and even the abandonment of the Christian faith. The Ripkens experienced death at the doorstep; Carey dealt with his wife's mental delusions; and Taylor buried seven children and two wives during his career. The threat of risk in the mind of global Kingdom workers calls for radical devotion to God's will.

The missionary examples in section three, *Risks*, leave you with this question: Is Jesus worth it? You will learn the startling statistics of missionary attrition, the unimaginable stress levels of cross-cultural workers, and how to thrive in your calling despite tragic setbacks. You will discover the benefit of self-care, the merit of missionary member care, and the value of linking hearts and hands with those who serve around the world. The missions enterprise is composed of ordinary, run-of-the-mill individuals who said "Yes" to God. By their examples, you will see that despite risk and difficulty, the Holy Spirit was an ever-present help in time of trouble. With such an understanding of God's love for His children, you might find that there is no such thing as "risk" when you remain in the safety of His embrace.

Chapter Seven

PHYSICAL CHALLENGES

Is Jesus Worth It?

Timothy Ripken battled asthma since he was seven years old. It typically flared up when he moved with his family to a new environment. As a missionary kid growing up in multiple foreign environments, his medical condition was of serious concern.

In 1991, Timothy's family moved from Johannesburg to Nairobi. After two years in Malawi and five years in South Africa, they felt strongly that they needed to go where the Gospel had not yet gone—where people had little or no access to Christ. "While there was certainly important work yet to be done in South Africa," Timothy's father later said, "we did not feel called to continue working in a country where Jesus had already been proclaimed for centuries."[1] Kenya bordered Somaliland (now Somalia)—a "failed state" marred by brutal war and abject poverty. Timothy's parents felt that Nairobi, the Kenyan capital, was a better staging point for their new ministry to the Somali people.

But a new environment meant new physical challenges for Timothy. Conscious of his health issues, Timothy's parents took every precaution to alleviate health risks for their son. For five years, no serious attacks came to him until a school trip to Mombasa in 1996. He stayed in a damp hotel room where the mold triggered a severe reaction. His throat began to close, and he gasped for air. The darkness settled in, and he saw stars. Before he passed out, one of the chaperones rushed him to a hospital emergency room where the medical staff quickly got his breathing stabilized. It was a close call for the teenage missionary kid.

The doctor assured his parents that Tim recovered well, but he said that they were right to be concerned. The good news: Tim's lungs and heart grew strong from fighting off asthma-causing infections for years. He was now robust and healthy. The bad news: Tim was so resilient and his body so good at fighting off asthmatic events that, by the time he evidenced serious symptoms from another attack, he might already be on the verge of cardiac arrest.

His parents took the doctor's warning seriously. They stocked up on epinephrine pens in case of emergency, but for the next year, no further episodes occurred. Everything returned to normal. Timothy and his brothers attended school while their father took multiple trips to Somalia. The family happily engaged in the missionary community; they felt hopeful about how God might use them to reach the unreached. What happened next blindsided the Ripken family and altered the course of their lives forever.

In the early hours of Easter, March 28, 1997, tragedy struck. At 1:30 in the morning, Tim stumbled into his parents' room. He struggled to breathe and could not talk. The epinephrine pens were useless, and so his father rushed Tim to the nearest emergency room. Halfway to the hospital, Tim went into cardiac arrest.

Their lone vehicle sped through the dark streets of Nairobi. Scattered streetlights cast a dim glow on the potholed boulevard. Tim's father frantically struggled to revive his son. After what seemed like an eternity, they finally arrived at the hospital. By this point, Tim was unconscious but breathing. Medical staff rushed the boy into the emergency room. Tim's father felt powerless. He wished there was something he could do to help his son, but he could only watch and wait and pray. Within an hour, Tim's mother arrived at the hospital. Shaken and alarmed, she threw her arms around her husband. They embraced under the sterile, fluorescent hospital lights. But it was too late. An inexplicable sadness spread through them as the doctors informed them that Timothy was gone. He was only sixteen years old.[2]

"Time stood still as we leaned over the bed to hold him," Nik Ripken said. His fatherly heart broke into pieces. "At that moment, something inside me died." Nik and his wife, Ruth, knew that Tim's spirit bounded to heaven that Easter morning. They were certain of this reality. But the loss overwhelmed Nik. "Ruth used the word 'resurrection' that night," Nik recalled. "I was fixed on the crucifixion."[3] The pain was unbearable. Nothing could be done to restore their son's life. Shocked and traumatized, the Ripken's drove back home, called family members in America, and informed them what had happened on the day of their Lord's resurrection.

Faced with the tragedy of their son's death, a single question lingered in the Ripkens' minds: "Is Jesus worth it?" How would they respond to what seemed like a Good Friday without an end? Was Jesus' resurrection power still available to them? The answers did not come easily; only time and the gentle whisper of the Holy Spirit could quell their quandary.

Three months after Tim's burial in Nairobi, Kenya, Nik and Ruth and their two other sons, Shane and Andrew, returned to America in June 1997. By this time, they had spent seven years in Malawi and South Africa before moving to Kenya to work among the Somali people. Now, after years of humanitarian aid and evangelistic outreach in the Horn of Africa, it seemed that their missionary journey had come to an end. "As I looked down from the plane," Nik said, "I saw a hostile land consisting mostly of dry, lifeless desert and hard, rocky terrain." He wrestled with the doubts that haunted him day and night. "After all the time, the expense, the energy, and the sacrifice expended by so many people, what (if anything) had our years in Somalia really accomplished?"[4] he wondered.

The Ripkens were not the first overseas missionaries to face such physical challenges. The mission fields of the earth are laden with peril and unpredictability. Fully conscious of this reality, the healthy missionary mind postures itself on the promises of God. Setbacks are superfluous and the many losses seemingly unbearable. Still, a mind set not on earthly things but on a Heavenly vision advances with God-given tenacity.

Missionary Life Is Simply a Chance to Die

"Are we prepared to stand firm in the cause we have undertaken at all risks?"[5] questioned legendary missionary to China, Hudson Taylor. This challenge comes from a man who lost four of his seven children and two wives during his missionary career. At face value, the matter seems simple. But tragedy has a strange way of transforming our response.

"Tim's death had changed us," Nik Ripken admitted. "After all that we had been through, we wondered if we were still willing to risk ourselves and our family to do what God had called us to do. Honestly, I thought that question had already been settled—but, now, I wasn't sure."[6]

The Ripkens were not alone in this conundrum. Throughout history, global Kingdom workers wrestled to understand God's purposes in the midst of great difficulty. *Is reckless abandon to the will of God worth the risk?* they wonder. *Is God's infinite worth more significant than my present troubles?* In the early 1990s, the Hogans were about to find out.

When all the world seemed brilliant, and the budding Mongolian Church was on the cusp of arguably one of the greatest revivals the nation had ever known, Brian and Louise Hogan tragically lost their newborn infant, Jedidiah.

On a frigid night in 1994, the Hogans showed off their newborn son, Jedidiah, at a Christmas party put on by the Foreign Language Institute. Joy swelled in their hearts as friends and disciples gathered around the infant. They pinched his cheeks and cooed gleefully. The room filled with laughter and thanksgiving. Jedidiah was the center of attention. Little did his parents realize that his short life would unwittingly play an integral role in the growth of the Mongolian Church.

After the party, Brian and Louise walked back home in the sub-zero degree temperature. Jedidiah slept soundly, bundled in the baby sling tucked against his mother's chest.

The city slept; Christmas was not widely celebrated in Mongolia; the Institute had wanted the Christmas party merely for a cultural experience. As the missionary catalysts of the Mongolian church planting movement walked along the deserted main avenue, they talked of the Christmas party, which was to be the very next night. "Louise had written a song called *Lullaby for the Baby King*," Brian said. "We were excited at the added meaning of holding a new baby while singing these lyrics."[7]

When they returned home, Louise nursed Jedidiah and prepared to tuck him in bed. Satisfied, he beamed the biggest smile at his parents—his first ever. Brian grabbed his camera, snapped a photo, and the couple laughed with delight. Louise told Brian to leave the camera out to take more pictures in the morning. But there would be no more happy photos.

At six in the morning on December 24, 1994, Louise woke with a start, sensing something was wrong. She hurried to Jed's bedroom and found him lying face-down. His body was ice-cold and stiff. Louise coiled into a fetal position and moaned, "God is good, God is good, God is good." Grief took over the Christmas season; Brian and Louise barely knew how to respond.

On Christmas Eve, Jedidiah died of SIDS (Sudden Infant Death Syndrome). Shocked beyond belief, Brian penned a letter to their families back home on December 25, 1994:

> Today is Christmas Day. Yesterday our son died. This letter will be tough to write. I usually enjoy writing to you, and the words flow easily. There are no words for this. Yesterday morning Louise woke to find a perfect baby boy lying dead in his bed. Jedidiah was 52 days old. I wish you could have known my son. I wish you could have held him and seen how beautiful his hands, eyelashes, lips, everything was. He learned to smile in his last week. He had a smile more gorgeous than a sunrise. Jed used to stare so intently at our faces—just as if he was memorizing every detail.[8]

Several years later, Brian learned that the way they grieved the death of their son had a significant impact on the Mongolian people. The Mongolians had never seen hope in the midst of grief until witnessing it through the Hogans' loss of their only son, Jed. For many Mongolians, this confirmed their faith in Jesus Christ and a supernatural church planting movement found its momentum.

Brian said,

> I was filled with extreme joy and overwhelmed with love as I realized how far out of His way God had gone to make sure we understood [the effect our lives had on the people]. It was all worth it. God had redeemed even our deepest sorrow and turned it into glory and [Mongolian] worshipers. As tears ran down my cheeks, all I could think was 'Jesus is worthy.'[9]

Some might call this response laudable; others would consider it laughable. How can joy be found amid such loss? Was Jesus truly worth it? The complicated losses that global Kingdom workers face cannot be understated. Far from their family, friends, and homelands, these privations are magnified and seemingly unmanageable. Yet, the Hogans show us that when the missionary mind mirrors the mindset of Christ, supernatural hope arises. Their eyes fixed not on the temporal but on an eternal reality—the Kingdom of God in their midst.

While serving in India, Amy Carmichael received a letter from a young lady who was considering life as a missionary. She asked, "What is missionary life like?" Amy responded by writing, "Missionary life is simply a chance to die."[10] Carmichael was not facetious with her remarks. She served in India for fifty-five years without returning home to Ireland. She abandoned temporal comforts for Kingdom rewards. She hurled herself into God's desires and laid her dreams by the wayside. She placed her life on God's altar, set fire to her wishes, and said, "Not my will, but Yours be done."

"Radical obedience to Christ is not easy; it is dangerous," wrote David Platt.

> It is not smooth sailing aboard a luxury liner; it is sacrificial duty aboard a troop carrier. It's not comfort, not health, not wealth, and not prosperity in this world. Radical obedience to Christ risks losing all these things. But in the end, such risk finds its reward in Christ. And He is more than enough for us.[11]

The risks that global Kingdom workers undertake are no trivial affair. Those who set their minds upon building the Kingdom of God in foreign lands often suffer great loss. They are often disdained by those they minister to and misunderstood by those who send them. "Why go to the far side of the world when there are so many needs here at home?" people question. "Timothy might not have died if you just stayed at home," they taunt. "Jedidiah had a promising future," they remark. "You should have left Mongolia sooner."

The radical growth of the first-century Church was wrought through the fires of tribulation, hardship, and persecution. Stephen, the first Christian martyr, was stoned to death for his fervent words. John was beheaded because he wouldn't shut up. Peter was imprisoned because he publicly preached the name of Jesus. Paul was beaten because he blazed new trails for the Kingdom of God. The long list of personal sacrifice for the sake of Jesus goes on.

Persecution is not a new phenomenon. One must merely open *Foxe's Book of Martyrs* to understand the tales of ultimate sacrifice throughout history. In the year AD 67, Nero commenced his barbaric eradication of Christians.

Some he sewed up in the skins of wild beasts, after which he released dogs to chew away at the flesh until the Christians expired. Others, he dressed in shirts made stiff with wax, fixed them to trees, and set them on fire in his gardens in order to illuminate them. Yet, the centuries of brutal torture that followed sparked the rapid advancement of the Christian faith. Historic persecution ebbed and flowed well into the modern era. Unbeknownst to many believers, present-day Christians still undergo physical torment because of their commitment to Christ. The recently-released *Open Doors' 2018 World Watch List* revealed "The 50 countries where it is most dangerous to follow Jesus."[12] Today, the Ripkens' Somalia ranks number three on the report.

Accounts of Christian persecution have always been a theme of radical commitment to Christ. In 1956, the Auca Indians speared to death Jim Elliot and his missionary counterparts in Ecuador. In 1962, the Motilone Indians of Colombia pierced arrows into Bruce Olson. In 1999, a gang of Hindu fundamentalists burned to death Graham Staines and his two sons (ages ten and six). In 2017, Pakistani extremists kidnapped and killed Chinese missionary couple Meng Lisi and Li Xinheng.

You don't really think that advancing the Kingdom of God on earth is easy, do you? Listen to the voices of the past. If you want to thrive on mission, you will suffer setbacks and face physical, emotional, and spiritual challenges. You will have to die to yourself so that the life of Christ might be evident in you. By embracing the reality that in a fallen world, bad things happen to good people, you will discover the path to victory lies not in your own power, but in the power of God in and through you.

Modern-day missions include a wide array of other unique dilemmas. Global Kingdom workers cross into an alien culture, navigate unfamiliar customs, and seek to influence people by using a foreign language. Thriving on mission is already a difficult endeavor; now they must raise funds for their work, safeguard themselves from physical fatigue, and deal with homesickness. They must avoid the many sexual temptations that seek to entrap them. Their emotional state is consistently under attack; their spiritual health is confronted at every turn. Without the help of the Holy Spirit, the missionary venture is an impossible task. The forces of evil rise against the missional Christian. The enemy will not release his grip on countries, communities, and individuals without a fight.

Thankfully, God already knows this, and He provides every opportunity to experience victory and breakthrough. But even with the promise of God's presence, a staggering number of global Kingdom workers will cut their losses and throw in the towel.

Many of the Losses Were Preventable

George Verwer, the founder of Operation Mobilisation, said, "Sending Americans for overseas ministry is a time-consuming, costly, and hazardous undertaking. If they come home prematurely for preventable reasons, it causes hardship on families and cost to the Kingdom."[13] This reality applies to overseas workers of all races, ethnicities, and nationalities.

Jesus commanded His followers to go. He promised the empowerment of the Holy Spirit to share the good news with every tribe, people, and nation. God loves to include His people in His global missions mandate. He desires that every individual might have the opportunity to hear of His unconditional love; that none should perish but that all should come to repentance. And His instrument of choice to accomplish this challenging task: weak and unassuming misfits; broken jars of clay.

The physical challenges of the mission field directly affect the emotional and spiritual health of the global Kingdom worker. Some of the difficulties are more menial than others. Whereas adapting to a new language, culture, and climate, and dealing with food allergies, digestive troubles, pollution, bizarre insects, chaotic traffic, and bumpy buses are troublesome, serious illness, substandard medical care, and risk of violence can all create substantial stress.

This cumulative exposure to unforeseen circumstances influences the decision-making process of people on the mission field. This year, more than 7,000 missionaries will quit. That means roughly twenty global Kingdom workers will pull the plug today. Nearly half of those will have managed only one term on the field. But that's not the worst part. Many of those who quit are lost not only to the cause of missions but to their faith as well. Disillusioned beyond belief and wounded beyond recognition, they turn their back on everything that reminds them of their pain. But that's still not the worst part. The worst part is that seventy percent of those losses are preventable.[14]

Many Christians have taken up the missions call. They have crossed cultural, linguistic, and geographic boundaries to make Jesus famous among the nations. But for all the eagerness and zeal of the missionary task force, we are often confronted with the unfortunate question: Why do so many people fall flat when they finally make it to the mission field? Why do some missionaries prematurely leave the mission field and abandon their missions call?

In 1994, the World Evangelical Fellowship Missions Commission launched the Reducing Missionary Attrition Project (ReMAP) to address specific issues related to undesirable attrition from active field service. The overall goal of the study was to reduce undesirable attrition in the long-term missionary body and thus increase the effectiveness of the global mission task force.

Between 1994 and 1996, ReMAP received surveys from 551 missionaries from fourteen sending countries.[15] In 1997, William Taylor edited and published the results in the book, *Too Valuable to Lose: Exploring the Causes and Cures of Missionary Attrition*.

The missionaries were asked to indicate the seven most important reasons why missionaries they knew had left their agency during the previous five years. Excluding retirement, the top seven reasons for attrition were listed in this order:

1. Child(ren): One or more of their offspring were unable to adapt to a new culture or had needs related to education, health, or behavior.
2. Change of job: They had completed an assignment or moved to a new post.
3. Health problems: They had issues in mental and/or physical health.
4. Lack of home support: They had inadequate financial, prayer, and/or other support from their passport country.
5. Problems with peers: They had relationship problems with mission field leaders or fellow missionaries.
6. Personal concerns: They had low self-esteem or were dealing with stress, anger, unrealistic expectations, singleness, loneliness, etc.
7. Disagreement with the agency: They had disagreements with their missionary sending body over policy, authority, etc.[16]

Gone are the days when missionaries pack their belongings in coffins knowing that they will most likely die on the foreign mission fields of the world. Modern-day global workers have multiple escape routes back home. Even those who choose to tough it out can be physically present overseas but mentally and emotionally insulated from their host culture. Today it is easier than ever to connect with family and friends back home and become detached from the very people they once sought to impact. Unprepared for the immense culture shock they face, abandoning their station often feels like the only option. What is really taking place in the mind of a missionary? How does the missions flame that once burned so brightly dwindle so quickly?

In the physical realm, the brain helps the body respond to dangerous situations. Three main parts of your body control your stress response: your hypothalamus and your pituitary (both in your brain), and your adrenal glands near your kidneys. The brain responds to stress or danger by sending immediate nerve signals down your spinal cord to the adrenal glands, telling them to release the hormone adrenaline. Once released, adrenaline increases the amount of sugar in your blood, increases your heart rate, and raises your blood pressure (amongst other actions). One might say this is the origin of the adrenaline rush of short-term missions or the "high" of the initial months on the mission field.

Your brain's remarkable hypothalamus also sends signals to your pituitary gland at the bottom of your brain, telling it to release factors that within a few minutes have traveled through your bloodstream and stimulated your adrenal cortex to produce the stress hormone cortisol. Cortisol is very important in your stress response. It keeps your blood sugar and blood pressure up to help you escape from danger.

Your body's stress response is perfect in the short-term but damaging if it goes on for weeks or years. Raised levels of cortisol for prolonged periods of time can damper your immune system and decrease the number of brain cells, impairing your memory. It can also affect your blood pressure and the fats in your blood making it more likely you will have a heart attack or stroke.[17]

The brain is the mechanism through which our thoughts pass. In chapter four, we learned that our brain is changing moment by moment as we are thinking. Our thought patterns and subsequent behaviors redesign the landscape of our brain. We cannot control life's circumstances, but we can control our response to them. Still, this can be particularly difficult in a setting foreign to our upbringing. When striking cultural differences challenge our worldview, we comb the area for something recognizable.

The way we think, what we experience, and what we do every day is very much a matter of metaphor.[18] Martin Gannon said that when humans cross into a new culture they "compare a new and uncertain situation to something with which they are thoroughly familiar in order to understand it."[19] "If the familiar is not similar to the new and uncertain," David Selvey, executive director of Faith Global Missions goes on to explain, "misunderstanding results. Living and working in a cross-cultural environment complicates individual life, family life, and work."[20]

Attrition is a genuine problem in the secular world as well. Note this insight from the business world: "Approximately thirty-percent of managers from the United States return home early from an overseas assignment."[21] Observers recognize that the primary factors are personal and family stress. What is the financial cost to business? For a single, middle-level professional, the figure is close to $150,000; for a senior professional with a family, it is $350,000 or more. But there are different price tags also. One article stated, "The human costs defy calculation. Emotional havoc, broken families, derailed careers, and illness are the price of neglecting personal well-being on the global circuit."[22]

Concerning the global missions force, it is estimated that one career missionary in twenty (5.1 percent of the mission force) leaves the mission field to return home every year. Of those who leave, 71 percent abandon post for preventable reasons. If we estimate the current long-term, international, cross-cultural missionary force at 150,000 strong (a very conservative number), an annual loss of 5.1 percent would be 7,650 missionaries leaving the field each year. Over a four-year term, this figure jumps to 30,600. Of these missionary losses, 71 percent (almost 22,000) could be prevented.[23]

Over twenty years have passed since ReMAP findings appeared in the book *Too Valuable to Lose*. Researchers admitted that the data they collected "should be seen as a starter study, not a definitive answer to the causes of attrition."[24] That's why in 2003, World Evangelical Alliance conducted ReMAP II, with the results discussed in *Worth Keeping: Global Perspectives on Best Practice in Missionary Retention*. ReMAP II expanded the pool of respondents to the administrators of approximately six hundred mission agencies in twenty-two countries, representing nearly 40,000 missionaries. Eager to understand the deeper reasons why global Kingdom workers leave the field, Craig Thompson wrote, "While ReMap focused on individual reasons for attrition, ReMAP II looked at the organizational practices that lead to retention. But something is still missing," Thompson admitted. His challenging remarks led to new research focused on "the viewpoints of returned missionaries."[25]

On November 10, 2017, Andrea Sears, the co-founder of giveDIGNITY and a missionary-in-residence at John Brown University, responded to Thompson's urge for updated data about missionary attrition. Sears and her husband opened the *Missionary Experience Survey* to returned global workers. Seven hundred forty-five former missionaries representing more than 140 foreign fields responded. Two of the nine categories for leaving the field ranked significantly higher than others: family factors and team/agency factors. Of the team/agency factors, the highest-rated factors in the decision to return to a passport country as perceived by former missionaries were "lack of missionary care, lack of integrity on the team, lack of freedom to pursue calling, team conflict, and confusion over role on the team."[26]

While these results point to some intriguing conclusions, there is still much left to discover. However, the initial results show that unlike previous studies, today's global Kingdom workers require intentional missionary member care. This new study hopes "to uncover valuable stories that will ultimately help missionaries better serve and be served in the future."[27]

Nik and Ruth Ripken could have allowed the death of their son, Timothy, to derail their missionary call. Indeed, with so many missionaries abandoning their posts each year, who would have blamed them? Yet, though they felt an overwhelming sense of loss and were tempted to throw in the towel, they plodded on. They rode the wave of God's glory, uncertain where the tide might take them, becoming advocates for the missions endeavor.

A Plane Ride to Hell

The idyllic, fertile green Nairobi hills faded in the distance as the twin-engine Red Cross plane glided along its flight path toward Somaliland. The landscape shifted quickly. The plane soared past the parched brown terrain of northeast Kenya and over the forbidding mountains and desolate desert of southern Ethiopia. The aircraft finally descended into "hell" by way of a bombed-out, single-landing-strip airport on the dusty outskirts of a city called Hargeisa.[28]

In early 1992, when Nik Ripken disembarked the plane, he was appalled at the first sights of Somalia. Every man working as airport security carried an automatic weapon. Nearby, women and children poked wearily through piles of refuse in search of food. Two Somali guards napped inside a shed, lounging atop stacked cases of hand grenades, AK-47s, rocket launchers, landmines, and assorted other ammunition.

"Ripken!" the Red Cross pilot called to Nik, "I can't promise when I'll be back to get you out of here." Weather conditions and the ongoing conflict in Somalia dictated his schedule. "I might be able to get back next week," the pilot said. "Or it could be two or three weeks, maybe even a month. Things get crazy sometimes. We don't make definite plans."[29]

One year earlier, the government collapsed as the Somali Civil War broke out. Virtually all Westerners and international groups pulled up stakes and left the country before the end of 1991. In the power vacuum that remained, various armed factions competed for influence. The nation was in ruins. Abject poverty evidenced in every alley, and death loomed over every street. Heaps of brick, rebar, and rubble situated where schools, hospitals, police stations, and sports fields once stood. Cardboard boxes and pathetic patchwork camps housed thousands of rural refugees.

Emaciated mothers scratched at the dry earth with nothing but bony fingers and broken sticks. Ripken wondered what they were doing. Shivers went down his spine when he realized the horrific reality. "Out of that hard, unforgiving ground," he said, "they were gouging out graves deep enough to gently lay a child's dead body and cover it with rocks." Words failed him. He watched in utter disbelief. "Hell" was the only relevant description of such a torturous misery.

"The Bible doesn't describe hell in great detail [and] Scripture does not ever pinpoint its precise location," Nik later wrote.

> Many theologians contend that the worst thing to be endured in hell is eternal separation from God. I had only been in [the country] for a few days. Yet I had already seen enough of evil and

its effects to decide that this place felt like total separation from God. It seemed to be a complete disconnect from all that was good in the universe.[30]

Nik was shocked with sensory overload, and his mind was spinning. On the third night of his arrival, he rested in a sleeping bag spread out on a concrete floor. "Lord, why me?" he questioned. "Why here?" Nothing in his upbringing, education, or professional experience equipped him to live or work in a place like Somalia. "What in the world do You expect me to do here, Lord?" he demanded.

> There are no churches and hardly any Somali believers. There are no pastors, no deacons, no elders, no Sunday schools, and no Bible studies. There is nothing here that I recognize! There is nothing that I know how to do here! I am hopelessly lost. I am all alone behind enemy lines. Please, Jesus, get me out of here![31]

The handful of Christians living among Somalia's seven-million Muslim citizens could hardly fill one small country church in Ripken's rural Kentucky hometown. In the midst of such suffering, what could one man do? He had no answers, and wasn't sure where to find them.

But God glories to dispatch His people into the depths of a fallen world where suffering is the standard system. He revels not in the affliction of His people but in their potential to overcome the kingdom of darkness. He equips His sons for battle and qualifies His daughters for combat. The Holy Spirit is an ever-present help in time of trouble. He beckons believers to follow Him into the darkness that His light might shine through them, illuminating the atmosphere with His glory.

When Nik found himself surrounded by the shadowy presence of evil, he could have caved. Instead, he discovered that the Source of supernatural strength is manifest through weakness and inability. God has rigged the world in such a way that victory can only be experienced through risk. So, he began to dream big, and his dreams evolved into defiance. Dead set against the opinions of the masses, he gave interviews and published articles advocating an immediate response to the growing crisis in Somalia. Churches and Christian organizations agreed that something must be done. "But until there is improved security," they argued, "there is little anyone can do."

Nik was frustrated by this response. Secular humanitarian groups and Western construction companies established inroads in the country, but the faith community was nowhere to be found. "How is it," Nik wondered, "that so many people are willing to die for financial or humanitarian reasons while many Christian groups insist on waiting until it is safe to obey Jesus' command to 'Go' into all the world? [He] commanded His followers to go into 'all the world'— not only into all 'the safe places in the world.'"[32]

Despite the challenges, in mid-1992, Nik and Ruth established a small business venture in the capital city of Somalia. With his family still based in Nairobi, Kenya, Nik made multiple trips in and out of the country. Stocked with basic medical supplies, their mobile clinics provided the first health care that some Somali villages had seen for years. As the fledgling operation grew, the United Nations' administrators approved them as a partnering non-government organization. Suddenly, they were asked to transport millions of dollars' worth of international aid to the Somali people.

Between 1991 and 1992, a staggering 300,000 Somalians are believed to have died of starvation.[33] Another 1,500,000 people became displaced refugees. As the complete breakdown of civil order ensued, violence and anarchy reigned supreme. In response to a public outcry for action, in August 1992, the United States launched Operation Provide Relief in partnership with the United Nations. The initiative aimed to secure and facilitate the delivery of humanitarian relief to starving Somalians. Over the next five months, ten military cargo planes delivered almost half a million tons of food and medical supplies. However, most of the relief supplies were looted by militants shortly upon arrival.

On December 5, 1992, president George H. W. Bush committed 25,000 American combat troops to Somalia to spearhead the newly renamed United Nations' relief effort, Operation Restore Hope. The goal of this deployment was "to prepare the way for a return to peacekeeping and post-conflict peace-building"[34] and authorize the use of "all necessary means to establish as soon as possible a secure environment for humanitarian relief operations in Somalia."[35]

As the first wave of United States Marines arrived, the Ripkens intensified their efforts and established five feeding centers in and around the capital city. Their team distributed food for 10,000 people each day at each center, keeping 50,000 people a day from starving.

Even though their mom-and-pop relief venture mushroomed into a professional, multinational organization, Nik wondered if they were making any difference at all. There was so much physical, emotional, and spiritual hurt to heal. He desired to raise Christ-followers, but in the Islamic environment, he could not openly share the Gospel.

On October 3, 1993, the United States Task Force Ranger was dispatched to Somalia to root out rebel forces. The seventeen-hour battle at the Olympic Hotel resulted in the loss of eighteen American soldiers and seven hundred Somalis. The engagement—named the "Battle of Mogadishu"—took place one mile away from the Ripkens' headquarters. The story was later made famous by the book and movie entitled *Black Hawk Down*.

The Ripkens continued to minister relief, but the next two years brought more death and destruction. A handful of their staff members—some of the only known Christians in the country—were murdered. The people in their organization invested blood, sweat, and tears, but with so few tangible results.

In the spring of 1995, the United Nations pulled its staff out of the country. Uncertainty filled the atmosphere. The poor still struggled to acquire the basic necessities of life. Local clans still fought. The desperation was inexhaustible. After six years in Somalia, each morning only brought more tears. "Certainly, we had eased suffering and saved tens of thousands of lives," Nik said. "But for how long? And to what end? Was Somalia better off now than when we had first arrived?"[36]

As security worsened toward the end of 1996, the Ripkens were forced to leave the unstable environment. They closed their organization and wondered if the last six years had been worth the effort. Life was about to take a new turn, and questions about God's sovereignty would become more personal. The death that loomed over the hellish Somalian atmosphere followed Nik home to Nairobi.

Months after the Ripkens closed their organization, they awoke in the early hours of Easter morning, 1997. Their son, Timothy, stumbled into his parents' room, gasping for air. Nik grabbed his keys, helped his son into the car, and sped toward the emergency room. The world spun at a dizzying pace as the pervading darkness enclosed around Timothy. Clutching his seatbelt, he panted for air. He exhaled. His eyes rolled back, and he slipped out of consciousness. Everything fell silent—the voices of doctors and nurses, father and mother—like a pantomime of speechless gesticulations. The day of his Savior's resurrection darkened tomblike on earth as Timothy's spirit bounded toward the brilliant light of a Heavenly Kingdom.

Do all things truly work together for good for those who are called according to God's purpose? After all the horrible sufferings that Nik and Ruth witnessed, the death of their son felt like insult upon injury. But in the strange way that time heals all wounds, the scars of their suffering would remind them of their Savior's triumph. Soon, God would grant the Ripkens an extra measure of grace to ease the suffering of Christians around the world.

Our Witness to the Power of the Resurrection

Some risks that we are called to take are worthier than others. Behind us stands a great cloud of witnesses—a host of Christian men and women who have gone before us. While on mission, many of them lost family and friends. They buried their children on foreign soil or in the ocean waters they crossed during long voyages abroad. Their sacrifices do not negate the physical challenges that modern-day missionaries face, but they do call into question our commitment to the commands of Christ. Are the occasional illnesses we encounter credible enough to crash our calling? Are the inconveniences of traffic and transportation reason enough to throw in the towel? And what if God asks us to lay down our loved ones for the sake of the Gospel? Is Jesus worth it? Will we put our hands to the plow and not look back? These are valid questions. They cause us to consider the underlying motivations beneath our behavior. They call us to contemplate the foundation of our expectations. They dare us to discover to what extremes we will go in our risky endeavors. They ask us to anticipate whether the establishment of God's Kingdom on earth is our primary goal.

In 1998, the year after Timothy Ripken passed away, the Holy Spirit led Nik and Ruth on a global pilgrimage to learn from believers in persecution. They hashed over their years of service in the Horn of Africa, pondering what they could have done differently. They thought about the sacrifices they made and the struggles they encountered. Could they rise from such loss and continue to minister in difficult environments? Could faith survive and thrive in a place like Somalia? Undoubtedly, wherever believers suffered for their faith, the Kingdom of God effectively advanced. They embarked on a journey to find out how persecuted Christians thrive on mission.

Nik's first trip brought him to Russia and half a dozen former Iron Curtain countries. There he met a man named Dmitri who was imprisoned for his faith for seventeen years. "Dmitri's story [was] one of the most remarkable and life-changing testimonies I have ever heard," Ripken said.[37] The Russian man recounted his imprisonment in a tiny jail cell where he was the only believer among 1,500 hardened criminals. Every morning at daybreak, Dmitri stood by his cot, raised his hands, and worshiped aloud. His fellow prisoners laughed and jeered, banging metal cups against the iron bars in angry protest. Some threw human waste to try to shut him up.

For years, his jailers threatened him with death if he did not recant his faith in Jesus. They promised to torture his family unless he signed a confession of his supposed crimes against the state. When he would not renounce his faith, the guards dragged him down the prison corridor to execute him. But the strangest thing happened then: 1,500 hardened criminals stood by their beds, raised their hands, and began to sing. The guards were shocked as worship resounded through the prison. "Who are you?" one of them demanded to know. Dmitri responded: "I am a son of the Living God, and Jesus is His name!" Caught off guard, his jailers returned him to his cell. Sometime later, Dmitri was released, and he returned to his family.[38]

Most of us will never be imprisoned or sentenced to death for our faith. The question is: Will we stand in freedom the way Dmitri did in confinement? If true discipleship is a dicey undertaking, why is it that many Western believers live such lackadaisical lives? Why do we who enjoy religious freedom find it so difficult to make a public stance for Christ?

Stoyan, an energetic and friendly sixty-year-old man in an unnamed Eastern European country, challenged Ripken's paradigm. At age twelve, Stoyan's father was imprisoned for his faith. For years, he underwent unimaginable difficulties, and in his absence, his family suffered. Still, Stoyan committed his life to Christ and he, too, was later jailed. Nik listened to his story, wondering how it applied to American believers. With a passionate, prophetic-like gesture, Stoyan leaned forward and poked Nik in the chest with his forefinger. "Don't ever give up in freedom what we would never have given up in persecution!" he said. What must a Christian never give up? To Stoyan it was simple: "That is our witness to the power of the resurrection of Jesus Christ!"[39]

What Nik and Ruth found was that Christians are persecuted for two reasons: they chose to follow Jesus and they decided to not keep Him to themselves. This is, in effect, the crux of our conversation about life's physical challenges. Struggles come to every human being in some form or another, but amidst tough circumstances, Christians have an eternal hope. We identify with believers in chains when we accept Christ and share Him with others. When we keep Jesus to ourselves, we identify with the ones who chained them. How dare we forsake the chance to preach about Jesus' resurrection power openly! Believers in persecution are presently proclaiming this truth, undeterred by the inevitable negative repercussions.

Do we believe that the resurrection power of Jesus is available to us today? We read about the radical accounts of His followers in the first-century Church. The New Testament shows us the power of the Gospel released through uncompromising men and women of faith. Is this power still promised to us today? Our brothers and sisters undergoing persecution emphatically pronounce this truth: God's grace enables us not only to survive but to thrive in our mission to make His name known.

The Ripkens went from Eastern Europe to China, India, and Central and Southeast Asia. They traveled to the Persian Gulf, the Middle East, and finally returned to the place it all started for them: the Horn and across Northern Africa. They spent time in over seventy-two countries and interviewed more than six hundred believers in persecution.[40] "There is no such thing as the 'free Church' and the 'persecuted Church,'" Ruth said. "There is just the Church. Believers in chains are as much a part of my body as the person sitting next to me on Sunday morning. When they're in pain, I should be in pain."[41] When we experience the physical challenges of life, it is comforting to know that we are a part of the body of Christ. Global Kingdom workers who are thinking about throwing in the towel would do well to remember this truth. Jesus' resurrection power is available to every single believer. We are more than conquerors through Christ Jesus our Lord. Still, the process of pain is never easy.

"After Tim's death," Nik said, "I left Africa wondering how my faith applied—or *if* it applied—in brutal places like [Somalia]." He said they went to Somalia believing in what the Bible proclaims about the resurrection power of Jesus. "Six years later," he continued,

> I fled home, doubting that power, and wondered if perhaps evil was stronger than God. If that kind of resurrection power couldn't be found in the world today, I had a problem... I had important questions to answer... What was the point of the last fifteen years of my life? And what was I going to do with the rest of my life?[42]

These questions formed the basis of Nik's book, *The Insanity of God: A Story of True Faith Resurrected*.

If we want to thrive amidst the physical challenges of life, our prayer must be, "Lord, protect us from harm but not from the lessons we need to learn." We utter this kind of prayer when we realize that we are sojourners awaiting our eternal dwelling place. We are *in* the world but not *of* it. Though we are *sent into* the world, it is not our home; we look forward to a Heavenly Kingdom.

Dear missionary, are you thinking about throwing in the towel? Pause to consider the eternal implications of that decision. Dear Christian, are you wondering what affect your witness makes? Remember that God is always working behind the scenes to accomplish His purposes. When you decide to seek first the Kingdom of God and allow Him to work through your willing obedience, you essentially accept the fact that you are a transient in this world. "People who live this way make it plain that they are looking for their true home," Paul wrote in the book of Hebrews. "If they were homesick for the old country, they could have gone back any time they wanted. But they were after a far better country than that—Heaven country. You can see why God is so proud of them, and has a City waiting for them."[43]

Though we now encounter pain and difficulty, God promises us a glorious future. In the meantime, He gives us the gift of the Holy Spirit—an ever-present help in times of trouble. Reliant on God's promises, we are overcomers committed to making Christ known whenever we go. How, then, can we reconcile the fact that 7,650 missionaries will leave the field this year? Why is missionary attrition so prevalent among the global task force? Are we so homesick for our country of origin and its conveniences that we forget about our transient state as Christians on the earth? And what about the physical challenges of the mission field? Does Jesus' resurrection power lead to longevity in the missions calling? Those who endure the difficulties of cross-cultural service and recognize they are pilgrims on the earth encourage us to expand God's Kingdom despite the difficulties.

Samuel Zwemer, known as "The Apostle to Islam," once wrote:

> [The great pioneer missionaries] all had 'inverted home-sickness'—this passion to call that country their home which was most in need of the Gospel. In this passion all other passions died; before this vision, all other visions faded; this call drowned all other voices. They were the pioneers of the Kingdom, the fore-lopers of God, eager to cross the border-marches and discover new lands or win new empires.[44]

Does such a fervent zeal burn in our hearts today? In a time when nationalism bleeds into the margins of faith, it can be difficult to decipher the difference between the Kingdom of God and the kingdoms of man. Led to believe that loyalty to country is our primary obligation, many Christians misunderstand correct Kingdom values. God's dominion knows no boundaries. His global plan includes every territory on earth. The Great Commission task summons every believer to lift their eyes toward higher ground; to recognize that people are precious to God's heart—even those whose cultures, customs, and countries contrast our worldview. In short, the missionary life is no easy assignment.

Brian and Louise Hogan buried their infant, Jedidiah, in the sloping plains of Mongolia. Nik and Ruth Ripken laid their son, Timothy, to rest in Kenyan soil. So, too, has the blood of Christian martyrs soaked the entire globe, giving life to scattered Gospel seeds sown in faith. They knew that this was not their home, so they lifted their gaze to the cross. Sadly, that is often where our watchful eyes stop—at the place of suffering and crucifixion. The life of the missional Christian often feels more tomblike—as if framed in the fate of Good Friday—than teeming with resurrection power. However, this notion could not be farther from the truth.

In the early hours of Easter, March 28, 1997, Timothy Ripken passed irrevocably beyond the veil. The secret of God's sovereignty, however, was that he was now more "at home" than he ever had been before. Though his body stopped breathing, his spirit rejoiced in the presence of God Almighty. Nik and Ruth's hearts broke, but Timothy grasped a long-concealed reality. Paul articulated this truth best when he wrote:

Who shall separate us from the love of Christ? Shall trouble or hardship or persecution or famine or nakedness or danger or sword? As it is written: 'For Your sake we face death all day long; we are considered as sheep to be slaughtered.' No, in all these things we are more than conquerors through Him who loved us. For I am convinced that neither death nor life, neither angels nor demons, neither the present nor the future, nor any powers, neither height nor depth, nor anything else in all creation, will be able to separate us from the love of God that is in Christ Jesus our Lord.[45]

Past the veil between this and the afterlife, on Easter Day, Timothy saw his risen King. And looking back beyond space and time, he witnessed the power of the resurrection.

CHAPTER EIGHT
EMOTIONAL STRUGGLES

A Tragic Heroine

History has not been kind to Mrs. Dorothy Carey. The portrait painted of the woman who accompanied her husband to India and remained there until the end of her increasingly unhappy life has often been unseemly, even loathsome at times. Early biographers often presented Dorothy as a stumbling block and millstone to her great husband. She was, however, a typical woman of her age and social class, a woman who possessed some exaggerated fears; a woman of sheltered experience who was asked to take on the gargantuan task of being the partner of a workaholic genius.[1]

For her, the missionary endeavor was a certain death to self. In fact, physical challenges, poverty, and death loomed over William and Dorothy. In 1783, disease struck. Before her second birthday, their daughter Ann died of fever. That fever nearly took William's life as well, leaving him bald the rest of his life. This unwanted intimacy with death was, perhaps, what became the origin of Dorothy's deep depression and mental fog.

Poverty was an ever-present companion to the Careys. The meager wages of a cobbler's salary hardly garnered enough to survive. But the community of 800 inhabitants in the obscure, rural village of Paulerpury, in the middle of England, respected the shoemaker. Every other Sunday, William Carey was invited to preach at a church in a nearby village; and in 1785, he was appointed the schoolmaster for the Moulton village. He also served as pastor of the local Baptist church.

It was during this time that he became deeply concerned with prop-
agating the Christian Gospel throughout the world. In 1787, at a small
Baptist ministerial association, the chairman asked the members to
propose a subject for discussion. Without hesitation, William Carey, one
of the newest members, suggested that Jesus' command to go into all the
world with the Gospel was a charge fit for every Christian present. The
chairman, surprised by such a radical notion at the time, responded with a
harsh rebuke: "Young man, sit down!" he quipped. "You are an enthusiast.
When God pleases to convert the heathen, he'll do it without consulting you
or me."[2] But the young enthusiast's missions zeal burned all the more, and
the fiery passion he possessed would be felt around the world.

Two years later, Carey became the full-time pastor of Harvey Lane Baptist
Church. Three years later, in 1792, he published his groundbreaking missionary manifesto, *An Enquiry into the Obligations of Christians to Use Means for
the Conversion of the Heathens*. The book arrived at a time of hyper-Calvinist
belief then prevalent in the Baptist churches, which suggested that all men
were not responsible to believe the Gospel. The temptation to domesticate
the Gospel is prevalent in every generation. Church leaders at the time did
not comprehend their role in the Great Commission. They left the ends of the
earth to God, unaware that men are God's means of proclaiming His message.

Antagonistic toward this mindset, the flame of Carey's missionary fervor
provoked his parishioners toward radical compassion for the lost and obedience to the commands of Christ. "Expect great things from God; attempt
great things for God," he said.[3] This epigram became his most famous quo-
tation. His words were not for his hearers only but also for himself. William
Carey made a conscious and calculated risk to leave home and country for
the goldmine of souls in India.

Carey, along with a small band of Baptist pastors, formed the Baptist
Missionary Society on October 2, 1792. One of the pastors recorded the
event from which came the famous "rope holder" story. He wrote:

> Our undertaking to India really appeared to me, on its com-
> mencement, to be somewhat like a few men, who were delib-
> erating about the importance of penetrating into a deep mine,
> which had never before been explored, [and] we had no one to
> guide us; and while we were thus deliberating, Carey, as it were,

said, 'Well, I will go down, if you will hold the rope.' But before he went down... he, as it seemed to me, took an oath from each of us, at the mouth of the pit, to this effect—that 'while we lived, we should never let go of the rope.'[4]

In April 1793, Carey uprooted his family from all their familiarities in England. Dorothy was pregnant with their fourth son at the time and so refused to leave England. She had never been more than a few miles away from home. Now she was pressured with the arduous task of international travel by ship to Calcutta. Not long before they were to set sail to India, Dorothy conceded and reluctantly boarded the ship.

William, Dorothy, and their four sons arrived in Calcutta on November 11, 1793. With little support and dwindling funds, they soon found themselves dependent on others for food and shelter. The early transition took its toll. Over the next seven months, they moved five times.

Subjected to new and unforeseen tropical diseases, Dorothy's health deteriorated as she struggled with bleeding. Then the family sustained a bitter blow on October 11, 1794, when their five-year-old son, Peter, died. In the next three months, the unimaginable ensued. Shortly before March 1795, Dorothy passed beyond the nebulous border between sound rationality and mental insanity. For the remaining twelve years of her life, she was to remain bound in the devastating grip of psychosis. "I have greater affliction than any of these in my family," William wrote to his sisters in England on October 5, 1795.

> Known to my friends here, but I have never mentioned it to anyone in England before, is my poor wife, who is looked upon as insane to a great degree here by both native and Europeans... I have been for some time past in danger of losing my life. Jealousy is the great evil that haunts her mind.[5]

Visiting friends shockingly witnessed the appalling state of the Carey household. Dorothy uttered the most blasphemous and foul things against her husband and became physically abusive. One morning at breakfast, she grabbed William by the hair, held a knife to him, and screamed, "Curse you! I could cut your throat!" It was not the first attempt made on his life.

Three months later, John Thomas, a medical missionary and friend of the Carey family wrote, "Mrs. C[arey] has taken it into her head that C[arey] is a great whoremonger; and her jealousy burns like fire unquenchable." Thomas added that Dorothy obsessed with Carey's supposed unfaithfulness and would follow him every time he left the house. "[She] declares in the most solemn manner that she has [caught] him with his servants, with his friends, with Mrs. Thomas, and that he is guilty every day and every night... In all other things she talks sensibly."[6]

James Beck, author of *Dorothy Carey: The Tragic and Untold Story of Mrs. William Carey*, writes, "Today we would diagnose Dorothy's condition as a Delusional Disorder (formerly paranoia), Jealous Type. The prognosis for intense delusional conditions is poor today, just as it proved to be for Dorothy 200 years ago."[7] Several friends encouraged William to commit his wife to an insane asylum. But Carey refused to assign her to such a place for fear of the treatment she might receive. Instead, he took the responsibility to keep her at the family home, even though his children witnessed her ongoing fits of rage.

Amidst such familial turmoil, it is astonishing that William Carey, often called the Father of Modern Missions, accomplished all that he did for the modern missions movement. During his missionary career, he translated the complete Bible into six languages and portions of 29 others. His service marked a turning point that sparked a new era in missions. It marked "the entry of the English-speaking world on a large scale into the missionary enterprise," writes historian Tom Payne, "—and it has been the English-speaking world which has provided four-fifths of the [Protestant] missionaries from the days of Carey until the present time."[8]

Dorothy Carey faced a tremendous amount of mental stress on the mission field. She encountered emotional struggles that many global Christian workers face when adjusting to new foods, customs, and climates. Yet she failed to adjust emotionally and mentally, though no fault of her own.

We can only hypothesize about the reasons for her unremitting psychosis. She had buried two daughters in England before traveling to India. She lost touch with extended family back home. Within a year of her arrival in Calcutta, her five-year-old son, Peter, died of dysentery. She had not chosen the missionary life; only under great pressure did she change her mind and abandon the normalcy of England. Her temperament was prone to fearfulness, and the triggers that elicited her mental anxiety and eventual nervous breakdown were bold and unambiguous.

In some ways, it feels befitting, then, that historians and biographers painted her in such a poor light. Yet one cannot help but feel a sense of compassion for the would-be Mother of Modern Missions. Perhaps she might better be recognized as a tragic heroine who unwittingly gave her sanity, and ultimately her life, for Christ and His cause.[9]

Dorothy's long battle with psychosis came to an end when she died on December 8, 1807 at the age of 51. Few back home knew anything about her emotional and mental struggles. A telescoped notice in the 1808 *Periodical* informed the public of her passing with these brief words: "Mrs. Carey, after having been ill about a fortnight, died."

What Kind of a Missionary Am I?

The Frasers look like fashion models on an H&M advertisement. With hair combed up into a wave crest above his high forehead, Drew is reminiscent of Conan O'Brien with the addition of a handsomely-trimmed ginger beard. Deanna is the ultimate hipster-creative-meets-soccer-mom, sprinkled with an ample measure of eager optimism evidenced by her warm smile. They both alternate between contacts and quirky, thick-rimmed glasses that scream "relevant Millennial." I have always known the Frasers to be jovial and enthusiastic about God, faith, family, and life in general.

Drew and Deanna left for the mission field right out of Bible school. Their hearts burned with a passion to reach the unreached in China. They knew it wouldn't be easy, but they longed for God's Kingdom to manifest to those who had never heard the Message before.

Though the contrasts between Ontario, Canada and Kunming, China were striking, the Frasers welcomed this new adventure. They hit the ground running. They enrolled in language school and studied Mandarin. They explored numerous possibilities for ministry. Drew immediately found his niche as a professional skateboarder while Deanna struggled to find her place in China.

"After six years on the mission field, I saw and experienced things that shook me to the core," Deanna told me.

> I had two children and a miscarriage. Two of my family members passed away while we were overseas. The environment was

unhealthy, and the humidity was stifling. We dealt with stressful tensions in our team. My kids and I were constantly fighting sickness, and the area where we lived did not have proper healthcare. Even everyday errands and visits to the grocery store filled with drama and inconceivable conflict.[10]

Deanna's words trailed off, and her sigh evocatively expressed the enigmatic circumstances of the mission field. Her forehead revealed the thoughtfulness that comes not only with age but by weathering the demands of life. I thought I recognized a trace of sorrow on her cheekbones and in her folded hands.

She continued: "Our son, Aaron, started pre-school and we found out one of the teachers was physically abusing the children in his class. Luckily, we found this out before Aaron was hurt, though several times he had been bitten to the point of bleeding by a classmate." This was common in China. Deanna knew many others who had experienced worse treatment than her son, but she had no idea how to cope. She assumed everyone else just sucked it up and "got through" this sort of thing.

She woke up one morning to the sound of her son coughing uncontrollably with pneumonia. She rushed to the store to restock her medicine supply. "I spent the entire time talking to myself. *Calm down, Deanna, I told myself. Aaron is going to be fine. It's going to be okay. Everything is going to be fine. You're okay.* But I was not okay." When she returned home, she saw her brother, who had come to China for a visit. He wore Deanna's recently deceased grandfather's coat. She collapsed on the floor, shaking and unable to catch her breath. "I began crying uncontrollably," she told me. "My heart was beating so profusely, I could almost hear it."

Deanna began to have multiple panic attacks per day. Some days, she sobbed uncontrollably; other days, she felt absolutely nothing. "I was scared. I thought I was going insane. I was afraid to go outside. Crowds terrified and overwhelmed me. I could no longer take care of my kids. I just sat on the couch or laid in bed, unable to function."[11]

Author and missionary coach, Sarita Hartz, is an avid proponent of missionary health and wholeness. She writes that

> many missionaries experience cumulative trauma, which is not tied to one specific event, but many difficult events over

time which range from vicarious trauma, conflict on the field, rejection, to guilt and feelings of failure. However, missionaries rarely admit depressive symptoms because they view depression, brokenness, or Post Traumatic Stress Syndrome (PTSD) as a sin or lack of faith.[12]

Research confirms that an astronomically high percentage of missionaries experiences trauma on the field. In a survey by the *Journal of Psychology & Christianity* in 1983, 91 percent of women and 88 percent of men said they were more stressed working as missionaries than they were beforehand, with women bearing a higher brunt of that stress.[13]

The widely accepted definition of stress (mainly attributed to Richard S. Lazarus) is this: Stress is a condition or feeling experienced when a person perceives that "demands exceed the personal and social resources the individual is able to mobilize." Otherwise stated, we become stressed when we feel that "things are out of control."[14]

In 1967, psychiatrists, Thomas Holmes and Richard Rahe, began to study whether stress contributes to illness. They surveyed more than 5,000 medical patients and asked if they had experienced any of a series of 43 stressful life events in the previous two years. Each of the events in the survey, called a Life Change Unit (LCU), had a different "weight" for stress. The patients marked the events that they experienced and tallied their marks to find their overall score. The higher the score, and the larger the weight of each event, the higher the probability that the patient would become ill. The Holmes-Rahe Stress Scale included the death of a spouse, divorce, marital separation, jail term, death of a close family member, personal injury or illness, marriage, etc.

The original 1967-1970 study found that if a person reached a level of 200 on the scale in a year, the cumulative stress would have consequences for some time to come. In fact, they found that 50 percent of those who reached this level were hospitalized within two years. The reasons included heart attack, diabetes, cancer, and other severe illness. If a person reached a level of 300, they were almost certain to end up in the hospital within two years.

In 1999, doctors Lois and Larry Dodds of Heartstream Resources began to study the levels of stress on the mission field using a modified version of the Holmes-Rahe Stress Scale. First-term missionaries were found to have scores peaking at a whopping 900, while veterans maintained 600-plus year after year. Remember, according to the research, people with a score above 200 will likely have serious, long-term health problems within two years.

This evidence clearly concludes that the "normalcy" of the missionary lifestyle is three times higher than the average "danger level" of stress. That means while the average person requires a decent amount of self-care, rest, and rejuvenation, and a person in the danger zone requires even more, a missionary realistically requires a bare minimum of at least three times the amount of attention to self-care than the average person.

Ron and Bonnie Koteskey, member care consultants with Go International, state that the three main causes of missionary burnout are: Social, System, and Self.[15]

- Social: The "problem people" require much more of the missionary's attention than do the "pleasant people." As a result, they begin to see even good people as problem people. They are supposed to be polite, tactful, and caring, so they feel like they cannot express the disappointment and frustration that they feel deep down inside.

- System: The missionary's job setting may be a source of burnout, as can language acquisition. There are so many people to get to know, so much to do, and so little time to do it. The missionary is busy doing God's work, and there is such a need everywhere they look that there is no time for breaks or for vacations. Team differences and lack of finances are also a huge part of the equation.

- Self: The missionary mind itself may be a source of burnout. If a missionary lacks self-confidence or has low self-esteem, he is a candidate for burnout. If missionaries are unassertive, submissive, passive, anxious, and blame themselves for failure, they are a candidate. If their needs for achievement, approval, and affection are too high, they are a candidate. If they are impatient, irritable, and do not know how to handle anger and conflict, they are a candidate for burnout.

Do you recall how we learned in chapter four that most missionaries possess a strong Belief theme? They sensed the call of duty and have responded by going where many Christians dared not. But global Kingdom workers must understand that this driving sense of Belief simply serves to reveal God's ability amidst their own inabilities. "Not only can committed missionaries burn out, but the more committed they are, the more likely they are to burn out," Koteskey says.

> If people slip through the screening process with major motives of travel and excitement, they can succeed at that quite readily. However, the more 'ideal' missionaries are, with hearts to win people to Christ, concern for others, and high expectations, the more likely they are to burn out.[16]

"I expected to be impacting hundreds of locals in their native language," Deanna told me,

> but after six years, I could barely manage simple conversations with the people in my apartment complex. I expected to love the lowly, but I was often uncomfortable and repulsed by their smells and lack of manners. I wanted to be the best mom, but I was screaming at my kids on a daily basis. I wanted to be the perfect wife, but I was always angry with Drew, laying loads of guilt on him. I wanted to please God, but I felt angry at Him. What kind of a missionary am I?[17]

It's Like We Live in a Fishbowl

The missionary task is a unique and often misunderstood endeavor. The misconceptions usually occur when the body of Christ readily recognizes what we learned in chapter three: that every Christian is a "sent one" who is "on mission" and is called to "live missionally;" yet the Church forgets to differentiate the unique role that an overseas Kingdom worker plays. The role of a missionary must not be elevated above the task of every Christ-follower. The charge that Jesus gave to His disciples was the same—"Go, therefore, and make disciples of all nations." Some are called to their respective "Jerusalems," some to the "Judeas," others to the Samarias," and others to "the ends of the earth."

Still, upon crossing cultural, linguistic, and geographic barriers, global missionaries are faced with tremendous and often unforeseen pressures unknown to those who remain at home. When asked about the emotional struggles on the mission field, one of my missionary friends, who wishes to remain anonymous, responded with a barrage of one-liners that she confronts: "Rejection, betrayal, territorialism, competition, and homesickness. Guilt of not being with family during crises; guilt of never doing enough or doing well enough; disillusionment and fear of failure." As if that list were not long enough, she went on to say, "Unrelenting standards and unrealistic expectations have been a huge factor in my struggle with perfectionism and the role it has played in my depression, anxiety, and burnout."

As I hear about the multifarious difficulties that missionaries face, a deep sense of compassion for global Kingdom workers grows inside me. "It's like we live in a fishbowl," my friend in China, Michelle Blackman, told me.

> Everyone seems to have an opinion about what we do. Sometimes we feel forgotten by our home church and supporters because they don't communicate as often as we'd wish. But on our part, we feel obligated to communicate everything we do because our support drops if we stay silent.[18]

William Carey went down into the goldmine of souls in India, expecting Christians on the home front to hold the ropes. This is still the desire of global Kingdom workers today. They desire a covering of prayer from sending churches, a sincere interest in their unique fields, and a tug on the end of the rope when they are surrounded by the darkness of a distant missionary life.

Unfortunately, this is not always the reality between Christians at home and abroad. "Loneliness is a harsh reality for every missionary I know," Claire Henderson, missionary to the Philippines said. "We have such a longing for deep friendship that can be difficult to find on the mission field. I realize that the friends I left behind in Ireland still love me. It's just hard to feel the depth of our relationship when we have been detached by time and distance."[19]

Missionaries are normal people who minister in abnormal settings. Yet not every global Kingdom worker deals with the struggles of the mission field in the same way. Dozens of cross-cultural missionaries contributed to this book by taking *The Mind of a Missionary Survey*. When asked if they "have a tendency to feel anxious and become discouraged with themselves or others," Mike Pettengill, a seminary trainer in Equatorial Guinea simply said, "No chance."[20]

Andrew Braze, who does leadership development in China, Laos, Myanmar, and Thailand said, "Not very often. I keep myself busy on the goal of God's mission."[21]

"I rarely feel anxious or discouraged," said Cornelius Groenewald, a strategy coordinator for Northern Thailand's unreached people groups. "I am so focused on the unreached who have never heard the Gospel that I don't have time to give in to discouragement."[22]

These succinct responses may be admirable. But realizing that no one is immune to stress in the long run, we would do well to guard our hearts and minds while living on mission.

Overseas missionaries ought to remember that they are not the only ones who face the struggles and difficulties of life. Indeed, the difficulties on the mission field often feel compounded in a cross-cultural fishbowl, but we must regularly remind ourselves to fix our eyes on Jesus, who is the Author and Perfecter of our faith. Christ—not missions— is meant to be the life and sustenance of every Christian, whether home or abroad. For as David Platt says, "Missions is the overflow of a life in love with Christ."[23]

One of the obstacles of thriving on mission within our own contexts is taking on unwarranted responsibility. The overwhelming needs around us can snuff out our joy. Meanwhile, Jesus says, "Come to Me, all of you who are weary and carry heavy burdens, and I will give you rest."[24]

Is His promise not truth for us today? Can God truly be trusted when the world feels like it is falling apart? When Timothy Ripken died in Nairobi and infant Jedidiah Hogan passed away in Mongolia, was not the grace of God enough for their missionary parents? And what about when Chinese missionary couple, Meng Lisi and Li Xinheng, were kidnapped and later killed by extremists in Pakistan? Was Jesus worth it in such calamity? Dorothy Carey buried her daughters before her missionary journey began, only to feel the tragic loss of her son in India. Deanna was no stranger to the numerous complications of her cross-cultural mission field. When her children were sick and the medical situation dire; when her loved ones passed away and she was far from home; when the cultural adjustments became too much to bear—was not her Heavenly Father there with her amid it all?

The promise of Jesus' presence was given in the context of the Great Commission, that Christians living and operating on mission might thrive both in ministry and in personal satisfaction. Matthew 28:18-20 reads:

Then Jesus came to them and said, 'All authority in Heaven and on earth has been given to Me. Therefore, go and make disciples of all nations, baptizing them in the name of the Father and of the Son and of the Holy Spirit, and teaching them to obey everything I have commanded you. And surely, I am with you always, to the very end of the age.'[25]

Does God require compliance to His mission at the expense of His children's wholeness? Or is it His joy that we link our hearts and minds with His passion for the nations to experience the deep satisfaction of partnering with Him?

"I told God that I don't want to go back to China at this point in my life," Deanna said. "I don't want to do ministry. I need to take a break because I feel awful. I'm angry, hurt, and broken. I have nothing left to give God." Thankfully, He is a loving Father, concerned both with Chinese people who live without a witness of the Gospel and about the well-being of global workers. Deanna felt the Lord respond by saying, "I don't want you to go back to China or do ministry right now, either. I want your anger, your frustration, your fear, your pain, and your brokenness. Take My yoke upon you and I will give you rest."

In 2016, after undergoing intensive counseling in Thailand, Drew and Deanna Fraser returned to Ontario, Canada. Initially, they felt like failures. They wondered what their supporters thought of their transition back home, and they felt like they had let God down. The role of their missionary identity was stripped away, and they were no longer in the limelight. They struggled to start over in their new context.

Drew wished to remain in China, so he grappled with his own emotions at home, while Deanna sought to recover from her wounds on the mission field. "I put so much of my life into the dream of becoming a missionary that this role transformed my identity," Deanna said.

"Then I went home. If all I am is a missionary and I'm no longer on the mission field, then what am I? The expectations that others have of me and, more importantly, my expectations of myself, cannot be the basis of my identity. I am not simply the sum of what I do."

In chapter one, we learned about the role that identity plays in the mind of global Kingdom workers. When their identity is fused with their role as a missionary, the tendency is to prove their inherent worth by work and human effort. This, in turn, affects the integrity of their missions motivation, the basis of their ministry expectations, and their response to such risky endeavors; it even impacts the quality of the rewards they hope to reap. "Two years into this new season of our post-missionary lives, we are still working through the pain and loss," Deanna admitted. "But I am so thankful for what the experience produced in my marriage and my life. I spent so much time trying to be this person I thought God wanted me to be," Deanna continued. "Maybe I had to experience such disillusionment and failure so I could find out who I really am in God's eyes; so I could help others experience wholeness in their missional callings."

An enormous number of missionaries crash and burn after reentry into their passport countries. Many become jaded by their missions experience, and it is not uncommon for them to abandon their faith after such fatiguing events. I was happy to hear that Deanna began to understand the reasons for her suffering. She plans to return to school and study psychology with hopes to enhance the global missionary cause. After her extended time in China, she has grown passionate about intentional self-care, missionary member care, and the health and wholeness of Kingdom workers.

I believe Deanna's burnout story will empower the next wave of global missionaries. With more joy in her voice than sorrow, she told me, "Maybe I won't go back, but I can still help the people who will."[26]

God's Cause Will Triumph

Judged by almost any standard, the modern missionary movement, spearheaded by William Carey, was the most important historical development in the last two-hundred years. Through it, the Christian faith spread to every country and almost all the peoples of the world.[27] Stephen Neill, in the conclusion to his *History of Christian Missions*, wrote, "The cool and rational eighteenth century [which ended with William Carey's departure for India] was hardly a promising seedbed for Christian growth; but out of it came a greater outburst of Christian missionary enterprise than had been seen in all the centuries before."[28]

But the path was not without its potholes, and the man used to usher in this mighty move of God was not without plight. During the first seven years of his arrival in India, during which time he buried his five-year-old son and witnessed the beginnings of Dorothy's psychosis, Carey completed the first revision of his Bengali New Testament. His prodigious labors appear all the more remarkable when we remember how depressing must have been this domestic trial. "It will serve," says J. C. Marshman,

> to give some idea of the strength and energy of Dr. Carey's char-
> acter that the arduous biblical and literary labours in which he
> had been engaged... were prosecuted while an insane wife, fre-
> quently wrought up to a state of the most distressing excitement,
> was in the next room but one to his study.[29]

If we pause to consider Carey's stress levels according to the Dodds' modified version of the Holmes-Rahe Stress Scale, we could unequivocally surmise that his score would top the charts at an easy 900—nearly five times higher than the average "danger level" of stress. We can only speculate how his mind parsed the layers of tension that overpowered his wife, Dorothy.

At the height of this distress, Carey formed a missionary community from the workers who began to arrive in India. The growing mission community purchased a house large enough to lodge all the families and a school. He established a print shop, and from the printing press came translations of the Bible in Bengali, Sanskrit, and other major languages and dialects that had never been printed before.

On March 11, 1812, irreplaceable manuscripts, including much of Carey's translation of Sanskrit literature, burned in a fire that broke out in the print shop. Thus began the arduous task of salvaging what remained, and within six months, the mission was able to continue printing. In Carey's lifetime, the mission printed and distributed the Bible in whole or part in 44 languages and dialects.

At the turn of the nineteenth century in India, only children of a certain social class received education, and even that was insufficient. Their learning was basic and focused predominantly on Hindu religion. Carey started Sunday Schools in which children learned to read using the Bible as their textbook.[30] He also opened what was considered the first primary school in all of India. His influence in social reform marked a turning point in Indian culture. His translation work and literary labors added much value to the county, and his teaching, writing, and publications transformed educational establishments. "[Carey] saw India not as a foreign country to be exploited," wrote Indian Christian philosopher, Vishal Mangalwadi,

> but as his Heavenly Father's land to be loved and saved... He believed in understanding and controlling nature instead of fearing, appeasing, or worshipping it; in developing one's intellect instead of killing it as mysticism taught. He emphasized enjoying literature and culture instead of shunning it as maya.[31]

Carey expressed,

> When I left England, my hope of India's conversion was very strong; but amongst so many obstacles, it would die, unless upheld by God. Well, I have God, and His Word is true. Though the superstitions of the heathen were a thousand times stronger than they are, and the example of the Europeans a thousand times worse; though I were deserted by all and persecuted by all, yet my faith, fixed on the sure Word, would rise above all obstructions and overcome every trial. God's cause will triumph.[32]

By the time the Father of Modern Missions died, Carey had spent forty-one years in India without returning to England for a furlough. "I can plod," he later wrote. "I can persevere in any definite pursuit. To this I owe everything." Though not the recommended course of action—perhaps one which even contributed to his wife's mental state—the legacy of Carey's ministry reached far and wide. The results of his career missionary effort may have felt meager at the time (some 700 converts in a nation of millions), yet he laid an impressive foundation of Bible translations, education, and social reform.

More than two-hundred years have passed since Carey ushered in the great outburst of the Christian missionary enterprise. Yet modern-day missionaries still deal with a wide array of emotional struggles on the mission field. The conflicts are real and have the power to impact a future generation of missionaries.

Missionary attrition rates continue to soar, and missions agencies and sending churches would do well to consider the strength of their screening processes. Global Kingdom workers ought to be aware of the stressors they will encounter. As Christians who remain at home seek to thrive on mission in their own contexts, the body of Christ would do well to link hearts and hands in the global missionary endeavor. Some have gone down into the goldmine of souls; those who remain above must hold the ropes, for every believer has a part to play in the global missions mandate.

God, in His wisdom, chooses to use weak and unassuming misfits to accomplish His mission to redeem mankind. To the human mind, this choice seems illogical and counterintuitive, and even a bit nonsensical at times. But He has no plan B; we are His instruments of choice.

God desires that none should perish but that all should come to repentance. The modern missionary movement has its shortcomings, and the vessels through whom He uses to display His glory are cracked jars of clay. Yet God sits enthroned in Heaven, confident that His redemptive plan will succeed. He is certain that every tribe will one day stand before His throne, clothed in white robes with palm branches in their hands, and cry out with a loud voice, "Salvation belongs to our God who sits on the throne, and to the Lamb!"

CHAPTER NINE

SPIRITUAL HURDLES

Missionaries Are Not the Church's "Special Forces"

Recently, in a public post on social media, I asked people to tell me who their favorite historical missionary is. Many people responded with a host of different names: William Carey, Gladys Aylward, Amy Carmichael, Eric Liddell, the Ecuador Five, Adoniram Judson, and Hudson Taylor were some of the people mentioned.

I then asked why they selected these missionaries. They elaborated with short explanations:
- "Carey was creative and committed."
- "Aylward obeyed God rather than men. She was brave, determined, and didn't fit into the box of predetermined expectations."
- "Carmichael was all in. She loved Jesus above all else. I could go on and on."
- "Liddell abandoned fame and fortune at home and laid down his life for others."
- "The Ecuador Five dared the impossible for the people they sought to reach and gave up their lives for the cause of Christ."
- "Judson was obedient and faithful for years without converts. He was convinced of his calling no matter what the circumstances."
- "Taylor was versatile and unwavering in his desire to become like the Chinese in order to reach them with the Gospel."

God used men and women throughout history to accomplish incredible things on the earth, and many of their examples are worth following. But should we think of missionaries as heroes? Are their lives worthy of such admiration? When we esteem global Kingdom workers, do we essentially diminish the role of believers who are not called to cross-cultural service?

Jonathan Trotter is a missionary in Southeast Asia where he provides pastoral counseling at a local center. In the popular online blog, *A Life Overseas*, he says when we think of missionaries as the cream of the crop or the special forces of the Church, there are damaging consequences both to the Church at large and to the missionary himself. "When the missionary realizes he isn't superman (or super-missionary), confusion, discouragement, and maybe even depression will set in," Trotter says.

> He may be forced into secrecy, covering up and hiding the fact that he is, in fact, human. He may feel like a failure because he now realizes he's not the best of the best, like all the 'real' missionaries. He may create a thin veneer of perfection and hide behind it for a very long time. If a missionary believes these lies, and continues to believe them, she may become extremely arrogant, judgmental, and condemning. The judgment and condemnation will be aimed at other missionaries who 'just can't hack it,' as well as all the lesser people back home who never even tried. After all, she's the top of the class, the one called and equipped for greater works. Again, these attitudes make sense if she starts with the basic assumption that missionaries are better.[1]

It should be stated clearly that missionaries *are not* better Christians than those who stay at home. Each member of the body of Christ has a specific role to play, and every one of these roles is necessary. The missions venture requires that some go and some stay behind. Those who go seek to advance the Kingdom of God where it is not; those who stay at home hold the ropes in prayer and support, shining the light of Jesus in their local context. Many Christians worldwide share the missionary's heart for the advancement of God's Kingdom in the earth. Their faithful prayers often open doors for the overseas missionary to walk through unhindered. But the blessing goes both ways. The home church experiences spiritual benefits while extended family abroad witnesses breakthrough. The richness of God's spiritual outpouring cannot be contained within geographical coordinates. The soldiers who go out to battle and those who remain back to guard the supplies all share in the spoils of war.

In chapter three we learned that every Christian is a "sent one" who is "on mission" and is called to "live missionally." Hence, missionaries are not the Church's "special forces" sent into enemy territory to do battle on the front lines of the mission fields of the world. They are not the cream of the crop or the elite of the Christian Church. They are just normal people, called—like every believer—to give testimony of the greatness of God.

Trotter goes on to say that when the Church unwittingly believes these lies by aggrandizing missionaries, "It effectively keeps missions *out there*. Missions becomes something missionaries do somewhere over there. The great call of God becomes disconnected from the Church of God." Trotter is convinced that his job of loving and serving people across cultures is what he is called to do. He also knows that other people are called and equipped to do work other than overseas missions. "I sure hope they realize their work isn't second-class," he says. Because "serving cross-culturally is definitely a valid response to the Gospel, but it is not the *only* valid response to the Gospel."[2]

God is searching for dependable disciples to whom He can say, "Well done, My good and faithful servant." When each member of the body of Christ operates in their God-given talents, beautiful things happen. The lost are located, the ill get well, the violated experience victory, and the broken become beacons of hope in the world.

In epic stories such as *The Lord of the Rings* or *Star Wars*, the heroes are not the untouchable warriors, but rather the seemingly ordinary and flawed characters. They are called from their comfort place to a greater task, one of which they feel unworthy. This is what Carl Jung and Joseph Campbell call the monomyth, or the hero's journey. In this common template, the hero goes on an adventure, and in a decisive crisis, wins a victory, and then comes home changed or transformed.

In his 1949 work, *The Hero with a Thousand Faces*, Campbell describes the basic narrative pattern as follows:

> A hero ventures forth from the world of common day into a region
> of supernatural wonder: fabulous forces are [then] encountered

and a decisive victory is won: the hero comes back from this mysterious adventure with the power to bestow boons on his fellow man.[3]

It follows, then, that the overarching narrative or the aim of the journey, not the protagonist, is the focus of the narrative. The "hero" is the character through which some victory is won, or some grand purpose is accomplished.

True heroes are never self-sufficient. They need guidance and aid from others. Their task requires bravery and often highlights their weakness. Doubt and fear are always an element of their story. Sam stood by Frodo and Gandalf guided him to victory. Obi-Wan Kenobi taught Luke Skywalker the ways of the Force. In fact, all our classic heroes achieved success not by an inborn power, but through their inabilities and willingness to learn from others.

Cross-cultural missionaries live no normal lives. They venture to distant regions with the mission to make known the glory of God. They face incredible spiritual hurdles on the mission field. And as missionary pastor to Thailand, Jonathan Vickers says, "They may not be heroes, but their lives are truly heroic!"[4] Beyond belief, God provides all of His children the same potential to thrive and overcome. He delights when His whole Church breathes bravery, inhabits heroism, and perceives His pervading power.

Missionary pioneer and China Inland Mission founder, Hudson Taylor, points not to the human aspect of the missionary venture but to God as the central focus of the plot: "It is always helpful to us to fix our attention on the God-ward aspect of Christian work; to realize that the work of God does not mean so much man's work for God as God's own work through man." Taylor probably would not have considered himself a hero of the faith but rather a servant of the King, and thus a small part of the story. He goes on,

> In our privileged position of fellow-workers with Him, while fully recognizing all the benefits and blessings to be bestowed on a sin-stricken world through the proclamation of the Gospel and spread of the Truth, we should never lose sight of the higher aspect of our work—that of obedience to God, of bringing glory to His Name, of gladdening the heart of our God and Father by living and serving as His beloved children.[5]

Again, we are taken back to the underlying role of identity in the mind of a missionary. "Do you want to thrive on mission?" query global Kingdom workers. "It's not that mysterious. When you understand your identity in Christ, it is only natural that you step into your destiny as a witness of God's glory."

History's heroes of faith should be viewed as an extension of *Christ's* missionary work. Are they superheroes? By no means. Their flaws and inadequacies were often more visible than their achievements. God's work in and through them was the central focus of the grand missionary narrative.

Should we, then, view missionaries as heroes? Inevitably, we will choose our heroes somewhere: athletes, actors, or entertainers. Our search for a hero is written in our code. Young adults today desperately need role models to look up to—people who live selfless lives and do great exploits for God. It is better to cultivate a culture where our heroes call us to a life of service, faith, and sacrifice rather than to greed and pride. In essence, we ought to give honor to whom honor is due. But the danger comes when we erect exaggerated mental images of missionaries, place them on pedestals, or aggrandize their role as more important than other parts of the body of Christ. "Missionaries are a sort of art gallery of God's work in their lives," says Thailand missionary Jacob Bennett. "Do you go to a Van Gogh exhibit and view Van Gogh? No, you go to view his works. So, is it dangerous to view missionaries as heroes? I think it's more dangerous to think that Christ can't produce true heroes."[6]

My Only Claim Will Be on God

In the middle of the nineteenth-century, an unassuming hero was miraculously produced. In 1847, Amelia Taylor, stirred by a solemnity that only the Holy Spirit can elicit, rose from the dinner table, went to her room, turned the key in the door, and pleaded for hours for her only son's salvation. There, she stayed on bended knee until at length she could pray no longer, but was constrained to praise God for that which His Spirit told her had already been accomplished.[7]

Seventy or eighty miles away, Amelia's son, fifteen-year-old James Hudson Taylor, browsed through the pages of a little Gospel tract. He read the booklet in an utterly unconcerned state of mind, believing at the time that if there were any salvation, it was not for him.

A little statement in the booklet struck the boy: "The finished work of Christ." Without warning, the room filled with the presence of God, and Taylor fell to his knees. In his own words, Taylor described the moment of his conversion:

> Then came the thought, 'If the whole work was finished and the whole debt paid, what is there left for me to do?' And with this dawned the joyful conviction, as light was flashed into my soul by the Holy Spirit, that there was nothing in the world to be done but to fall down on one's knees, and accepting this Saviour and His salvation, to praise Him for evermore. Thus, while my dear mother was praising God on her knees in her chamber, I was praising Him in the old warehouse to which I had gone alone to read at my leisure this little book.[8]

Not many months after Taylor's conversion, on a leisure afternoon, he spent hours in prayer and thanksgiving. It was a momentous occasion of communion with God. Later in life, Taylor recalled that afternoon as the moment of his missionary call. "Well do I remember that occasion," Taylor said.

> I besought [the Lord] to give me some work to do for Him, as an outlet for love and gratitude; some self-denying service, no matter what it might be, however trying or however trivial; something with which He would be pleased, and that I might do for Him who had done so much for me.[9]

The time of worship concluded with Taylor prostrate on his bedroom floor, stretched out before God in an awed silence. For what service he had been accepted he knew not, but, he recalled, "a deep consciousness that I was no longer my own took possession of me, which has never since been effaced."[10]

Into the mind of the sixteen-year-old boy, the Holy Spirit spoke "China." This impression stirred his heart and thus began his search for the hard-to-come-by information about the mysterious country. Taylor learned that a minister in his native town possessed a copy of Medhurst's *China*,[11] and he requested the man to loan him the book. The man kindly obliged, asking why he wished to read it. Young Taylor told the minister that God had called him to spend his life in missionary service in the land. The man replied, "Ah, my boy, as you grow older you will get wiser than that. Such an idea would do very well in the days when Christ Himself was on earth, but not now."[12]

Taylor grew older but never so wise as to deny Christ's call on his life. The young man was single-minded and resolute. Every task to which he concerned himself was in preparation for his missionary service. He distributed Gospel tracts, taught Sunday School, and regularly visited the sick and poor. Taylor disposed of his feather bed to sleep on the floor in order to prepare himself for rougher lines of work. He examined his material life, wondering if there were any earthly possessions he could live without. He browsed his library and wardrobe for excess, giving away his books and clothing. "The result was that the library was considerably diminished, to the benefit of some poor neighbors, and to the far greater benefit of my own soul,"[13] he later wrote.

Medhurst's book on China emphasized the value of medical missions there, so in 1852, as a valuable mode of preparation for working in China, he began studying medicine at the Royal London Hospital. While studying medicine, motivated both by the spiritual needs of the Chinese and for the global glory of God, he immersed himself ever deeper into the Bible and prayer.

But for all his altruistic missionary motives, Taylor knew that going to China was a grave matter. He would have no human aid. He would rely on God alone for protection, supplies, and help of every kind. In this preparatory state of mind, Taylor said, "When I get to China, I shall have no claim on anyone for anything; my only claim will be on God. How important, therefore, to learn before leaving England to move man, through God, by prayer alone."[14]

Modern-day missions preparation generally does not include sleeping on the floor, discarding excess books, or giving away used clothes. The physical risks of the modern missions endeavor may pale in comparison to Kingdom workers of the past, but the extreme risk of the mission field is still palpable. Spiritual attacks carry over to the physical and emotional dimensions of missionaries as well. Career missionaries, Dennis and Kathy Balcombe, founders of Revival Chinese Ministries International in Hong Kong, experienced the kingdom of darkness in very tangible ways. "When the doors began to open for my husband, Dennis, to go to the rural countryside in China in the late 1980s, an all-out spiritual warfare came to our family to try to stop him,"[15] Kathy told me. Christian ministry was a dangerous undertaking at that time. The government imprisoned, tortured, and even killed Chinese Christians for their faith; yet Christians hungered for the Word of God above all else. Undeterred, Dennis brought their daughter with him to the mainland. "Sharon was fifteen-years-old at the time," Kathy said. "It was a precarious age; even though she was a missionary kid, she questioned if God was real." Their trip to China's rural countryside quelled her quandary.

As Dennis and Sharon planned the inland trip, Kathy suddenly fell ill with sarcoidosis—a rare and incurable autoimmune disease. Kathy believed it was an attack from the enemy to stop the work of the Holy Spirit in China. Yet, full of faith, she encouraged her husband and daughter to proceed with the trip, knowing that God would do something miraculous. Her only claim, like that of her missionary predecessor Hudson Taylor, was on God.

The ten-day, father-daughter trip marked a new beginning of revival in China. Dennis and Sharon made their way through China's interior by dilapidated trains and antiquated trucks. They stealthily plodded over rice paddies and through villages to remain undetected by the authorities.

The fire of the Holy Spirit fell and a passion for souls spread through the house Church network. "When Sharon returned to Hong Kong, she was a completely different person," Kathy marveled. "She described to me the numerous miracles she witnessed—the blind could see, the deaf hear, the lame walk, and even the dead were raised!"

The advancement of God's Kingdom on the earth comes at a cost. "If this is a real work for God," Hudson Taylor wrote, "it is a real conflict with Satan."[16] God has not left us alone in this work. Indeed, it is His work to begin with. While the spiritual attacks are real and powerful, God's presence and promises never fail. "Satan may build a hedge about us and fence us in and hinder our movements," Taylor said, "but he cannot roof us in and prevent our looking up."[17]

Miraculously, the disease that had attacked Kathy's body went into remission and never returned. "God heard the intercession from the body of Christ," Kathy told me. "Christians around the world stood with us in prayer, set their minds on things above, and believed with our family that China was worthy of Christ's suffering."[18]

The Balcombes—covered in prayer by Christians around the world—experienced God's outpouring in a marvelous way. Their ministry grew, and many souls were added to the Kingdom. But this revival did not come without a fight. In the midst of physical challenges, emotional struggles, and spiritual hurdles, they witnessed God's faithfulness. The attacks brought them face to face with the sufferings of Jesus; the victories edged around the bend. They saw the preciousness of God's lost children and realized their salvation was a fight worth joining. As their minds fixed on the promises of Heaven, they delighted to be instruments He chose to use.

You may have heard the popular expression: "Some people are so Heavenly-minded that they are of no earthly good." The problem is that this statement is completely unbiblical. And, in any case, the statement is wrong-headed. C. S. Lewis pointed this out by saying, "If you read history, you will find that the Christians who did most for the present world were just those who thought most of the next."[19]

The Bible says, "Set your minds on things above, not on earthly things."[20] Contrary to popular opinion, being Heavenly-minded always inspires us to be more earthly good. Dennis and Kathy Balcombe attest to this truth. Indeed, their daughter, Sharon, is a living example of a life transformed by the Kingdom of Heaven.

So, too, Hudson Taylor's focus on the coming Kingdom transformed the world that we now know. His radical concepts were ahead of their time. During his later missionary journey, his emphasis on Gospel contextualization by way of "adopting the costume of the country" as a courtesy to one's hosts vexed missions agencies and missionaries alike. His attitude about sending single women to the mission field caused heated debate, which later reshaped perceptions about gender roles on the mission field. The risks Taylor took by sending missionary recruits into dangerous territory produced no small amount of doubt—even in his own mind. Meanwhile, a million a month were dying without God in that land. This reality was burned into his very soul. So palpable were these perilous and Heavenly-minded considerations that in 1865 he wrote in his diary, "For two or three months, intense conflict... Thought I should lose my mind."[21] After an intense time of seeking God's direction, a breakthrough came. Taylor wrote, "...the Lord conquered my unbelief, and I surrendered myself to God for this service. I told Him that all responsibility as to the issues and consequences must rest with Him; that as His servant it was mine to obey and to follow Him."[22]

This Heavenly-mindedness marked Hudson Taylor's missionary career, making him a prominent figure in God's global plan. He commenced his journey on September 19, 1853. Taylor was twenty-one-years-old when he boarded the *Dumphries*, the ship secured for him by the Committee of the Chinese Evangelisation Society, under whose auspices he was going to China. The journey was an arduous one. Over five months later, on March 1, 1854, the ship finally arrived in Shanghai, China, where he was immediately faced with civil war, throwing his first year there into turmoil.

All God's Giants Have Been Weak Men

"China is not to be won for Christ by quiet, ease-loving men and women," Hudson Taylor said. "The stamp of men and women we need is such as will put Jesus, China, [and] souls first and foremost in everything and at every time—even life itself must be secondary."[23] For "Unless there is the element of extreme risk in our exploits for God, there is no need for faith."

Without a doubt, global Kingdom workers face significant spiritual hurdles on the mission field. But are their obstacles greater than those Christians face at home? After all, every individual resides in the duel dimensions of the spiritual and the material, seeking to successfully navigate the precarious passage of life.

One could say the human body houses a soul and a spiritual being. Or better stated, humans are spiritual beings whose spirit and soul are encompassed within a physical frame. In other words, we are not human beings having a spiritual experience; we are spiritual beings having a human experience.[24]

The biblical picture of a spiritual person is one who is "led by the Spirit of God"[25] and "live[s] by the Spirit."[26] The Apostle Paul, writing to the Romans connects the body, the mind (soul), and the spirit:

> Therefore, I urge you, brethren, by the mercies of God, to present your bodies a living and holy sacrifice, acceptable to God, which is your spiritual service of worship. And do not be conformed to this world, but be transformed by the renewing of your mind, so that you may prove what the will of God is, that which is good and acceptable and perfect.[27]

Paul reminds us that while our human experience includes the elements of body, soul, and spirit, the battle for the souls of men is not merely a physical fight. He writes to the Church in Ephesus: "For our struggle is not against flesh and blood, but against the rulers, against the authorities, against the powers of this dark world, and against the spiritual forces of evil in the heavenly realms."[28]

Some Christians might say, "Doesn't the greatest place of spiritual warfare reside between our ears?" Indeed, the enemy constantly plagues our minds with ungodly, twisted, and self-serving thoughts and ideas. Some of these mind games are subtler than others. In C. S. Lewis' classic satirical book, *The Screwtape Letters*, we gain a certain knowledge of the enemy's workings in the form of a series of letters from senior demon Screwtape to his nephew Wormwood. In the thirty-one letters, which constitute the book, Screwtape gives Wormwood detailed advice on various methods of undermining faith and of promoting sin in "the Patient." The senior demon relays the subtle stance that the fallen spirit world ought to take to tempt Christians away from "the Enemy" (God): "Indeed the safest road to Hell is the gradual one," Screwtape writes to Wormwood, "—the gentle slope, soft underfoot, without sudden turnings, without milestones, without signposts."[29]

This kind of gradual descent is one of the most dangerous pitfalls on the mission field. Faced with blatant spiritual strongholds and outright deception, the global Kingdom worker can easily be lured into thinking the battle is somewhere "out there" in another realm. Indeed, there are territorial spirits and rulers of darkness at every geographical location bent on sidelining their missionary efforts. However, if they are not alert to the enemy's subtle entrapments, they risk losing the spiritual authority to effectuate God's dominion in the earth.

In an earlier letter, the senior demon writes, "It is funny how mortals always picture us as putting things into their minds: in reality our best work is done by keeping things out."[30] The battle of the mind is again discussed in this excerpt: "There is nothing like suspense and anxiety for barricading a human's mind against the Enemy. He wants men to be concerned with what they do; our business is to keep them thinking about what will happen to them."[31] Indeed, the greatest battles of life are fought out daily in the silent chambers of the soul.

But we would be remiss to not look beyond the spiritual battle in the mind of every believer. The constant fight for a God-centered mindset is a task every Christian is called to engage. The mind is, no doubt, a serious battleground that cannot be overlooked. But this mind battle is for self-defense, not for overcoming darkness and taking regions for Christ.

Though every Christian will face their fair share of spiritual hurdles, each geographical environment possesses its own unique strongholds. The Bible clearly tells us that there are regional rulers of darkness over each geographical location. The enemy is a master at assembling the history, strengths, weaknesses, and tendencies of a particular place, and successfully disrupting the mindset and worldview of the said culture's inhabitants. In other words, there are distinct territorial strongholds in every culture on earth, each boasting its own unique difficulties. And as the pervading values, beliefs, underlying assumptions, attitudes, and behaviors of that culture evolves, so too, these strongholds shift over time.

Hudson Taylor's China is radically different from the China of today. From the Boxer Rebellion to the communist takeover, from the Cultural Revolution to the modern-day economic boom, the pervading mindset of the people altered through generations. This is as true of China as it was of Elliot's Ecuador, Dober's St. Thomas, Moffat's South Africa, Pullinger's Hong Kong, Eubank's Burma, the Ripkens' Somalia, and Carey's India. Name the country where you are reading this book. The enemy has uniquely tailored his tactics and spiritual strongholds in such a way as to overwhelm you and your neighbors by optimal means.

Screwtape writes to Wormwood:

> The humans live in time, but our Enemy destines them to eternity. He therefore, I believe, wants them to attend chiefly to two things, to eternity itself, and to that point of time which they call the Present. For the Present is the point at which time touches eternity. Of the present moment, and of it only, humans have an experience analogous to the experience which our Enemy has of reality of whole; in it alone freedom and actuality are offered to them.[32]

God has set eternity in our hearts. With an awareness of this timeless perspective, Christians are called to focus on the "God-ward aspect of

Christian work," as Taylor called it; to tear down strongholds and help restore mankind to their original purpose as the dwelling place of God.[33]

My friend in Thailand, Jonathan English, told me,

> As missionaries, we live in a culture not our own. We need to be students of the culture that we are in and also students of God's Kingdom culture. It is easy to slip into our host culture and operate by such natural means that our Christian impact becomes passive and powerless. We need to be aware of the spiritual strongholds around us so that we can point to a different Way of life.[34]

The spiritual strongholds over Thailand—where I reside among a population of ninety-five percent Buddhist adherents—is drastically different from the strongholds in my birth country. So is the case with my wife. She grew up in the Philippines, a predominantly Catholic country with a fast-growing evangelical Christian population. The moral frameworks of our cultures are strikingly different than that of Thailand. Our Judeo-Christian context shaped our worldview in radically different ways compared to the Theravada Buddhist worldview of the Thai. Satan, a constant student of culture, adapts his attacks accordingly. His ultimate goal is to separate man from God.

Missionaries are called to be students of culture—both their host culture and the culture of God's Kingdom. (The Kingdom of God was the central aspect of Jesus' message and a major theme of the Bible. In chapter twelve, we will explore why it is so rarely understood, and see examples of God's Kingdom manifested on the earth.) "Naturally speaking, Satan is way too strong for us," Steve Braselton told me, "but he is no match for Jesus Christ!" The longtime missionary in Malawi reminded me to keep the main thing the main thing. He said, "We must remain in Jesus and allow His Spirit to lead, guide, and direct our steps as we advance the Kingdom of God in the earth."[35]

We have a wonderful example of this in Hudson Taylor. He was sensitive to the Holy Spirit's plans. Despite the spiritual difficulties he encountered on the field, he joined God's heart for the lost. He was a true student of culture. There were countless spiritual hurdles for him to overcome. China's strongholds poised against him and his work, but his faith rested upon a powerful God. He said, "All our difficulties are only platforms for the manifestations of His grace, power, and love." So, the man went forth in zeal and confidence, knowing that through his inadequacies, God's power would be manifested. "Many [Christians] estimate difficulties in the light of their own resources, and thus attempt little and often fail in the little they attempt," Taylor wrote. "All God's giants have been weak men who did great things for God because they reckoned on His [power and presence with them]."[36]

Are you expecting great things to happen through your Christian witness? Your expectations should be married to momentum. It is difficult for God to steer a parked car. As you follow His footprints in the sand and take the path less traveled, your weakness may just be transformed into a force for good in the earth.

Let Us Give Up Our Lives

Hudson Taylor arrived in Shanghai in 1854 during a time of great turmoil and civil unrest. The spiritual forces of darkness poised against bearers of the Gospel in hopes that China would forever remain in darkness. The Taiping Rebellion, waged from 1850 to 1864, ranks as one of the bloodiest wars in human history. Casualties of war are estimated at twenty to seventy million, with millions more displaced.[37] It is notable that the uprising commenced when Hong Xiuquan, leader of a fanatic religious sect known as the God Worshipping Society, sought to upend the moral and social order of China. Hong (who was arguably mentally ill) believed himself to be the younger brother of Jesus Christ.

This was the bizarre, anti-Christian milieu in which Taylor's missionary journey began in Shanghai, one of five "treaty ports" China had opened to foreigners following its first Opium War with England. Taylor desired to win the Chinese to the truth of the Gospel, and immediately took the controversial stance to "become all things to all men" by adopting the local costume. He attracted criticism and ridicule from other foreigners for wearing Chinese clothes and a queue pigtail. Taylor believed that the locals would be more likely to listen to his message if he blended in. "The foreign dress and carriage of missionaries," he said, "the foreign appearance of chapels, and indeed the foreign air imparted to everything connected with their work has seriously hindered the rapid dissemination of the Truth among the Chinese."[38]

Ridicule was not his only concern. Taylor spent his first few months dodging the cannon balls of the Red Turban rebels who had taken possession of the native city in Shanghai. But the young man was not to be deterred. He dreamed of living among the Chinese—a thought unheard of among Western residents. Taylor paid no heed to the expatriate community and soon secured a home in a Chinese neighborhood. But when cannon balls pelted the nearby homes and a fire broke out next to his room, he was left with no choice but to abandon the house and return to the Foreign Settlement. "[It was] a step that was taken none too soon," Taylor said, "for before the last of my belongings were removed, the house was burnt to the ground."[39]

The horrors, atrocities, and misery connected with war encompassed young Hudson Taylor on every side. An intense loneliness grew inside him, and the enemy repeated his age-old lies. Like all his predecessors and the missionaries who would come after him, Taylor battled his negative internal monologue, the fatalistic chatter around him, and the discouraging whispers of the spirit world. Yet, he remained expectant for the promises of God to be accomplished.

Despite all odds, the young missionary pressed forward. In the autumn of 1854, Taylor traveled inland on a seven-day journey with his missionary counterparts. It was during this first inland trip that Taylor's eyes were opened to the enormous spiritual needs of the Chinese. Few had ever heard of the saving knowledge of Christ. "I wish sometimes that I had twenty bodies," Taylor said, "that at twenty places at once I might publish the saving name of Jesus."[40]

In 1857, the Chinese Evangelisation Society, strained with lack of funds, was no longer able to support Taylor. "Not infrequently, our God brings His people into difficulties on purpose that they may come to know Him as they could not otherwise do,"[41] Taylor wrote. He resigned and became an independent missionary. Without promise of financial support, he trusted God to meet His needs. Later that year, he married Maria Dyer, the daughter of missionaries serving in China. The couple poured themselves into the ministry and witnessed a steady growth in their church. This expansion ensued alongside Maria's bouts of illness. Taylor would have lost his wife but for the miraculous arrival of much-needed medical supplies. Her life thus spared, their ministry to the Chinese continued.

On July 31, 1859, Maria gave birth to their first child, Grace Dyer Taylor. A season of joy came upon the family, and over the next year, many souls were added to the Kingdom. However, their Christian labors provoked the rulers of darkness. For millennium, Satan held captive the occupants of the land, and his grip would not loosen without a fight.

In 1861, illness attacked Taylor during one of the most fruitful seasons of his ministry. He filled with sorrow to leave his field, but he was forced to return to England. The long separation from China, however, proved providential. It was a necessary step in the formation of the China Inland Mission. The forced furlough allowed him to view China from a distance, thus realizing the breadth of need he never before noticed while in his small corner of the country.

After his recovery, Taylor remained in England for six years. There, the conviction came to him that a special agency was essential to evangelize China's interior. To new missionary recruits he said, "Let us give up our work, our thoughts, our plans, ourselves, our lives, our loved ones, our influence, our all, right into His hand, and then, when we have given all over to Him, there will be nothing left for us to be troubled about, or to make trouble about."[42]

On June 25, 1865, Hudson Taylor founded the China Inland Mission. Months later in October, and with Maria's help, he published *China's Spiritual Need and Claims*, which revealed the country's urgent necessity of the Gospel message. In the hearts of its readers birthed a missions flame, and more recruits committed to return to China with the Taylors in 1866. Prior to their departure, Maria bore three more children: Herbert, Frederick, and Samuel. So, on May 26 of the same year, Hudson and Maria, their four young children, and sixteen of the China Inland Mission's first global Kingdom workers departed London for the Orient.

A number of distinctive features marked the organization. Missionary recruits had no guaranteed salaries, nor could they appeal for funds. "God's work done in God's way will never lack God's supplies,"[43] Taylor explained. Missionaries would be required to adopt the Chinese dress to contextualize the Gospel to their hearers. The mission also accepted female recruits, both married and unmarried—an approach both far ahead of his time and widely criticized. "Hudson Taylor makes extraordinarily ample use of the services of unmarried ladies," German missionary Julius Richter wrote in the *Missionary View of the World* in 1898, stating that he found this idea "unbecoming and repellent."

The radical band of missionaries saw great breakthroughs because of their willingness to meet the Chinese where they were. As students of the culture, the Taylors and the China Inland Mission workers labored for the locals' salvation. Maria entered a period of deep victory and peace. "It [is] just resting in Jesus," she said of her source of strength, "and letting Him do the work."[44] That such blessing should be tested by increasing trials is not to be wondered at. The period they entered surged of unprecedented distress. They experienced the power of the adversary as never before, while in personal matters, new and deep sorrows awaited them.[45]

Mere months after arriving in China, Maria gave birth to another girl, Maria, only to lose their firstborn soon after. Nine-year-old Grace died in a temple near Hangzhou on August 23, 1867. This became the story of their lives: gaining one child only to lose another. Charles was born in 1868. Samuel, their fourth child, died in 1870. Noel was born in July of the same year, but died thirteen days after his birth on July 20. "I could not but admire and wonder at the grace that so sustained and comforted the fondest of mothers," Hudson wrote of Maria's fortitude. "The secret was that Jesus was satisfying the deep thirst of heart and soul."[46]

Maria herself chose the hymns to be sung at Noel's little grave, one of which, "O Holy Savior, Friend Unseen:"

> *Though faith and hope are often tried,*
> *We ask not, need not, aught beside;*
> *So safe, so calm, so satisfied,*
> *The souls that cling to Thee.*
> *They fear not Satan nor the grave.*
> *They know Thee near, and strong to save;*
> *Nor fear to cross e'en Jordan's wave,*
> *While still they cling to Thee.*[47]

The burial took place amid riots, civil unrest, and governmental pressure. On top of that, the summer heat was excessive, which added to the unrest of the native population. During that time, the missionary families huddled in the small room of one of their mission stations and prayed for relief. Taylor slept on the floor so that Maria might share the bedroom with the other ladies.

During her last son's birth, an attack of cholera left her body frail. At daybreak on July 23, 1870, ten days after the burial of her son, Noel, Maria awoke with serious symptoms. She called Hudson to her side. He was shocked by her appearance. "By this time, it was dawn," he later wrote, "and the sunlight revealed what the candle had hidden—the deathlike hue of her countenance."[48]

Husband and wife exchanged the most loving final conversation:

"My darling, do you know that you are dying?" he asked.

"Dying?" she replied. "What makes you think so?"

"I can see it, darling. Your strength is giving way."

"Can it be so?" Maria asked. "I feel no pain, only weariness."

"Yes, you are going home." Hudson tried to compose himself. "You will soon be with Jesus."

"I cannot be sorry to go to Him," Maria admitted, "but it does grieve me to leave you alone at such a time. Yet, He will be with you and meet all your need."

Little was said after that beside a few last words about the children. She drifted out of consciousness and seemed to fall asleep. The summer sun rose higher and higher over the city, the hills, and the river. The busy hum of life came up around them from many a court and street. But within one Chinese dwelling, in an upper room from which the blue of God's own Heaven could be seen, there was the hush of a wonderful peace.

Though the loss was immense, God empowered the Taylor family to move forward and to thrive on mission. Unrest in China continued to rise and fall, the country ever in a precarious state. Yet, the global Kingdom workers at the China Inland Mission advanced to the farthest regions, proclaiming the grace and glory of God to the Chinese. Taylor himself worked tirelessly to see the name of Jesus preached among these lost communities. He took a total of eleven voyages across the seas to speak in Europe, North America, and Oceania. His plodding led to nationwide Kingdom advancement and unlocked the door to China's future Christian revivals. "I have found that there are three stages in every great work of God," Taylor once said. "First, it is impossible, then it is difficult, then it is done."[49]

His statement compels us to consider the impossibilities we presently face in our Christian outreach. With God, nothing is impossible. We admit that we believe this reality, but do our actions state otherwise? Man's impossibilities are the avenues through which God proves Himself mighty. These impossibilities become simple difficulties. Then, through the working of the Holy Spirit in and through us, God accomplishes His Kingdom purposes in ways we never thought possible.

The China Inland Mission grew steadily, and in 1876, its fifty-two workers constituted one-fifth of the missionary force in China. In 1881, Taylor pleaded with God for seventy more missionaries to respond to the call.

Seventy-six came.

In late 1886, he prayed for another one hundred within a year, and by November 1887, 102 missionary candidates were accepted for service by the China Inland Mission. This trend continued. By 1888, 294 missionaries served in fourteen provinces at the China Inland Mission. Between 1898 and 1900, during the Boxer Rebellion, hundreds of foreign ministers and thousands of Chinese Christians were put to death. The mission lost fifty-eight missionaries and twenty-one children. Through this time of persecution, the China Inland Mission grew in number to 933 people. By 1939, almost 200,000 Chinese and minority people had been baptized.[50]

A turning point came in 1949 when Mao Zedong and his communist party took power in China. A "reluctant exodus" ensued; in 1950, the missionaries left the country. By providential design, God used the organization to impact neighboring nations and regions beyond. The China Inland Mission established headquarters in Singapore; workers spread out to proclaim the Gospel message in Asia's vast harvest fields. Today, unofficial estimates number China's professing Christian population at over one-hundred million.

Though Taylor never solicited funds or appealed for financial support, his ministry inspired nearly 1,000 people to give up their comforts and ambitions for the cause of Christ in China and beyond. Long after the man was buried in 1905, the China Inland Mission continued to make the Christian message known. In 1964, the name was changed to Overseas Missionary Fellowship, and then to OMF International in the 1990s. Taylor's ministry continues to this day with 1,400 workers from over forty different nations serving among approximately one-hundred people groups in East Asia. The organization also ministers among the Asian diaspora in Europe, Africa, the Americas, New Zealand, Australia, and in Asia.[51]

One hundred fifty years have passed since Hudson Taylor stepped foot in China. His sacrificial service opened new horizons to global missionaries, transforming Asia as we now know it.

Not Machinery but Men

The Bible says that the eyes of the Lord search the whole earth to strengthen those whose hearts are fully committed to Him.[52] He is more concerned with our availability than with our abilities. In fact, the Christian's inadequacies display God's might and power in ways man is unable.

That being said, global Kingdom workers are nothing more than simple men and women who responded to the missions call of God. Should we, then, applaud this act of obedience? Are their lives more heroic than others? The Church often paints the missionary life in idealized hues, embellishing the tale of sacrifice, and idolizing the role of global Kingdom workers. However, the reality most missionaries attest to is that their service is simply a natural response to the magnanimous grace of God.

Hudson Taylor paints an honest picture of the task by saying, "The work of a true missionary is work indeed, often very monotonous, apparently not very successful, and carried on through great and varied but unceasing difficulties."[53] In historical missionary biographies, we rarely read words like these. Missions stories have inspired thousands of people to preach the Gospel of Jesus around the world. Their examples encourage us to thrive on mission in our own ministries and contexts. Yet, many times, by no mistake of their own, their courageous obedience induced the idolization of a role, a title, or a task.

In 1900, Taylor spoke on "The Source of Power" at the Ecumenical Missionary Conference in New York City. Despite great advances on the mission field, he cautioned the delegates about the pitfalls of a faulty focus:

> We have given too much attention to methods and to machinery and to resources, and too little to the Source of power—the filling with the Holy Ghost. This, I think you will agree with me, is the great weakness today, and has been the great weakness of our service in the past. Unless remedied, it will be the great weakness in the future.[54]

Many men and women are searching for a hero; God is looking for men and women willing to live heroic lives. We marvel at courageous acts; God seeks to empower us with His Holy Spirit that even greater works might be accomplished. We are enamored by daring escapades; Christ calls us simply to be witnesses of His Kingdom on the earth.

In a *Christianity Today* article entitled "Farewell to the Missionary Hero," Amy Peterson, author of *Dangerous Territory*, describes the recent historical shift in missionary communication. As an advocate of honesty about the real challenges of the mission field, Peterson writes,

> We need to hear stories about the real struggles and joys of missions work. These kinds of stories have the power to improve our missiology; unless we are honest about the challenges missionaries face, we won't find realistic solutions. But if we are forthright about what the job requires, we'll stand a better chance of attracting the right people and preparing them adequately for long-term service, rather than sending them home early, disillusioned and depressed.[55]

Do you desire to thrive on mission? Do you long to experience breakthrough in your life? Do you want to discover what God is calling you to do with your life? It is in the secret place of prayer and sensitivity to the Holy Spirit that God wields broken vessels into glorious instruments that He can use.

For as E. M. Bounds wrote,

> What the Church needs today is not more machinery or better, not new organizations or more and novel methods, but men [and women] whom the Holy Ghost can use—men of prayer, men mighty in prayer. The Holy Ghost does not flow through methods, but through men. He does not come on machinery, but on men. He does not anoint plans, but men—men of prayer.[56]

Seemingly daunting dangers pepper the mission fields of the earth. Global Kingdom workers count the physical, emotional, and spiritual risks they will indubitably face when going to serve abroad. But intimacy with God through prayer bolsters the mind of a missionary. Many come to realize that in the light of eternity, the risks they take are no risk at all. Those whose minds focus on a heavenly Kingdom know that there is no safer place than in the center of God's will.

SECTION FOUR
REWARDS

God rewards those who earnestly seek Him. You live in the "now" and the "not yet" of the Kingdom. As a follower of Christ, you wait expectantly for His consummate reign in the earth. In the meantime, He graciously grants you joy on the journey. This is one of the rewards in the mind of missional Christians. Other rewards include supernatural ministry breakthroughs and the manifested presence of God in and through your life. All the prizes for Kingdom service begin at the feet of Jesus; a high regard for the Holy Spirit's presence directs you deeper into a relationship with Him.

In section four of *The Mind of a Missionary*, the lives of Amy Carmichael, Don Richardson, and Heidi Baker prove that God chooses weak and unassuming vessels through which to display His Kingdom. Despite unmatched opposition, Carmichael exuded joy in her difficult mission field; Richardson found relevant cultural keys to explain the Gospel message to cannibalistic headhunters; and Baker continues to experience the tangible presence of God in the most unlikely spots.

The missionary examples in section four, *Rewards*, point you to God's fingerprints in culture. You find that He is always at work in the world, moving in the hearts of the people you seek to reach. You are an integral part of His glorious missions narrative; He is arranging every piece of the puzzle to fit perfectly in His Divine sequence of events. The overarching plan: every nation, tribe, people, and language worshiping before His heavenly throne.

In God's "upside-down Kingdom," He raises the lowly to honor and bestows His glory upon the humble. His presence changes everything; His

Kingdom transforms earthly atmospheres. As you willingly give your life to God's desires, He paints a portrait of His glory in and through you. God grants you the mind of His Son, Jesus, that you might display His light in the darkest of places.

CHAPTER TEN

JOY ON THE JOURNEY

Global Goers Are Not Mindless Gears in the Missions Machine

In this section, we will examine the rewards for which the missionary mind yearns. Everyone desires to experience success in their endeavors, and global Kingdom workers are no exception. They long for a joyous missional journey, a breakthrough in ministry outreach, and a witness of God's Kingdom being established in their respective fields. Consequently, these rewards generally arise in the wake of great difficulties and obstacles.

In the previous section, we looked at the risks that cross-cultural missions entail. Global Kingdom workers face real physical challenges, emotional struggles, and spiritual hurdles in foreign lands where they serve. These struggles evidenced themselves in the lives of Nik and Ruth Ripken, William and Dorothy Carey, and Hudson Taylor. Because of these difficulties, many missionaries return to their home countries, otherwise known as missionary attrition. Those who continue on the field live in particularly high-stress environments—usually three times higher than the average "danger level" of stress. The kingdom of darkness wields an all-out attack on Christians who seek to diminish their strongholds within a particular place or people group.

During the initial weeks or months of their first-term (some organizations use the phrase "mid-term," which lasts between one to three years on the field), missionaries often sense a growing excitement in their new environment. Their assignment imbues with the thrilling buzz of the strange and unfamiliar. Christian theologian H. Richard Niebuhr presented the "love of the distant" as one of the manifold motives for overseas missionary service. The allure of the far, the strange, and the foreign contrasted with "love of the near."[1] But the allure of the distant exotic inevitably wanes with time. It may instill initial intrigue, but this fleeting feeling is woefully shallow.

Unfortunately, the incessant bombardment on the physical, emotional, and spiritual fronts often lead to the loss of joy in the missional endeavor. Jesus promised His followers abundant joy, yet we do not always reside in this reality. When the initial buzz of cross-cultural service wears off, can we truly find long-lasting satisfaction? Is joy on the journey still a promise for us today?

These thoughts lead us back to the underlying motivation in the missionary mind. The first three chapters in this book questioned the starting point of our compassion for the lost and our obedience to the commands of Christ; they challenged us to measure our passion for the glory of God. Jim Elliot showed us that individuals who are intrinsically motivated to pursue the call of God experience a deep pleasure in Christian service. This inherent drive far outweighs man's praise, accolades of the masses, or external rewards. It then infuses us with a passion for souls. We see this reality in the life of C. T. Studd. A determined focus on God getting the glory He deserves leads Christians to a deep sense of satisfaction. The first Moravian missionaries obeyed the call so that the Lamb who was slain might receive the reward of His suffering: people from every nation, tribe, and language. In turn, an otherworldly joy in the presence of a glad God became the reward for Zinzendorf and the Moravians.

God does not want global goers to be mindless gears in the missions machine. A missional fervor devoid of relational intimacy is not His ultimate goal. God invites every believer into the joy of partnership with Him. The Great Commission enterprise is not comprised of commonplace Christian cogs, but integral, God-ordained components in the body of Christ. God thinks highly of His children, esteems our uniqueness, and values our individuality. Every spiritual gift matters; every missional offering carries importance. Every citizen of God's Kingdom is significant. Though He is sovereign and all-knowing, He grants us free will. The mystery of God's omnipotence and our freedom of choice baffles human understanding; yet without such freedom to obey or refuse, our acquisition of personal joy is but a fleeting fantasy.

I Don't Want to Fail

"Don't let your mind dwell on sadness as it saps the soul of strength," Amy Carmichael once wrote. "There is more blue sky overhead than clouds. The clouds will pass. I often think how sad we shall be at the end, if we have failed in joy. I don't want to fail."[2]

Amy was born on December 16, 1867, to the Missionary Generation[3] in the wee village of Millisle, County Down, in Northern Ireland. Her parents, David and Catherine, were devout Presbyterians with a compassionate heart for people. They raised their seven children (of whom Amy was the oldest) in a godly environment with hopes of seeing them grow up to serve the Lord. At age fifteen, Amy wrote, "In His great mercy the Good Shepherd answered the prayers of my mother and father and many other loving ones, and drew me, even me, into His fold."[4] Her parents could not have imagined the global impact their God-centered values would have on their firstborn child.

When Amy was sixteen-years-old, her father moved the family to Belfast. In Millisle, he prospered as a mill-owner; he and his brother had just built a new mill in Belfast. However, in 1883, the business took a turn for the worst. A large loan he had made was not repaid, leaving the family in dire straights. Life changed for the Carmichael household when their father died suddenly on April 12, 1885 at the age of fifty-four.[5] Amy undertook the responsibility of caring for the younger members of the family. Even at a young age, a maternal heart birthed in her.

In Belfast, the Carmichaels founded a small gathering called the Welcome Evangelical Church. A pioneer at heart, Amy started a Sunday-morning class for local mill girls. Her Gospel work among children in a deprived area of the city bloomed until they needed a hall to seat 500 people.

At that time, the spiritual milieu among evangelicals in Great Britain stressed that "spiritual usefulness [was] related to personal holiness."[6] Founded two decades earlier in 1875, the Keswick Convention gathered annually to encourage God-directed holiness in the Christian sphere. Its message is perhaps best expressed in the terms of its original title, in which it was described as a "Convention for the Promotion of Practical Holiness."[7]

"Character, and not service, was the aim held closely before all who spoke and heard at those meetings," wrote Charles F. Harford in *The Keswick Convention*. "What we were intended to *be*, and not what we were called to *do*, was the prominent thought in the whole Convention."[8] It was believed that if the highest possible Christian character was developed, then fruitful service would naturally follow.

Into this age of spiritual awakening, and subsequent springboard for missions, Amy Carmichael entered early adulthood. At the age of twenty, Amy went to Glasgow to attend the 1887 Keswick Convention. Hudson Taylor, the founder of the China Inland Mission, was one of the speakers. There she sat and listened to a fervent appeal for global missions. Her heart filled with a sense of purpose; her eyes welled up with tears. Gripped by the call of God, the young woman dedicated her life to obedient service to her Master's will. "I cannot forget the flints on my own path and the thorns," she later wrote.

> But, looking back, I know I would not have chosen any other if I could have known… what it would mean of His companionship, and also of the power to enter into the griefs of others. It was all worthwhile, ten thousand times worthwhile.[9]

A rich, joy-infused love for Jesus marked her early years and became the bedrock of her missionary service. Yet, her life met with an equal amount of sacrifice and struggle, heartache and pain. Hers was a long journey over the rugged Golgotha slopes, cross in tow, body weary. Still, the gleam in her eyes and smile on her lips revealed her inner delight at her Father's ever-present comfort during times of struggle.

Amy continued at the Welcome until she received a call to work among the mill girls of Manchester in 1889. But the tug to minister overseas continued to bud in her heart. Amy was an unlikely candidate for the demands of missionary life. She suffered from neuralgia, a disease that stimulates the nerves, causing severe aches and pain. The disease often put her in bed for weeks on end. However, the call to service abroad only increased.

On January 14, 1892, she wrote to her mother:

> Everything, everything seemed to be saying 'Go'; through all sounds the cry seemed to rise, 'Come over and help us.' Every bit

of pleasure of work which has come to me has had underlying it the thought of those people who have never, never heard of Jesus; before my eyes clearer than any lovely view has been the constant picture of those millions who have no chance, and never had one, of hearing of the love which makes our lives so bright.[10]

But Amy was torn. Her "home claims" seemed to say "stay." She wrestled with the missionary call until at last, she wrote a short list of reasons why she could not go. Her first reason was of her mother's need of her; her final reason mentioned her frail health. But as her pen continued the heartfelt letter to her mother, the Holy Spirit spoke more plainly than ever before. She continued:

> ...though I seem torn in two, and just feel one big ache all over, yet the certainty is there—He said to me 'Go'. Oh, nothing but that sure word, His word, could make it possible to do it, for until He spoke, and I answered, 'Yes, Lord', I never knew what it would cost.

Her letter concluded with a tearful farewell: "Goodbye, my mother. May He come very near to you and strengthen and comfort you. Your own Amy."[11]

One can only imagine the heart-wrenching emotion Amy's mother must have felt. The prospect of giving up her daughter to the foreign field broke her heart in two. Yet, the comfort of the Holy Spirit swept over her emotions, and she submitted to God's will. Two days later, her mother wrote back to Amy. The letter opens with a poem by Frances R. Havergal:

He Who hath led will lead
All through the wilderness;
He Who hath fed will surely feed;
He Who hath blessed will bless;
He Who hath heard thy cry
Will never close His ear;
He Who hath marked thy faintest sigh
Will not forget thy tear.
He loveth always, faileth never,
So rest on Him today, forever.

Her mother wrote:

> Yes, dearest Amy, He has lent you to me all these years. He only knows what a strength, comfort, and joy you have been to me. In sorrow He made you my staff and solace, in loneliness my more than child companion, and in gladness my bright and merry-hearted sympathizer. So, darling, when He asks you now to go away from within my reach, can I say nay? No, no, Amy, He is yours—you are His—to take you where He pleases and to use you as He pleases.[12]

My heart bursts with emotion as I read these intimate letters. They remind me of the day I left my mother in Prescott, Arizona when I departed for China in 1998. Oh, what heart-wrenching sadness filled our hearts that day. Without question, every global Kingdom worker who left homeland and family resonates with such sentiments. The sacrifice to God's call is taxing; surrender to His global cause is a solemn undertaking.

This thought leads us to question: Where, then, is the merriment of the missionary task? Is not the lot of the global Kingdom worker filled with more sadness than joy? Make no mistake about it: grief is a two-sided coin. Behind the facade of sorrow, gladness grows—ever so slowly at first—until the bloom undergoes a complete transmutation. In His mercy, God injects joy into our pain. Godly gladness is, after all, the gift through which we find strength amid strain and struggle.

Amy's yearning for overseas service continued to swell. On July 26, 1892, she noted, "Definitely given up for service abroad."[13] The next month, she offered herself to the China Inland Mission; they accepted her. On September 10, 1892, Amy traveled to London for a character and missionary vocation assessment. Elated, she packed her trunks and expected to sail for China. However, it was a shock for her that the medical adviser of the China Inland Mission did not pass her for China. He felt that her health issues were too great a risk to send her to the East. In January 1893, Hudson Taylor wrote a letter to China, stating, "[A] Keswick missionary, Amy Carmichael, had not been accepted as a candidate, on grounds of health and temperament..."[14]

Amy felt the blow of rejection but tried to keep a steady head. She believed that her call to mission work was a divine commission. God must be the One to swing the ajar door wide open on its rusty hinges and thrust her out at the proper time.

Hudson Taylor's January thirteenth letter went on to state that Amy "was to sail with a [China Inland Mission] party to... Japan." Without proper contact having been established, and with a little mission training in London, Amy became the first Keswick missionary when she sailed to Japan on March 3, 1893. But her term would be shortened due to ill health.

On January 22, 1894, on one of her preaching tours, she suddenly could not go on. She wrote, "Within half an hour I could hardly think, with acute neuralgia."[15] On July 3, "a hot, hot afternoon," Amy's body gave way, and she collapsed. "I find myself environed by wet towels, doleful faces, and a general sense of blurs," she wrote.[16] She was advised to leave Japan. Her departure—a painful episode in Amy's life, from which was birthed great humility and attentiveness to the voice of the Holy Spirit—took place rather quickly. In July, she sailed to China. There, China Inland Mission workers attended to her medical needs. Again, however, the Holy Spirit spoke, and she set sail to Ceylon (now the nation of Sri Lanka).

By this time, she was very ill and questioned her Father's seemingly roundabout leading back to Great Britain. She questioned if this under-taking was of the Holy Spirit's leading. "I cannot attempt to explain this," she wrote. "I am prepared for much blame... but I cannot help it. One dare not anything but obey [and] follow in the Way, be it... a path in the great waters, footsteps all unknown."[17]

Had I been with Amy at the time, I, too, might have questioned the wisdom of her decision to crisscross the continents. However, do not every one of life's steps fill with uncertainty? And are not these uncertainties the exact means through which God guides His children? In retrospect, clarity forms. The providential sequence of events led her to a lifelong commitment in the neighboring nation of India. Amy later explained to the Dohnavur children that God's plan for her was for the children in India: "I was guarded and kept for you, my children,"[18] she wrote.

At the end of 1894, Amy returned home. Her mother met her on December 15, just one day before her twenty-seventh birthday. Back in England, she felt unsure of her next step; but she was willing that God could break her and use her in whatever way He saw fit. At present, however, she had no immediate explanation. What *had* occurred in her was the deep-ening of reliance on the Holy Spirit's leading and increased intimacy in her prayer life. "It does not matter how many questions fill the deep places of prayer," she wrote many years later. "We shall know the answers tomorrow. Today is enough that we may prove our God by the humble, the far-reaching energies of prayer."[19]

I find this reliance on the Holy Spirit's leading a paramount key to thriving on mission today. In our moments of uncertainty and confusion, God delights to lead us into our destiny. He reveals each step as it comes, guiding us along an unfamiliar path. Our only choice is to cling to His promises, draw closer to Him, and seek not His wonders but know His ways.[20]

In England, Amy's brief and turbulent missionary career seemed to be over. However, God providentially arranged His divine sequence of events. He had much more in store for the young woman. In fact, her missionary journey had barely begun.

The foreign field drew Amy once more. In 1895, she attended the Keswick Convention, a notable year due to the presence of Andrew Murray from South Africa. Murray's words captured Amy's heart and mind:

> But understand that your God longs to rule the world, and your Christ is upon the throne, leading you on as His soldiers, and wanting to bless you with victory upon victory... If you want to take a word as your motto and watchword, let it be, 'Sacrifice everything and anything for the glory of your God... Anything that I can do for that glory, Lord, here I am.' Give yourself up to God.[21]

Recently commissioned to Bangalore, India by the Anglican Church of England Zenana Missionary Society, Amy was welcomed to the stage at the Keswick Convention. Inspired by Murray's words, she spoke the following day, July 27, 1895, at the missionary meeting held in the big tent. She held up a red scroll, on which stated: "Nothing Too Precious for Jesus."[22] She urged her listeners:

> Let these words come home to the mothers and the fathers. Are they cherishing something—a son or a daughter, too precious for Jesus? He counted nothing too precious for us. If He calls any to leave all and follow Him, may it be in the power of His resurrection and in the fellowship of His sufferings. Whatever He calls us to do, let us do it in His might and for His Glory.[23]

The sporadic and turbulent years now behind her, new and unforeseen challenges lay ahead of Amy Carmichael. Her many experiences abroad matured her heart, and gradually she would become a well-respected missionary. Though she still suffered severe physical ailments, God's empowerment overshadowed her weakness. Questions about the future coursed through her mind. How would her sickness affect her missionary career? Could she ever settle somewhere? How might God use her? Rather than focus on the unknowns, she chose instead to follow step-by-step in the footprints of her Master.

In many ways, the magnitude of her story commenced at the end of the nineteenth-century. On October 11, 1895, Amy Carmichael sailed for India. She left Britain at the age of twenty-seven, never to set foot again on British soil.

You Will Carry His Happiness Wherever You Go

"Of the blistering days before I sailed and of the goodbye I will say nothing," Amy Carmichael wrote of her departure to India. "We shall all be together soon in the Father's Country. Such days will seem worthwhile There."[24]

Her family and friends lined the shore to see her off. Tearful farewells rose from the depths of each one's heart and passed between parted lips. Amy's mother wept. Slowly, the ship departed the dock, and the gap between land and sea widened. "God bless you all!" Amy called to her well-wishers; they echoed blessings back to her. The rudder churned the ocean below; swirling eddies formed on the water's surface. The sounds of the sea mixed with the crowd's refrain as their unified voices broke into song: "Crown Him, crown Him, crown Him Lord of All!" The distance between ship and land swallowed the sound of song. Amy gazed back at the people, the coastline, the city, and the mountains. Everything became vague—a blurred memory of her homeland. Overhead, seagulls cried.

During the 19th century, an explosion of Protestant missionary activity thrust global Kingdom workers into Asia. Through the efforts of the China Inland Mission, and largely in part by the work of the Anglican Church of England Zenana Missionary Society—by whom Amy Carmichael was commissioned—female missionary work expanded. The work done by women for women—who otherwise could not be reached by their male counterparts—saw remarkable effects.[25] The characterization of the "Victorian lady missionary" as "resourceful, self-sacrificing, dedicated, and willful"[26] meant that the influence and impact of their work were felt for decades in the countries where they served.[27] Female missionaries transformed the world of missions. The frontier advanced on the stepping stones of missionary graves, paving the way for modern-day ministers.

Over one hundred years earlier, in April 1793, William Carey (the "Father of Modern Missions") and his family set sail to India. They met with immense physical, emotional, and spiritual obstacles on the foreign field. During their first five-and-a-half-years of service, not a single Indian was converted. Yet, Carey said,

> I would not abandon the Mission for all the fellowships and finest spheres in England... The work, to which God has set His hands, will infallibly prosper. Christ has begun to besiege the ancient and strong fortress, and will assuredly carry it.[28]

In the 19th century, Carey's prophetic pronouncement materialized. Thousands of men and women, sensing that God was at work before they arrived, linked hands with the Almighty to win souls for Christ. The Gospel would "infallibly prosper" among unreached peoples. Carey wished that faithful missionaries should preach Christ in India; that the country would fill "with the knowledge of Christ." "We are neither working at uncertainty nor afraid for the result," he said. "[God] must reign, until Satan has not an inch of territory."[29]

The missionary task fills with uncertainty. Global Kingdom workers dive into a pool of unknowns. Confronted by cultural, linguistic, and religious (amongst many other) nuances, the task of Kingdom establishment in a foreign land is inarguably arduous. No wonder missionary attrition is at an all-time high. Yet, one thing is certain: God will reign over the earth. In 1793, Carey was convinced of this. At the name of Jesus, every knee will bow—of those who are in Heaven and on earth and under the earth—and every tongue will confess that Jesus Christ is Lord, to the glory of God the Father.[30] On October 11, 1895, Amy Carmichael sailed to India to join the great cloud of witnesses gone before her, this deep-seated conviction burning in her heart.

Physically frail yet mentally alert, twenty-two-year-old Amy landed on Indian soil on November 9, 1895. Illness immediately greeted her already weakened frame. She contacted dengue fever, a dangerous and often fatal virus that causes a skin rash, joint pains, fever, and headaches. The illness laid her low for a period, but her focus remained on things above. "Joys are always on their way to us," she wrote. "They are always traveling to us through the darkness of the night. There is never a night when they are not coming."[31] Despite the undesired physical setback, her heart settled on joy. More appropriately stated, her mind rested on Jesus. She found in His presence a fullness of joy.

Though out of sight, she was not out of mind. Back in England, faithful Christians prayed for their dear missionary. In the Keswick mission report of August 5, 1896, we read:

> Miss Carmichael, being unable to resume work in Japan, has been sent to Bangalore. Accounts of her arrival, and impressions of work there have from time to time appeared in the *Life of Faith*. Constant prayer is asked that the many opportunities allowed her may result in blessing, not only to the heathen, but to native Christians also, and that health may be preserved in this new climate.[32]

This report, sent in a time devoid of our present-day technological advantages, reveals the passion of that era for foreign missions. I immediately recall the rope-holding imagery encouraged by William Carey on October 2, 1792: "I will go down [into the goldmine of souls] if you will hold the rope."[33] Is not this summon still a necessity of the modern-day missions endeavor? I believe it speaks to the value of every citizen in God's Kingdom, each with a role to play in God's global masterplan.

A land of complexities and seeming contradictions, 19th century India posed formidable problems for foreign missionaries. "Almost inextricably religion is woven into the cultural setting of India," writes Hans Kommers in *Triumphant Love*. "The Hindu ideology as well as the social system affect every area of life and thought. Hinduism espouses the division of people into hierarchically placed groups, the 'castes.'"[34] The social structure of caste life oppressed the Indian people, separating the elites from the "untouchables." At the dawn of the new century, India's population was estimated at 210 million Hindus and 67 million Muslims. Out of the 145 million women and girls, only one million at the most could be said to be under any Christian influence whatsoever.[35]

Amy immediately gravitated toward the women and children, of whom the latter she wrote seemed to live "in a land where childhood ends almost as soon it begins."[36] Their hollow eyes beckoned her help. Perhaps the cry she heard on January 14, 1892—"Come over and help us"—issued from the hearts of these little ones. Here now she stood on Indian soil as a ministry budded, ever so subtly at first, that would initiate a far-reaching, transformative effect.

In an effort to respect Indian culture and scale societal boundaries, she wore the native Indian sari. Her decision opened doors otherwise closed to members of the foreign missionary community unwilling to take such measures.[37] Amy frustrated at the apathy she saw in the missionaries. She longed to enter the lives of the locals and pray with them. Immense need and opportunity evidenced themselves at every turn; she felt these met with shocking indifference. Still, missionary reports from her counterparts seemed to sparkle. The "stretching" and adjusting of the truth (so as not to discourage financial supporters) aggravated her. Amy resolved, whenever she might write something, to tell the truth, and the truth only.[38]

Her "controversial" stance caused others to view her with caution; they saw her as someone who "caused a stir among fellow missionaries." She was "something of a firebrand."[39] Inconceivably, some of her fellow missionaries and local Christians started the "Get-Amy-out-of-India movement."[40] Thankfully, her "rope-holding" Keswick friends encouraged her with a timely letter, in which they stated, "Do not cool; look to Him to keep you burning and shining."[41]

"It is easy to rejoice when everything is as one wishes it were," Amy wrote. "But when things are exactly as one wishes they were not, it is not so easy. Then is the time to prove the things we believe."[42] Later, she said,

> He has brought you into the company of the happy-hearted, and you will carry His happiness wherever you go. How we dishonour our good Master when we carry fogs and mists and a general sense of dreariness. The Lord of joy keeps us in the glorious way of joy.[43]

Too often, we allow our circumstances to dictate our temperament. As "sent ones" called to missional living, we do well to take Amy's words to heart. One of the principal keys to thriving on mission is to draw near to the Lord of joy. Cast off the fog and mist and dreariness! A gloomy disposition not only dishonors our happy God but steals our strength in the process. Joy hoists up the heavy-hearted to exhibit the good news of the Gospel; it compels us to steal into the dark regions of the enemy's territory, spread the glorious light of salvation, and reclaim those bound by Satan.

With Exultation, We Go Forth

In this day and age, we are in desperate need of pioneers: daring missional Christians who step beyond cultural convenience and comfort zones to open new horizons. We need trailblazers who hack new passageways in the wilderness; who do not go where the path may lead, but go instead where there is no path to leave a trail. This apostolic anointing invigorates the weary, inspiring courage from inaction. The pioneer we need is bored by the status quo and motivated by an intrinsic drive to make God's glory known in the earth. Christian pioneers encourage us to be all that God called us to be.

Twenty-year-old Amy Carmichael wrote: "Does it not stir up our hearts, to go forth and help them, does it not make us long to leave our luxury, our exceeding abundant light, and go to them that sit in darkness?"[44] Stirred by the power of love, Amy began her itinerating work in 1897, around the age of thirty. For seven years, she traveled with a band of local women and girls, known as the "Starry Cluster," who were inspired by the verse: "So that you may become blameless and pure, 'children of God without fault in a warped and crooked generation.' Then you will shine among them like stars in the sky as you hold firmly to the word of life."[45]

They toured through the southern tip of India, striving to reach the women who lived without a witness of the Gospel. Their caravan furnished with a flag made of folds of black, red, white, and yellow sateen—the four colors of the wordless book often used to tell the story of salvation. Utilizing Eastern musical instruments and a baby organ by way of attraction, their street-preaching drew large crowds. However, the pioneering work was not without opposition. "Being the first women's band of its kind in the district," Amy said, "we walked circumspectly. I used to feel like a cat on the top of a wall, the sort of wall that is plentifully set with bits of broken bottles."[46] They skirted areas known for its bandits and faced much persecution. In one village, they were pelted with ashes and rotten garlands from the necks of Hindu idols. In a stunning display of missional fervor, Amy counted it pure joy when faced with trials of various kinds: "Oh, for an enthusiasm for Christ that will... thrill us with joy if He allows us to share in the faintest measure in His dishonour and loneliness; that will set every pulse throbbing with exultation as we go forth unto Him."[47]

Do our hearts beat with such a godly fervency? Do we take joy in dishonor and loneliness? This counterintuitive mentality emerges from a mind stayed on the Author and Perfecter of our faith. When we fix our eyes of Jesus, we gain an understanding of our identity in Him, "Who for the *joy* set before Him endured the cross."[48] A glad heart issued from inglorious affairs opens unimaginable opportunities to thrive on mission. We recognize this paradigm in the life of Amy Carmichael. She plodded straight into precarious places, expecting God to open providential doors. In 1901, she crossed beyond an impossible threshold and entered into a new season of Christian ministry.

On March 6, 1901, a seven-year-old girl called Preena bounded into the mission station and pleaded for help. Her dark eyes filled with terror as she clung to Amy's sari. She had escaped from the nearby temple to which her parents had sold her for "service" to the gods. Having already attempted once before to run away to her home, some twenty miles away, a wicked woman caught her and threatened wrath from the gods should she refuse to consent to temple life. Fearing the Hindu deities, Preena's mother unloosed her daughter's clinging arms and sent her back to the temple where she was subjected to savage torture. Tied to a stone, her hands were branded with hot irons. Preena lifted her hands to reveal a horrific display of punishment. One of India's ugliest hidden secrets uncloaked before Amy's eyes: the underground traffic of young temple girls and boys. She wrote:

> When first, upon March 7, 1901, we heard from the lips of a little child the story of her life in a temple house, we were startled and distressed... The subject was new to us; we knew nothing of the magnitude of what may be called 'The Secret Traffic of India'—a traffic in little children, mere infants oftentimes, for wrong purposes.[49]

Her choice of words does not adequately describe to the modern reader the magnitude of the monstrosity. In *Triumphant Love*, Hans Kommers explains the situation:[50]

In the 19th-century, *devadasis* [servants of the gods] were widely reputed to be prostitutes, 'and were recognized essentially as temple equipment.'[51] In short, it was the secret system 'by which the temple altars were supplied with little living victims...'[52] The practice involved grooming girls, some of them only babies, for a life of ritualized prostitution. These girls were a valuable commodity since they would become the sex slaves of the Brahman priests who ran the temples. Considered as property of the gods, the girls had no rights of their own and could be sexually abused and tortured without censure. Parents giving children to the temple were taught it was meritorious and since there were often financial rewards to the parents who did so, many children were—even before birth—dedicated to the temple.[53]

A shocking number of government officials turned a blind eye to this direct path to sexual exploitation. Even the majority of missionaries disregarded the savagery, for who could put an end to a system that had existed for ages? In the year 1004, the temple of the Chola king Rajaraja at Tanjore included 400 women of the temple, who, "as servants of the gods [*devadasis*], were subsisting by dancing and music and involved in the oldest profession in the world."[54] But Amy could not ignore such a devastating reality. She grieved at the fate of these little ones, "perverted at the very spring of being." She wrote, "The shame that burns, the wrong that stings us as we are forced to regard it, is this awful perversion of sweet to bitter, pure to vile, this deliberate defacement of the Lord's image in the soul of an innocent child."[55]

After the arrival of Preena, Amy's itinerating work ended. "And so began that which was afterwards to be the Dohnavur Fellowship."[56] 1901 was also "the year which we look back upon as the year of beginning of battles."[57] The villagers, pressured by the temple priests (who had already paid a sum for the girl), wanted Preena back. But Amy hid herself with the child in the tower of the village church where they slept for one night. There, Preena encountered her Savior's newfound affection in the person of Amy Carmichael, who came to be known as *Amma*, Tamil for mother. Years later, after Amma's passing, Preena recalled the day she met Amy: "When she saw me, the first thing she did was to put me on her lap and kiss me. I thought, 'My mother used to put me on her lap and kiss me—who is this person who kisses me like my mother?' From that day she became my mother, body and soul."[58] Having thus felt such unconditional love, she did not want to return to the Hindu religion.

The rescue had begun; from the bowels of a bleak underworld, scores of bruised children would find their way to the Amma of Dohnavur.

Coming to the Feet of Jesus

In the summer of 2000, sixteen American college students traveled to Southern India. Arriving at the Dohnavur campus, they marveled to visit the site where Amy Carmichael commenced her ministry. The campus leader—the last girl Amy Carmichael rescued from temple prostitution— gave them a tour. The leader of the team, Andy Lepper (now the director at Shiloh Children's Home in Northern India) shared his experience with me.

"Enamored to be in Dohnavur, I innocently said to our guide, 'It's so wonderful that you are carrying on Amy's memory by continuing to do what she did.'" The sweet, elderly woman's response made a lifelong impression on Andy.

She said, "My child, do not think we are carrying on Amma's legacy or continuing what she started. We are simply doing what God called *us* to do." The Indian woman explained: "Amma was so close to the feet of Jesus that it looks as if we are doing as she prescribed when, in fact, all we are doing is coming to the feet of Jesus." Her words struck Andy to the core.

He told me, "Those words became a benchmark in my life. I no longer try to be like anyone else; I simply seek to be found at the feet of Jesus."[59]

Such is the mark Amy Carmichael made in the minds of believers worldwide. She encouraged the body of Christ not to emulate her example, but to strive to know Jesus more. That is, essentially, the message of this book. Many missionaries lived exemplary lives, but we do better to pursue the same God they sought. The mind of a missionary is often worth emulating, but the mind of Christ is our ultimate goal.

Amy's joyful life seeped into the margins of everyone around her, dissipated on the fringes, and displayed not her own importance but instead uplifted her Savior. Amy, the frontierswoman, trailblazed new pathways to publicize the Person of Jesus. Her life commended the words of John the Baptist who said of his Master: "This is the assigned moment for Him to move into the center, while I slip off to the sidelines."[60] She gave Jesus the entire limelight.

Amy and her fellow missionaries intended to use Dohnavur merely as a temporary base for their itinerant missionary activity, but God had other plans. After hearing about girls kidnapped and forced to spend the rest of their beautiful young lives as sex fodder in the Hindu temples, Dohnavur became the base for one of the world's most successful Christian rescue missions. There, girls (and eventually boys) found sanctuary from a life worse than death. Whenever Amy heard about children in danger, she went to extreme measures to rescue them. She traveled long distances on hot, dusty roads, often disguising herself by rubbing coffee powder onto her skin to darken it. Thus, she penetrated India's secret trafficking world to rescue hundreds of precious children.

"Ever since I was a child, Amy Carmichael discipled me into missions through her stories and writings." Amy Rhodes, an American missionary at Within Reach Global in Chiang Mai, Thailand, recounted the impact that the 19th-century Kingdom worker made on her life: "Her courage to champion the cause of rescuing unwanted children inspired me. She took in dying babies so they could expire in loving arms instead of perishing, forgotten and alone." I have often told Amy Rhodes that she reminds me of a present-day Amy Carmichael. The early pioneer's influence on her life is evident. Amy continued: "Almost every day, I read an excerpt from Amy Carmichael to encourage me away from mediocre missionary activity. Her words fostered in me an understanding of my identity in Christ and a passion for His global cause."[61] At the end of our conversation, she quoted the last lines of one of Amy's most famous poems:

> Give me the love that leads the way,
> The faith that nothing can dismay,
> The hope no disappointments tire,
> The passion that will burn like fire,
> Let me not sink to be a clod:
> Make me Thy fuel, Flame of God.[62]

In the first few decades of the 20th-century, God used an unassuming, physically frail, courageous young Irish woman to transform Southern India. Through her many books, she relayed to the world the shocking exploitation of young children trafficked as sex slaves. Thomas Walker, Amy's missionary counterpart, wrote in the preface of *Overweights of Joy*:

> It is true also, absolutely true, that here, in Southern India, we are 'skirting the abyss,' an abyss which is deep and foul beyond description... Growing knowledge and accumulating information are only serving to make the awful darkness of that fell abyss more and more visible to view.[63]

After years of advocacy, the world finally took notice.

In 1947, inspired by Amy Carmichael's work, Dr. Mutthu Laksmi put forward the Devadasi Act for implementation.[64] The State Legislative Assembly in Madras passed legislation prohibiting the dedication of female infants to Hindu temples. This prohibition extended in 1954 nationwide by the Central Government in Delhi. Since 1988, the *devadasi* practice has been forbidden all over India.[65]

Despite Amy's strenuous efforts, sex trafficking has once again surfaced as a primary concern for modern-day justice causes—hence, our need for daring missional pioneers with an apostolic edge. We need trailblazers who hack new passageways in the wilderness. For "our enemy is more aware than we are of the spiritual possibilities that depend upon obedience."[66] What might Amy Carmichael say to us who stare straight into the face of such injustice? I imagine she might choose these words: "Satan is so much more in earnest than we are—he buys up the opportunity while we are wondering how much it will cost."[67] Yes, dear Christian, there is a price for obeying the commands of Christ, but the rewards far outweigh the expense. For at the feet of Jesus is joy everlasting.

The Continuation of a Story

God glories to situate us somewhere between the beginning and the continuation of a story. With our limited view of eternity, one can never be quite sure of his or her placement. Regardless of the situations or circumstances you find yourself in, God bestows upon you a rich joy for the journey.

In 1908, Amy Carmichael published *The Beginning of a Story*, chronicling her work with the temple children of India. However, her readers wished to know what happened next. Thus came *The Continuation of a Story* in 1914, the first words of which begin:

> Is *The Beginning of a Story* never going to have a Continuation?
> This is the question which comes rather frequently and seems to
> expect an answer. The answer is that we are in the middle of the
> Continuation, and it is difficult to stop and talk about it, for con-
> tinuations, if they are to continue, insist upon steady work rather
> than over-much talk. [68]

These words reveal yet another key to thriving on mission today: cheerful labor marks the faithful and moves you toward your destiny. Joy is found in the lines within a chapter, the pauses between a play, and the interludes of a performance. Inevitable difficulties mark the drama, but the show must go on until the culmination of the plot. In the messy middle, better a merry heart than an anxious mind. The joy of the Lord is your strength today, here in the halfway moments, ever available for those who choose to accept it.

Ana Opungu, a Filipino missionary in Papua New Guinea, told me: "Remembering that this is God's work and not ours is a powerful key to maintaining equilibrium on the mission field." She relayed her family's experience of "hitting rock bottom" when their coworkers unjustly accused them of wrongdoing. "We welcomed the comfort of the Holy Spirit, knowing that God accomplishes His work in His own way and in His own time." Ana's family saw themselves as small parts of a Kingdom picture. "Each of us occupies a different space in the puzzle; He fits every piece in its rightful place."[69]

Perhaps you are unsure where you fit in God's Kingdom purposes. You know He wants to use you, but you're not quite sure how. May I encourage you to pause from your busy activity and press deeper into His presence? Fullness of joy is there, awaiting your arrival. And as you experience joy on the journey, faithful service follows. He guides your every step and will maneuver you to the perfect place of employment.

Picture a story as a tree. Its origins do not always evidence themselves in its low-hanging fruit, its leafy twigs, its broad branches, or its stalwart trunk. It does not even begin at the root; its beginnings are much older than the tree itself. Some might say such a story starts in a seed—an acorn, perhaps—from which grows a sturdy oak. But the mystery of its beginnings traces farther back to an era in which the whole forest did not yet exist.

A tiny, wind-blown seed from yet another tree fell to the soil, buried, and brought forth new life. Even the seed from that tree found its origins in another. Farther back in time the process goes—a steady succession of life to death and back to life again. The forest you now find yourself within simply breathes the whispers and carries the memories of its first dawning at the creation of time.

The pieces of a puzzle might also depict an ongoing story. I picture God hunched over a jigsaw, a serene smile hovered on His lips. He thoughtfully selects a puzzle piece, pinches it between forefinger and thumb, and places it in the proper location. The image begins to form—a masterpiece in the making.

As I consider the life of Amy Carmichael, I am struck by the providential sequence of events that makes up her story. "We have a God who thinks beforehand for His children," she wrote. "We have only to follow His thoughts."[70] Each fragment—sometimes a situation, often a person— played a part in the providential sequence of events.

Space does not allow—nor is human mind able to comprehend—God's divine weaving together of His glorious timeline. We recognize but the fragments—seemingly jumbled and disjointed bits. God views the macro narrative from outside space and time.

On June 28, 1875, Robert Wilson helped organize the first Keswick Convention in a tent on the lawn of St. John's vicarage in Keswick, England. Since the day Amy sailed to the East, on March 3, 1893, Wilson's weekly letters to Carmichael crossed the oceans. He encouraged her "to keep first things first"[71] and to "follow no voice, not mine or any other which is not His."[72] The Keswick Convention imprinted on Amy's ministry. Andrew Murray also played an important role in shaping Amy's missional fervor. His appeal at the 1895 Convention—namely, these words: "Sacrifice everything and anything for the glory of your God"[73]—helped her do just that. Her network of influencers included Arthur T. Pierson, who succeeded Charles H. Spurgeon in the pulpit of the Metropolitan Tabernacle in London. Pierson, along with Dwight L. Moody, inspired student Robert P. Wilder to form the Student Volunteer Movement, which we read about in chapter two. This movement sent the Cambridge Seven—"men of culture, education, and distinguished gifts"—to China where C. T. Studd and his counterparts assumed the baton passed by the prayerful Dr. Harold Schofield. Studd, after having been sent to China by the China Inland Mission in 1885, later felt the Lord directing him to India. It was there that Amy frequently met the Studd family, becoming lifelong friends. Though different people helped to shape Amy's mission view, some men seemed to rise above the others. In 1885, Amy met Hudson Taylor, the founder of the China Inland Mission, for the first time. She heard him pleading for the millions who, every month, passed away beyond the reach of the Gospel:[74] "If we would be soul-winners and build up the Church, which is His temple, let us not this: not by discussion nor by argument, but by lifting up Christ shall we draw men unto Him."[75]

The providential sequence of persons and events left an indelible mark on Amy Carmichael. She, in turn—a small yet integral piece of the puzzle—continued God's global narrative, inspiring scores of global Kingdom workers who followed in her footsteps. Perhaps the most notable of these were Jim and Elisabeth Elliot, who we read about in chapter one. Elisabeth Elliot first heard of the Irish missionary, "whose beautiful writings captivated my imagination,"[76] at age fourteen. Amy's selfless ministry indirectly affected Operation Auca and the Ecuador Five, whose martyrdom led to the salvation of the Huaorani tribe. Along with her three-year-old daughter, Valerie, Elisabeth Elliot moved in with the Huaoranis of Ecuador. In 1958, she wrote: "Just about ten feet away, sit two of the seven men who killed my husband. Gikita, one of the men, has just helped Valerie... roast a plantain."[77] Missionary outreach to the "savage" stone-age tribe transformed the Ecuadorian people group. So moved by the service of her predecessor, Elisabeth Elliot later wrote a biography of Amy Carmichael entitled *A Chance To Die*.

Today, the legacy is still felt around the world. A bronze sculpture of Amy Carmichael unveiled on December 16, 2017 at a private ceremony at Hamilton Road Presbyterian Church in Bangor, England. The sculpture portrays Amy in the tenth year of her life as she holds her diary where she recorded her dreams about the future. She is looking out from below her hat towards a purposed life of devotion to others, and a giving heart that would impact generations of children to come.[78] At the unveiling, Valerie Elliot Shepherd, daughter of Jim and Elisabeth Elliot, stood in attendance as part of the Irish missionary's ongoing effect. There it was said: "We hope that the many children and people who see the sculpture will be challenged by Amy's story and selfless sacrifice to travel and live and die in a foreign land, all in service to the Lord Jesus Christ."[79]

I, too, was indirectly affected by the life of Amy Carmichael. As a child, my father read the Elliots' story to me in *Through Gates of Splendor* by

Elisabeth Elliot. The missionary biography shaped my worldview. Years later, in 1998, my missionary career began when I moved to China. Had I followed a "call" to missions? Some might consider this. Instead, I see myself as a small part in a long succession of global Kingdom workers.

There are no commonplace Christian cogs in the Great Commission enterprise. Every Christ-follower is an integral, God-ordained component in His divine plot. God puts each puzzle piece in place to construct the timeless masterpiece of His story. True missional beginnings commence at the feet of Jesus and continue by His sustaining grace. And in the assembling process of divinely intertwined sequences, an unearthly joy undergirds our every step.

Joy, Not Suffering, Is Eternal

In 1906, Amy's mother came to Dohnavur to assist her for one year. "As for my mother, she would have gathered all India into her heart," Amy said. "For India's imperiled children she had only one word, 'Welcome.'"[80] At that time, Dohnavur filled with women and children. The mission was more like a family than an orphanage, and Amy's mother thrilled to take part in her precious daughter's ministry. The following year, a serious outbreak of dysentery followed the baptism of several girls. It was a vengeful attack from the enemy, infuriated by his loss of territory in Southern India. All hands were needed in Dohnavur to nurse the sick. With all the assistance that arrived, nobody could prevent ten babies from dying.

Struggle and difficulty mounted as the mission grew. Not a few babies died in Amy's loving arms; yet, amid such suffering, she found the strength to carry on. "If our God tells us to do a thing and we say we cannot, there is something wrong somewhere," Amy said. She quoted Philippians 4:13: "I can do all things through Christ who strengthens me."[81] The storms we must endure are "an eternal reminder of what we are all meant to be and do. We are not meant to be fair-weather Christians; we are never promised fair weather."[82] With so great a need all around her, she could do nothing but rely on help from her Heavenly Father. This dependence on God led to the rescue of hundreds of temple children who found refuge in Dohnavur.

On July 14, 1913, Amy's mother went to be with the Lord. Ten days earlier, she had written a letter to Amy that began: "My own most precious earthly possession." She posted her final loving letter on July 10, 1913, and her last act was to post a cheque for the Dohnavur work. Amy heard the sad news of her mother's passing on July 17. Everyone at the mission felt the loss, but celebration superseded sorrow. Years later, Amy wrote to the children in Dohnavur: "When my mother passed on we made the Praise Room bright with lights and beautiful with flowers, and you all stood in the dark courtyard and then came into the shining room, and we sang together the most Heavenly hymns we knew and were happy in her happiness."[83]

Amy's otherworldly joy calls our Christian work into question. Does the joy of the Lord jumpstart all our missional efforts? In victory and privation, God remains unchanging. The reward of joy is available to us today just as it was for the 20th-century Irish Amma.

Were it not for an accident in 1931, Amy might have stealthily entered every temple in Southern India in search of captive children. (An early member of the Starry Cluster once said that Amy was "not walking, nor even running but always *flying*, with many a glance at a wristlet watch 'lest we waste moments.'")[84] Instead, God had an even further-reaching plan.

Early morning, on October 24, 1931, Amy broke her ankle and distorted her back in a fall. From that day she was never without pain. Ten years before her accident, Amy had written: "To be ill in India can never be easy. It is a land to live for, and (most joyfully) to die in, but it is not a land to be ill in..."[85] Confined to her room, she hoped for a full recovery. But weeks became years; the injury left her bed-ridden for the remainder of her life. Sleep eluded her; she awoke each night in pain. Still, even in her suffering, she remained people-centered. A deep sense of empathy for the sufferings other people underwent furthered her offerings of comfort and refreshment. "Joy is not gush," she said. "Joy is not mere jolliness. Joy is perfect acquiescence—acceptance, rest—in God's will, whatever comes."[86]

Amy Carmichael served in India for fifty-five years without returning to her homeland. During her life, she wrote thirty-five books that still urge a deep devotion to the Lord and a fervent zeal for missions. Many of her masterful pieces of missions literature she wrote while confined to her bed. Her heart and mind founded on the promises of God, she championed the joyful Christian life, inspiring us to thrive on mission today. "Joy, not suffering, is eternal," she said. "And there are many joys now. May your day be full of joy, the kind that is strength."[87]

On January 18, 1951, Heaven called the Amma of Dohnavur away from her earthly battle. Amy Carmichael died in India at the age of 83. The reward she had long sought came at last: not only "the crown of converts won for Him,"[88] but a place at the feet of Jesus. The people in Dohnavur felt the grief, but not gloom; Amma was with Jesus, and her children joyed that they should meet her again in Heaven. As is still the custom, all the graves in "God's Garden" in Dohnavur (where many a child laid to rest) are equal, with no headstones to mark the graves; a single brick identifies each burial spot.[89] So it was with Amy's grave. However, shortly after her funeral, a humble bird bath was placed there, fixed with the single compelling inscription: "Amma."

CHAPTER ELEVEN

BREAKTHROUGH IN MINISTRY

An Immeasurably Greater Privilege

A one-thousand-mile beast rises westward from the waters north of Australia. Its clawed forelimbs skirt the sea. Its scaly tail situates south of the equator, stretching east toward the Pacific Ocean. 19th-century Dutch explorers likened the shape of the beast to a bird-of-paradise. However, upon closer look, the creature looked more like a Tyrannosaurus rex—its carnivorous jaw open, poised to attack.

This depiction is, in fact, of a geographical territory situated in Oceania. The eastern half of the island of New Guinea is the major land mass of the independent state of Papua New Guinea. The western half, referred to as Western New Guinea or West Papua (formerly Irian Jaya), is a former Dutch colony and the present territory of Indonesia. The large island is populated by almost one-thousand different tribal groups and a near equivalent number of separate languages, making New Guinea the most linguistically diverse area in the world.

A spine of east-west mountains dominates the geography of New Guinea, stretching over one-thousand miles from the "head" to the "tail" of the island. The western half of the island contains the highest mountains in Oceania, rising to 16,024 feet. The beast's head, neck, and northern mountain vertebrae are a kind of "Eden"—a mile-high landscape with moderate weather and flourishing agriculture. In the southern "belly" of the beast lies the wetlands, its "shimmering, emerald swamps, veined with turgid streams, lush with endless sago thickets,"[1] stretching as far as the eye can see. There resided a cannibalistic, headhunting tribe called the Sawi to whom, in 1962, God called Don and Carol Richardson with their seven-month-old son, Stephen.

In 1955, while studying at Prairie Bible Institute in Alberta, Canada, Don Richardson sat enthralled with 700 students. Richardson riveted as a visiting missionary speaker unburdened his soul before the student body with a strong sense of purpose. The white-haired man's grey eyes shone with intensity as he spoke about New Guinea's need of the Gospel. "Now the way is open to the interior!" he boomed.[2]

Despite the fact that law enforcement agencies "could not accept the responsibilities of protecting [the] missionaries from the cannibals,"[3] two couples had joined Regions Beyond Missionary Union to reach the unreached people groups. "I cannot believe that God has brought [us] to this great new threshold so that two men and their wives should cross it alone!" the speaker urged. He paused to scan the student body, then continued: "There must be others whom God will call to join them! There may be some such seated here before me now!" Across the auditorium, the Holy Spirit drew the hearts and minds of the young men and women in attendance. Many stepped forward to offer themselves to the foreign field. They joined hands with other volunteers from Christian campuses in North America, England, Germany, and Australia to swell the ranks of the organization's missionary task force in New Guinea to more than thirty by 1965.[4]

Richardson also felt the scrutiny of God upon him. Sensing the Holy Spirit's drawing to the foreign field, he eagerly returned to his dormitory room, fell to his knees, and prayed, "Is this it? Is this what You want me to do?"[5] God seemed to respond with a sweeping invitation into the unknown. For Richardson, a life of service to the cause of Christ signified eternal meaning. "If sharing Him where His name was already known was a privilege," he said, "sharing Him where His name had never been heard must be an immeasurably greater privilege!"[6]

Has the urgency of God's Gospel message for all peoples waned in the hearts of His followers? Certainly, there exists in many minds an altruistic desire to be used by God. Why, then, do nearly two-billion people wait hopelessly for a presentation of the Good News? Why is it that we talk of the second coming of Christ when so many have never heard of His first? I see two reasons for the plight of present-day unreached people groups: ethno-centrism and a lack of grit. We believe that Jesus called us to live and thrive on mission with Him; to give witness of His Kingdom wherever we go. But for all our zealousness, we have overlooked the "hard places" of the world, relegating the bulk of our ministry efforts to areas that already have access to the Christian message. It is hard for us to see the colossal needs that lay beyond the scope of our zip codes and country. And many of those who dare to cross cultural, linguistic, and geographic boundaries for the sake of the Gospel flounder on the foreign field. Publicizing the name of Jesus to elicit worshippers from every nation, tribe, people, and language is no easy task. The reward of ministry breakthrough will not transpire without daring risk and steadfast missionary grit.

The "guides" that appear in every chapter of this book—the missionaries who challenge us to recognize God's glorious global plan—do not downplay the unique roles in the body of Christ. After all, every citizen in God's Kingdom is crucial. However, they *do* challenge us to look beyond our spheres and remember the fringes that are equally important to our Heavenly Father. The mandate of our message matters because of the supremacy of God's glory. Our urgent mission, then, is merely a means to an end, namely: to worship. "Worship is the fuel and goal of missions," says John Piper.

> Missions is not the ultimate goal of the Church. Worship is. Missions exists because worship doesn't. Worship is ultimate, not missions, because God is ultimate, not man. When this age is over, and the countless millions of the redeemed fall on their faces before the throne of God, missions will be no more. It is a temporary necessity. But worship abides forever.[7]

I believe that if we passionately pursue the presence of God, compassion for people swells as a matter of course. So, it expanded in the heart of Don Richardson. Still another Prairie Bible Institute student was present for the stirring call to New Guinea. Carol Soderstrom trained as a nurse in hopes to serve on the mission field. She caught Don's eye, and in 1960, she became Mrs. Carol Richardson.

On November 23, 1961, after the Richardsons attended a linguistic course offered by the Summer Institute of Linguistics, Carol gave birth to their first child, Stephen. God's plan for the Canadian family swiftly transpired.

On March 19, 1962, they sailed from Vancouver aboard the Oriana, arriving April 13 at Sentani, an airfield on the north coast of New Guinea. Seven days later, they flew from the northernmost tip of the island to Karubaga, the main interior station of Regions Beyond Missionary Union in the Black Valley. They would soon find their way even farther south to the swampy wetlands of New Guinea: the belly of the beast.

I Am No Place for You

Backdropped by precipitous mountain ranges, nearly naked tribesmen sported stone axes, and string-skirted women dug with wooden sticks in their sweet potato gardens. The fertile hills sloped to meet the hutted settlements, home to the Dani people. "There is still much to be done here in the Black Valley," the Reach Beyond Missionary Union's host told Richardson. But a great deal of discussion about the needs of other tribes that were still unreached became forefront in the conversation. Richardson heard about a large area of the vast swampy plain south near the Arafura Sea where few missionaries dared to go. "The area is anything but hospitable," his host reported. "Many of the tribes in that region are still practicing both cannibalism and headhunting and are generally not to be trusted."[8]

Reports of the treacherous terrain, cruel climate, and bloodthirsty inhabitants pricked up Richardson's ears. Twenty-two feet of rainfall descended each year over the region. The mosquito-infested swamps mushroomed with malaria. Giant crocodiles, poisonous snakes, and bloodsucking leeches were of less concern than the cannibalistic headhunters. But Richardson welcomed the invitation to serve in the tough field. After two days of waiting on God in prayer, the Richardsons gave their answer: "Yes, we are happy to go to one of the tribes in the south!" they said. "How soon can we leave?"[9]

On May 19, 1962, Don, Carol, and six-month-old Stephen soared over the mighty ranges of Mount Wilhelmina, awed as they suddenly dropped from altitudes of 15,000 feet down to sea level. God's fingerprints evidenced in the panorama, proof that His presence predated their arrival. Their hearts thumped with nervous enthusiasm. Somewhere below, in the shimmering stretch of emerald grasslands, graceful palms, and dense sago thickets, they were to build a home and live among a cannibal-headhunter tribe.

As long as anyone could remember, the Sawi people warred with neighboring clans. They valued treachery and trickery as a way of dominating the territory. Presumably, in the late 1950s, Yae, a man from the Sawi village of Mauro donned his ornaments in preparation for his journey to an enemy village. He covered his naked loins with a narrow grass skirt—a symbol worn only by men who had slain an enemy in battle. Yae had slaughtered five, taking the heads from three of his victims. The three bracelets of wild boar tusks that hung around his elbow indicated his superiority in combat. His hunting prowess expressed by a six-foot-long necklace of animal teeth (those from the wild pigs, crocodiles, dogs, or marsupials he slaughtered) draped in two loops around his neck. He fitted bands of finely woven rattan tightly above and below the muscles on each arm and just below his knees. He proudly inserted into his pierced nose a six-inch hollowed bone, sharpened on each end, carved from the thighbone of a pig.

Yae's mission was purely diplomatic. An enemy warrior named Kauwan had demonstrated his friendly intentions by giving Yae a small piece of sharpened bamboo, woven by a lock of his stringy black hair, and wrapped in a leaf. With this token of safe passage in his possession, Yae agreed to journey to the upstream Sawi village called Haenam. If peaceful relations between Mauro and Haenam established, both Yae and Kauwan hoped to rise to new heights of prestige. The two communities might then join forces to inflict a decisive blow against the Asmat and the Kayagar, enemy tribes further downstream. Yae considered the prize his pact with Kauwan might incur: the Sawi ideal of a harem of five healthy wives.

Yae acted in a guarded manner; he needed to be sure of Kauwan's intent. Over the next seven months, Yae visited Haenam ten times, passing each time beneath a Kayagar skull suspended from a low-lying branch at the village entrance. At each arrival, the tribesmen received him with the same warm welcome, increasing his confidence with each successive visit. All signs seemed to point to peace and friendship between the warring villages.

On his eleventh visit to Haenam, the previous apprehensions he had felt now expired. Kauwan greeted Yae at the river's edge and warmly welcomed him into his hut. There he dined on freshly toasted sago grubs with his hosts as the room filled with jest and side-splitting laughter. The Sawi men heaped compliments on Yae, saying they had heard of his prowess in hunting and fighting. Smiling, Yae eased back onto his grass mat.

A sudden subtle raising of the eyebrows silenced the festivity in the hut. The secret signal passed from one man to the next as each stealthily drew forth long, needle-sharp bone daggers, barbed ironwood spears, stone axes, bows, and arrows. The men encircled Yae, pointing their weapons toward his body. He looked around at his new "friends" and saw the sinister smile of satisfaction. They duped him. "Tuwi asonai makaerin! We have been fattening you with false friendship for the slaughter!"[10] Kauwan jeered. As he looked at their faces, Yae knew those sinister grins was the last thing he would ever see.

Such was the social milieu that greeted the Richardson family as they arrived in Sawi territory. In June 1962, Don left his wife and son to the care of a missionary family on the southwestern coast of New Guinea. Along with his missionary counterparts, Richardson paddled in a canoe through the serpentine rivers to meet the Sawi. His goal was to establish a beachhead among the people, build a home, and return as soon as possible for his family. Don recalled that pivotal pioneering moment of his departure into the dense swamplands: "Carol was holding baby Stephen, who had just awakened," he said. "His tiny face was barely visible in the pale blue of early dawn as he snuggled close to Carol's blond hair."[11]

During his river journey, the wilderness of the locale seemed to taunt Richardson. Something in the mood of the place seemed to mock, "I am not like your tame, manageable Canadian homeland. I am tangled." The canoe drifted past the twisted vines and sago thorns that lined the dense banks, skirting death adders and taipans, leeches and crocodiles. The taunting whispers continued: "Your idealism means nothing here. Your Christian Gospel has never scrupled the conscience of my children. You think you love them, but wait until you know them, if you *can* ever know them!" Don was not worried for his safety, but thoughts about his family coursed through his mind. The region thronged with malaria and dysentery, filariasis and hepatitis. "Think again, before you commit yourself to certain disillusionment!" the voices seemed to continue. "Can't you see I am no place for your wife? I am no place for your son. I am no place for you."[12]

Whether these were the voices of the negative inner monologue or a challenge from the enemy that we read about in chapter four, global Kingdom workers are sure to experience similar discouraging rumination. The kingdom of darkness fills with terror at the advent of the missional

Christian. Satan understands the conclusion of God's narrative, often more than we do. He knows his end; his days are marked. Compelled to establish the Kingdom of God where it is still unknown, Christ's followers advance confidently into the shadowlands, certain that the victory is theirs.

A plan of divine proportions set into place. In 1949, when the rest of the Dutch East Indies became fully independent as Indonesia, the Dutch retained sovereignty over western New Guinea and took steps to prepare it for independence as a separate country. Tensions between Netherlands New Guinea and Indonesia escalated in the late 1950s and heightened after the Dutch endorsed the selection of a new national anthem[13] and new national flag[14] on December 1, 1961.

The year previous, in 1960, two canopied riverboats advanced through Sawi territory under a fluttering red, white, and blue flag of the Netherlands. Their mission: "to explore the little-known southern extremity of the Agats administrative district, which until now had been left without any kind of government supervision."[15] They hoped to put an end to the ceaseless headhunting and cannibalism prevalent in the wild area.

The Sawis had heard rumors of pale-skinned foreigners, called "Tuans." Their "super canoes" sailed past the banks of Sawi settlements, supplied with iron tools, nylon fishing lines, and modern technology unknown to the stone-age tribe. Again, we notice a providential sequence of events that the mind of man could never have surmised. The positive impression produced by the foreign presence was atypical in the underbelly of Netherlands New Guinea.

When Don Richardson's canoe slid onto the banks of Kamur Village in June 1962, the Sawi welcomed him nervously. They helped him build a thatch-roofed jungle home stilted six feet above the ground in case of flooding. The "thatch box," as Richardson called it, was to be the family's first home to themselves since marriage. Upon completion of his home, Richardson returned to retrieve his family, communicating to the Sawis as best he could that "In three days' time I'll return with my wife and child."[16]

On July 13, 1962, sun rays glimmered on wet paddles as the Richardson family traversed the long bends of the Kronkel River. Hour after hour, they skimmed the waterways toward their destination. At the final bend, the sun set; dusk settled over the settlement. Still a distance off, Carol spotted the "thatch box" silhouetted against the dim, blushing sky. As they approached the village, they were unprepared for what they saw next. About two-hundred armed warriors thronged on the shore, spears in hand, plumed feathers upraised, warpaint streaked across their faces. The Richardsons were now in range of their weapons; it was too late to think about retreating. The situation seemed grim. "The best we could hope for was that it would be over as quickly and painlessly as possible,"[17] Richardson later said.

The canoe slid up on the mud at the feet of the armed host; the Sawi looked down at the missionary family in silence. Don could hear his heart beating anxiously. He steadied Carol off the boat, Stephen tucked in his right arm; they walked straight into the midst of the Sawi crowd. Suddenly, a loud voice shrieked a high-pitched command; the people began leaping in the air, brandishing their weapons, and shouting at the top of their lungs. The synchronized rhythm of the drummers thundered as the crowd danced wildly, escorting the missionaries further away from the river and in the direction of the thatch box home. Carol's eyes met Don's; they sparkled with delight. Stephen reached out from Don's arm to grab white cockatoo feathers, golden bird-of-paradise blooms, and dog-fang necklaces.

"Suddenly, in the blue glow of twilight, a Presence stronger than the presence of the multitude enveloped us," Don recalled. The same Presence that had first drawn the Richardsons to trust in Christ, and then wooed them across continents and oceans to that very jungle clearing probed Richardson's motives: "Missionary," He was asking, "Why are you here?" Don breathed his reply: "Lord Jesus, it is for You we stand here, immersed not in water but in Sawi humanity. This is our baptism into the work You anticipated for us before creation. Keep us faithful. Empower us with Your Spirit."[18]

The dancing continued for three days as the Sawi celebrated the arrival of their new guests. This settlement was made for the Richardsons; they were home in Kamur. The peace of God poured over the family like a waterfall from Heaven.

Fatten Him with Friendship for an Unsuspecting Slaughter

Language is the key that unlocks the door to culture. Far too many missionaries are content to stand outside the entrance, peering through the ajar door, but never crossing beyond the threshold. They catch occasional glimpses of the pervading values, beliefs, underlying assumptions, attitudes, and behaviors of the culture, but only enough to keep them at the fringes. Make no mistake about it: language acquisition is the hinge upon which foreigners forge new frontiers, the passageway into a cultural worldview.

The definition of culture presented in *The Evangelical Dictionary of Missions* reads:

> We use the term 'culture' to refer to the common ideas, feelings, and values that guide community and personal behavior, that organize and regulate what the group thinks, feels, and does about God, the world, and humanity. It explains why the Sawi people of Irian Jaya regard betrayal as a virtue, while the American sees it as a vice.[19]

Without a grasp of the language, mystery shrouds our understanding of cultural values. And with little comprehension of the value system, finding the cultural compasses (what Don Richardson calls "redemptive analogies") is a complicated chore.

Contextualization is not only the task of the global Kingdom worker. We are all called to present the Gospel in a culturally relevant way, thus highlighting and not diminishing its potency. Don Richardson understood that to unlock the hearts of the Sawi, he must first master their language and penetrate its mysteries.

Without the help of an already-published grammar or dictionary and no bilingual helper, Richardson spent eight to ten hours each day learning the Sawi language. Through body language and gesturing, he accumulated nouns; he mimicked actions to elicit verbs. He then began to combine nouns and verbs to find out the correct order—subject at the beginning, object in the middle, verb at the end. "I felt like a linguistic Columbus," he said, "sailing an uncharted linguistic sea, making new discoveries in vocabulary and rules of grammar."[20] He hoped to eventually explain why they were there.

An inducement of novelty and practicality—and perhaps a certain prestige—drew residents from the neighboring Haenam and Yohwi villages to the missionaries' thatch box home on the clearing of Kamur Village. The Sawis believed the extremely rare "Tuans" to be a source of potentially limitless supplies of iron axes, steel machetes, knives, fishline, fishhooks, and other prized rarities. As the curious inhabitants swelled to hundreds, the missionaries delighted at the prospects.

The Dutch government was unwilling to send doctors and nurses into the dangerous territory, but Carol welcomed their offerings of much-needed medical supplies. Day after day, she treated patients suffering from malaria, dysentery, and hepatitis, and medicated hosts of wounded Sawis. Over the next several years, Carol saved an average of a life a day, and many more during peaks of epidemics and diseases. The Sawis called her "the woman who makes all the villages well."

Don focused intently on the language, longing to proclaim the Gospel message to the unreached tribe. One hot and humid day, he climbed a bamboo pole leading up a stilted hut where the men of Haenam and Yohwi gathered. Joining them around a smoky fire pit, he laid his notes on the mat in front of him and started in. He told about the Creator of the world, His dominion over the spirit world, and of His great love for the Sawi people. Some of the men seemed disinterested while others listened in open-jawed amazement. His narration weaved through the Bible and arrived at the Son of God. The men listened intently as he described Judas Iscariot's betrayal of Jesus. They noted the details: for three years Judas kept close company with Jesus, shared the same meals, and traveled the same roads.

At the climax of the story, one man whistled a birdcall of admiration. Several men touched their chests in respect; still others chuckled. A feeling of coldness gripped Richardson when he realized they were acclaiming Judas as the hero of the story! The exact opposite effect Richardson expected had occurred. Christ meant nothing to the Sawi men; they cheered for Judas the betrayer, a master of treachery. That was not the response the missionary expected. One man leaned forward and exclaimed, "Tuwi asonai man!" Soon after, Richardson would come to understand the Sawi worldview expressed in that short phrase, meaning: "To fatten him with friendship for an unsuspecting slaughter."

The missionary looked across the swampy grasslands. Carol dispensed medicine to the locals while baby Stephen played on a mat behind her. "Was this the limit of the good we could do for the Sawi?" Richardson wondered. "Bringing health to their physical bodies while the core of their beings remained remote and unreachable?"[21] He felt like a failure but decided to go back to the drawing board in hopes to find a way into the heart of the people.

God's Fingerprints in Culture

The notion that godly Kingdom principles are foreign concepts introduced into a culture is a fundamentally erred hypothesis. Don Richardson says that "God has been sovereignly working in a preparatory way by seeding cultures worldwide with foreshadowings of the Savior."[22] Facets of Christ's redemptive message can be found in every populace. These signposts help facilitate the fulfillment of the Abrahamic Covenant—"I am going to bless you," God said to Abraham, "and through you bring blessing to the whole world."[23] Christian, you are blessed to *be* a blessing.

The fallen aspects of mankind are evident in every culture on the earth; the broken bits are often easy to spot. As Christians, our task is to help shed light on the splendor of God's original intention: His salvation available to every nation, tribe, people, and language. This is not merely the job of foreign missionaries. Global Kingdom workers tell us that every member of the body of Christ is a minister. If we serve a God who bestows upon His creation a crown of beauty instead of ashes, the oil of joy instead of mourning, and a garment of praise instead of a spirit of despair,[24] it follows that His people do likewise. For God evokes holy calling from unassuming spots, pulling passion from the profane, wringing vision from vile waters. He is in the business of transformation, of altering atmospheres, taking the squalid and making it exquisite.[25]

When we look at culture through the lens of what Don Richardson calls "redemptive analogy," God's fingerprints upon humanity come into full view. A redemptive analogy harnesses the language, story, or tradition of a particular culture to facilitate the explanation and understanding of God's redemptive work through the Person of Jesus Christ. An excellent example of these "cultural compasses" is found in the Chinese word for "righteousness."

On September 2, 1998, I officially commenced my study of the Mandarin language in China's southwest city of Kunming. There I lived and ministered for the next fifteen years, and with my wife, later established a missions agency called Within Reach Global. Our vision, simply stated, is this:

"Honor God. Reach the unreached." We focus on evangelism, discipleship, and church planting among Southeast Asia's unreached people groups.

As I studied the Mandarin language, I came to see the many redemptive cultural compasses hidden within Chinese characters. The traditional character 義 (yì), for example, combines the characters 羊 (yáng, "lamb") and 我 (wǒ, the first-person pronoun "I" or "me") to form the word for "righteousness." The word essentially states that when "I" am under the "Lamb," I become "righteous." This is but one of myriads of examples of Gospel truth found in the Chinese language. Biblical truths like this interweave throughout the language, dispel the "foreignness" of the Message, and open natural pathways to God in the hearts of the Chinese.

In Romans chapter one, Paul wrote that "God's invisible qualities—His eternal power and divine nature—have been clearly seen, being understood from what has been made, so that people are without excuse."[26] The Creator seeded each society with secrets of Himself. He joys to see His children discover the mysteries of Heaven in their midst. As ambassadors of the Kingdom, our task is to unearth and make plain these Gospel truths hidden within our culture. Utilizing linguistic (and other) redemptive analogies, we have seen significant breakthroughs in Southwest China through the ministry of Within Reach Global.

Our job as believers is to give witness of God's glory in a culturally relevant manner; to unearth the cultural compasses that speak to the hearts and minds of our hearers. Redemptive analogy is not a new concept. Jesus often utilized parabolic metaphor in His storytelling, saying that the Kingdom of God is like "a mustard seed," "a pearl of great price," and "hidden treasure." He told Nicodemus that "as Moses lifted up the serpent in the wilderness, even so must the Son of Man be lifted up, that whoever believes in Him should not perish but have eternal life."[27] The Jewish ruler was familiar with the story of Moses lifting the serpent of brass upon a pole so that Jews, dying of snake bites, could look at it and be healed. The Apostle Paul also employed redemptive analogy as a bridge between the Gospel and Greek culture. While in Athens, he was greatly distressed to see that the city was full of idols.

> People of Athens! he said, I see that in every way you are very religious. For as I walked around and looked carefully at your

objects of worship, I even found an altar with this inscription: TO AN UNKNOWN GOD. So you are ignorant of the very thing you worship—and this is what I am going to proclaim to you.[28]

Many people recognized "the Lord of Heaven and earth" present in their cultural context and chose to follow Paul's Message.

After ministering in China for more than a decade, my wife and I felt the Holy Spirit directing us to Thailand. I am writing this book from my home in Chiang Mai, where we have been living for more than five years. Ninety-five percent of Thailand's 69,000,000 citizens adhere to Theravada Buddhism; after hundreds of years of Protestant missionary work, less than one percent claim to be Christians. "Our method of presenting the Gospel has been opposed to the Thai peoples' lifestyle, language, and culture," says Jiraphon Serithai, a leader of a Thai Christian Movement.

> If we had purposefully brought Jesus in a Thai way with Thai culture and language, Thai churches would be sending missionaries to Laos, Cambodia, and Burma by now. But the way things were done resulted in generation after generation recognizing that following Jesus Christ meant joining a Western religion.[29]

Troubled that so few Thai people believed in Jesus Christ, Serithai spent years examining the centuries of missions effort in Thailand. She now subscribes to a metaphoric approach to Gospel presentation among her people, contextualizing the Message to the Thai mindset. Instead of presenting Jesus as another religion, she says that "Jesus is the Way of release," "nirvana," and "the Truth and the Life." She does not tell people they are "sinners," but that they have "karma." She declares this year as "the golden year" because "if you are in Christ, every year is your golden year." Serithai expresses Gospel terms in the Theravada Buddhist framework and has seen a tremendous increase of Thai believers. Confident that God's sovereignty and holiness are unchanging, she says,

> We do not need to be afraid that God's name will be tainted, damaged, or disgraced. If we present Him for Thai Buddhists to choose, He will go and sit on the throne of their hearts, even though He might be sitting with all the gods that are hanging on their necks.[30]

If Serithai's evangelistic manner startles you, consider the following conundrum.

Many people deem John 3:16 as the "theme verse" for the entire Bible. "For God so loved the world" automatically evokes in the Christian mind the portrayal of an all-powerful, all-knowing, holy and compassionate God filled with love. But the text finds the minds of the Thai completely blank. Because there is no God in Buddhism, Thai Buddhists interpret the "God" concept in the light of their mental framework. The entire verse crumbles in their imagination. In the Thai Buddhist worldview, John 3:16 reads much differently than we are accustomed to hearing it: "This cruel or stupid Western God lusts after the world so much that he commits a sin by sacrificing his only son so that we will be caught in the wheel of suffering, death, and rebirth forever and never go to heaven."[31] If the "theme verse" of the Christian message can be so profoundly misunderstood, where must the missionary begin? How can we address the swiftly changing and pervasive worldview of unbelievers?

By now, you are probably beginning to understand some of the complexities that global Kingdom workers face on the foreign field. You may not be required to tailor your Gospel presentation in the same drastic fashion of missionaries seeking to reach Thai Buddhists, but you too must consider a creative approach to missional outreach. You must cultivate your awareness of the spiritual, social, and cultural milieu around you. Culture is alive and ever-changing; like fermenting wine, it breathes. It cannot remain for too long in old wineskins; it threatens to burst apart at the seams. The present age is pregnant with potential, necessitating new wineskins and an unconventional *modus operandi* for mission.

Redemptive analogy excites me. I thrill on the journey to unearth cultural compasses. I enjoy finding God's fingerprints in culture. My heart burns to see Christ transform culture—particularly among unreached people groups. However, the statistical data regarding the unreached world does not lie. Approximately 7,078 people groups are unreached; they comprise nearly forty-two percent of the world's population.[32] This sad reality reveals the global Church's lack of concern for finishing the Great Commission task. Clearly, we must examine our conventional methods of Gospel presentation. People need a living picture that captures their imagination and meshes their sensibilities with their need of a Savior. Why, then, do so few missionaries and ministers seek to contextualize the Christian message for their listeners? Why is the art of metaphor and redemptive analogy so rare among us?

The most obvious reason is the fear of syncretism, that is, the mixing of Christianity with something else such that they become a different Gospel. The Message of Jesus is counter-cultural: it transforms mindsets and world-views.[33] Thus, some Christians say that metaphors (redemptive analogies) are powerful but dangerous. Well, "Danger" happens to be Ben Fa'alafi Jones' middle name.

Born in Samoa in the Polynesian Islands, Jones moved to Thailand at age seventeen in the year 2000. He spent the next seventeen years learning to let the Thai Buddhist context guide his use of vocabulary, methods, and illustrations to explain God, the cross, and Jesus' resurrection. Jones felt that his non-Western upbringing gave him a head start. "I didn't have a lot to unlearn," he told me. "Truth debates are generally not the best way to make disciples. By understanding the host culture's worldview and felt needs, doors open by natural means." Our philosophically-charged theological chat helped me understand Jones' evangelistic success among Thai Buddhists: He listened, he learned, and thus he was able to introduce Christ in a culturally relevant context. However, his methodology drew skepticism from the missionary community and even from Thai Christians. "Some people call me the "Buddha guy!" They referred to his unconventional approach of sharing the Gospel to Thai Buddhists. This appellation often stated in a derogatory manner did not seem to bother Jones. Despite being labeled "dangerous" by many Christians, the provocateur saw an unmatched number of Thai conversions to Christ. I prefer to call Ben a "righteous deviant."

"Why did you see such incredible results?" I queried. "What did you do differently from the centuries of missionaries working in Thailand?" Our conversation continued onto the "touchy topic" of analogy.

"All of life is metaphor," Jones said. "The human experience is analogous."[34] He explained: "The only way to make sense of God is by using human concepts in language. This language originates from our worldview. But the Western viewpoint and Thai Buddhist worldview are completely opposite."

The Thai language reflects a Thai worldview that is underpinned by Buddhism. Key Christian words and doctrines are generally employed by missionaries in terms that are incomprehensible to Buddhists. Thus, our good news is not good news to Buddhists. "We're good at taking in facts and information to form our opinions. There's a lot of teaching going on in the missions world, but there's not a lot of learning," Jones admitted. As our conversation concluded, he left me with a final challenge: "God's fingerprints *can* be found in culture. He manifests what He is doing on many levels. Are we listening?"[35]

In the mid-1960s, Don Richardson searched for the fingerprints of God in the Sawi culture. His first presentation of the Gospel had flopped: Judas duped Jesus and unwittingly arose as the hero of the story. How could Richardson mesh their vicious sensibilities with their need of a Savior? Would he find a redemptive analogy to capture the imagination of the stone-age tribe?

Tomorrow We Are Going to Make Peace

The "social experiment" in Kamur Village began to break down as arrows pierced the sky. Sawi communities preferred to leave several miles of empty jungle as buffer zones separating them from even their fondest neighbors. However, the rare arrival of the missionaries had unwittingly expanded the settlement. The Richardsons did not yet realize the joining of three villages into one would inevitably lead to bloodshed.

The villages of Kamur and Haenam had previously been at war. They tried to forget the grievances of the past—the trickery and treachery, murder and cannibalism between them—but soon hostility broke out. A steady release of arrows arced overhead, slicing the ground near the Richardsons' thatch box dwelling. "Carol," Don shouted, "Keep Stephen away from the windows!"

Amidst the din that surrounded him, a voice seemed to whisper, "Blessed are the peacemakers, for they shall be called the children of God." Richardson dashed from behind the hut onto the battleground. He urged the Sawi to stop fighting. The Sawi tribesmen glistened with perspiration and rage. Warpaint streaked across their faces; with clamped fists, they clenched swords and spears. "Making peace is not a simple thing," they said. "We shed each other's blood, devour each other's flesh, cut off heads, and save skulls as trophies. When these things have happened, making peace is not the simple thing you seem to think it should be." It seemed there was no means of conflict resolution.

The Sawi idealization of treachery presented itself numerous times throughout the history of the people group. Tribesmen, wearied by the incessant fighting, sought to make peace. They passed jungle relics to warring neighbors as gestures of goodwill. Short periods of harmony ensued between the hostile clans but eventually ended in bloodshed. Countless victims "fattened for the slaughter" fell prey to the treacherous methods of rival communities. Richardson saw no end in sight. Don and Carol concluded that they had unwittingly deprived Kamur, Haenam, and Yohwi of the mutual isolation they needed to survive in relative peace. The combining of the villages triggered more friction than they anticipated. The missionaries decided it would be better if they left the settlement. They planned to go to the northern Sawi tribes rumored to be living in reasonable harmony.

The Richardsons did not want to leave but they struggled to find alternative ministry options. "Since you cannot make peace with each other," Don told the men of Haenam and Kamur, "it is clear to us that we ought to leave you. If we stay here, it is only a matter of time until men are killed, and then you will be locked in a blood-feud which may take still more lives."[36] His words sparked a tumult of frustrated discussion. Their decision to move, compounded with the fact that Carol, now pregnant with their second child, was a difficult one. Meanwhile, little Stephen was sick and pale with malaria. Beginning again in a new jungle home would be a struggle. The Sawi men had other thoughts in mind. Their source of medicine and steel axes threatened to dry up. The two villages continued their chaotic discourse for hours until the sun fell beyond the western ranges.

A million stars punctured the pitch sky and the murmur of distant dialogue died away. The missionary family prepared to sleep, unsure what would ensue on the following day. Suddenly, Richardson heard a loud shout outside their thatch box home. Startled, he grabbed his flashlight and walked out onto the back porch. His beam revealed a host of stony Sawi faces of leading men from the warring factions.

"Tuan," one of them pleaded, "Don't leave us!"

"You have left me with no other choice," Don replied.

"Tuan, we're not going to kill each other." The man took a deep breath, squared his shoulders, and gave the missionary his solemn vow: "Tuan, tomorrow we are going to make peace!"[37]

The Peace Child

The mind of a missionary is a complex and cavernous expanse permeated with faith, hope, and love. Yet, it is by no means perfect. Its broad sphere hosts an array of contrasting thoughts and emotions. It gathers data from a large body of uncommon experiences, aspiring to fit each sequence into some semblance of order. It seeks to walk by the Spirit so that the desires of the flesh will not be carried out. But the Spirit and the flesh are in opposition to one another; the natural mind doubts the inter-workings of the Divine. While it tries to walk by faith and not by sight, doubt and despair linger on the periphery. As the mind of the global Kingdom worker strives to be steadfast and joyful, heartache and disappointment dot its landscape.

The internal contention of the missionary mind subsists on the prospect of success; it hopes for a favorable outcome. But these intangibles can be challenging to recognize. What does true success look like in the Kingdom of God? Will the progress we hope to see through our missional efforts serve to populate Heaven? Amidst the murmur of the negative internal monologue and the incessant external chatter, the steadfast mind postures itself on the promises of God. Breakthrough in ministry is one of the rewards that the missionary mind pines for; but doubt and difficulty mark the messy middle between the present state of affairs and the future hope of glory.

The mind of a missionary is a land of striking contrasts. We notice this reality in the examples of Jim and Elisabeth Elliot, C. T. Studd, Nikolaus Ludwig von Zinzendorf, Robert Moffat, Jackie Pullinger, The Eubank family, Nik and Ruth Ripken, William Carey, Hudson Taylor, and Amy Carmichael. So, too, the lives of modern-day missionaries reveal a godly motivation mingled with shortcomings and inability. Such was the case in Don Richardson's mental and emotional state on the banks of the Kronkel River in 1963. Would the cannibalistic Sawi truly make peace or were the rumors merely a sham that would end in yet another gullible tribesman fattened with false friendship for the slaughter? Could the Gospel of Jesus Christ gather the broken shards of the tribe to fashion a glorious trophy? In view of well-remembered Sawi history, the prospects seemed unlikely.

The morning after the promise of peace, dawn returned color and life to the jungle settlement. Smoke from cooking fires sifted through thatched roofs, dissipating in skewed sun rays. The Richardsons watched from their thatch box home. An eerie silence pervaded the village.

The sudden sound of a mother's violent sobs echoed across the swamp. Kamur erupted in chaos. Men were running back and forth, shouting and waving their arms in wild gesticulations. Women clutched their babies close to their breasts, crying apprehensively. Richardson heard the men asking for a peace offering, but he was yet to understand the scope of the situation. He noticed a husky man named Kaiyo dart out of his hut and run toward the enemy camp of Haenam. Cradling Biakadon, his only child, Kaiyo ignored the hysterical sobs of his wife. He ran to the adjacent village and halted before a mass of enemy men.

Kaiyo could not bear to see the senseless violence of his people drive the Tuans away. He sensed blessing coming to his people. Though it would break his heart and break the heart of his wife, for the greater good of the many, the few had to suffer. He kissed his only son for the last time, faced the enemy, and challenged, "Will you accept the peace of Kamur?" Kaiyo lifted Biakadon as a peace offering.

"Yes!" came the reply, "I will plead the words of Kamur among my people!"

The crowd shrieked, "Eehaa! It is enough!"

The enemy hurried back to his hut, picked up one of his children—Mani—and returned to face Kaiyo.

"Kaiyo! Will you receive this child as a reconciliation for peace among your people?"

"Yes!" cried Kaiyo, holding out his hands to receive the offering.

The entire population of Haenam village clamored around the child. One by one, they laid their hands on Biakadon, accepting him as a basis for peace. Meanwhile, across the bank that separated the two villages, the people of Kamur received Mani, the enemy's child, by laying their hands on his chest as a token of peace.

Biakadon and Mani were adorned with armbands and legbands of braided vine and feathers; a celebration ensued. The combined villages danced jubilantly to the sound of drums and cheering. Three-hundred Sawi had a peace child. Happy songs rang across the valley and mingled with laughter. "This was the key we had been praying for!" Richardson said.

"Among the Sawi, every demonstration of friendship was suspect except one. If a man would actually give his own son to his enemies, that man could be trusted! That, and that alone, was a proof of goodwill no shadow of cynicism could discredit."[38]

Two months of harmony passed after the "peace child" exchange. Richardson had found a moving, cultural analogy to use in his second telling of the Gospel story. He climbed into the hut where the men of Haenam and Yohwi gathered, and braced himself with excitement.

God had only one Son to give, and like Kaiyo, He gave Him anyway! This revelation began to form in the minds of the Sawi men. Richardson explained that unlike the "weak" Sawi peace children, God's Peace Child is called "Wonderful Counsellor, Mighty God, Everlasting Father, and Prince of Peace."[39] The Sawi tradition stated that when the peace child died, the warring villages were freed from the peace contract. God's rules were different. Because His Son lives forever, the token of His peace is everlasting!

The lightbulbs flicked on. A Sawi man looked at Richardson and asked, "Is He the one you've been telling us about? Jesus?"

"He's the very one!" Don replied.

"But you said a friend betrayed Him," the man continued. "If Jesus was a peace child, that's the worst thing anyone could do!"[40]

"You're right again," Don said. He mused inwardly. At the first telling of the Gospel, Judas had been the hero. Now he was a villain.

Beginning in March 1963, Richardson accented the peace child analogy, expounding on the Sawi's need of a Savior. The tribesmen contemplated their decision to accept God's Son. Only the eternal Peace Child could transform their people. Richardson felt that he adequately presented his case; he now hoped for a mighty turning to Christ. Still, he would have to wait. God was working behind the scenes to stir hearts and reveal Himself to the Sawi people.

A turning point came on July 7, 1963 when a young man named Hato said, "Tuan, your words make my liver quiver (You have aroused longing within me)."[41] Hato continued, "I want to receive the Peace Child of God." Richardson laid his hands on the young man's shoulders. Hato's eyes glinted with a startling new radiance. A spiritual joy came over him.

"Has He come in?" Richardson whispered.

"He has come in!" the young man responded. "It is Jesus!"

The long-awaited ministry breakthrough had finally arrived. Hato became the first of many Sawi to put his faith in the Prince of Peace. Father God ran across the grasslands to hand them His only Son: the eternal Peace Child. "Will you receive this Child as a reconciliation for peace among your people?" He asked. "Yes!" came their reply, followed by a jubilant "Eehaa!" Celebratory dancing ensued; the beating of drums echoed throughout the valley. From this point on, nothing could remain the same.

Never the Same

On June 23, 2012, fifty-year-old Steve Richardson boarded a propeller plane bound for Kamur Village on the southern tip of New Guinea. His destination: the same Sawi settlement where his parents had taken him as a seven-month-old baby. Steve's two brothers, Shannon and Paul, joined him on the journey. Their seventy-seven-year-old father, Don Richardson, boarded the plane with them. "It's been fifty years since that day," Steve said, referring to the time Hato met the Peace Child, Jesus. His words kick off the riveting narrative in a documentary entitled *Never the Same*.[42] "We are very anxious to see how the Sawi are doing."

The aircraft climbed over the green archipelagos and fertile wetlands. Labyrinthine rivers snaked through the jungle below, partially obscured by a blanket of cumulous clouds. The plane descended steadily and Steve saw Sawi settlements for the first time in twenty-five years.

Throngs of Sawi men, women, and children descended the sloping plains to meet the missionaries who led them to Jesus. Warpaint streaked their faces; their heads adorned with woven vines and bird-of-paradise feathers. Toothy smiles spread across joyful faces; the crowd began to dance. The nostalgic pulse of beating drums brought Don back to the day he first arrived on the banks of the Kronkel River in June 1962. "Normally you wouldn't hear someone say, 'It's great to see so many old people,'" he mused. "Now to come back and see throngs of people with gray hair—old enough that they have trouble walking along the trail—that's a special joy."[43]

In 1974, when Richardson released his widely acclaimed book *Peace Child*, he estimated the population then at 2,600 people in eighteen villages. Sawi population is now reaching toward 6,000.[44] In those days, disease and warfare took its toll on the former cannibal-headhunting tribe. Two out of every three babies born to Sawi mothers did not reach five years of age; today, the villages fill with healthy children. Entire populations experienced a dramatic release from spiritual oppression, historic savagery, and crippling superstition. They now enjoy not only the blessings of spiritual wholeness through the Gospel, but also a social peace and security that their forefathers never knew. Education entered Sawi settlements to secure them against unsympathetic exploiters who might otherwise take advantage of their simplicity, as has so often occurred amongst primitive peoples in other parts of the world.

The Sawi are now literate; they can read Richardson's translation of the Sawi New Testament and the entire Bible in Indonesian. The "literacy-in-Sawi" classes that Don and Carol launched are still being taught today. In fact, one of the two peace children later became the first Sawi graduate of higher education. He completed his college education and now serves as a primary school principal. Other sons of former headhunters are now following in his footsteps.

The Christian worldview penetrated every facet of Sawi culture; they are now an evangelistic witness to former enemy communities. In June 2012, the Sawi of Kamur invited two-thousand people from thirty-seven villages representing five neighboring tribes to join them in celebration. Don officiated a mass wedding ceremony for 102 couples and dedicated 130 new babies to the Lord. The same day, 325 Sawi joined a public baptism. Fifteen groups of twenty-five new believers each waded into the river, closed their eyes, and lifted their hands in prayer; Don personally baptized fifteen people. Joshua Project, a research initiative that highlights ethnic peoples worldwide, now estimates the Sawi Christian population at eighty-five percent.[45]

"One of the things that struck me the most," Steve recalled of that day, "was how many people grabbed my hand or gave me a hug—often with tears in their eyes—and said that they had been my close friend or playmate when I was little. The emotion was overwhelming." Steve paused to consider the providential sequence of events that led to the salvation of the Sawi. "It's amazing the see the legacy of God's grace through my parents in their obedient step of faith fifty years ago."[46]

The remarkable ministry breakthrough among the Sawi people continues to stir the hearts and minds of Christians worldwide. The faithful labor of the Richardson family resulted in eternal fruit. They followed in the footprints of their Master, searching for God's fingerprints in the Sawi culture. They helped unearth the age-old peace child tradition to reveal the Prince of Peace. For God so loved the Sawi that He gave His one and only Son, that whoever believes in Him shall not perish but have eternal life.

When we look at culture through the lens of redemptive analogy, God's fingerprints upon humanity come into full view. In the same regard, Paul charged us to become all things to all men that by all means we might win some.

Do you wish to witness the transformative power of the Gospel through your missional efforts? You must become a student of culture and a master of metamorphosis. You must meet people where they are and thus prove your concern for them. The age-old proverb rings true today: People don't care how much you know until they know how much you care.

In light of God's lavish grace, how vigorous is your compassion for the lost? What measures are you willing to take to witness a breakthrough in your missional efforts? Are you chasing the current of the Holy Spirit's movement and following the flow of God's activity? He is already at work in the hearts of those you serve. The peace that passes understanding comes to those who comb the landscape for the stamp of His presence.

The 19th-century Dutch explorers were right. As I look at the contours of New Guinea's topography, I realize that the beast looks less like a Tyrannosaurus rex and more like a bird-of-paradise. I once saw its mountainous vertebrae covered in scales from head to tail; now I find a pattern of florid feathers. It's fierce, carnivorous jaw turns out to be a bird's beak opened in mid-song. As I recognize the fingerprints of God on the Sawi culture, I find that New Guinea is, indeed, a thing of beauty.

CHAPTER TWELVE

THE KINGDOM OF GOD ON EARTH

The Upside-Down Kingdom

After nearly two decades of pioneer missionary work among Southeast Asia's poorest of the poor, I was tired. I had traveled thousands of miles in rickety Chinese sleeper buses, crisscrossing the mountainous terrain to minister to Gospel-deprived communities. Thousands of people came to Jesus; hundreds received biblical training; over twenty-five rural churches planted. I witnessed the Kingdom of God advance among unreached people groups through the ministry of Within Reach Global. I knew the supernatural work of the Holy Spirit eclipsed the occasional setbacks. My twenty-two interrogations, ongoing threats of governmental persecution, and general difficulties in pioneer outreach paled in comparison to the power of God that I witnessed. Still, I was weary. My efforts felt feeble; I edged toward the brink of burnout. Surrounded by the enormous need, I wondered what impact my life had made—if any.

I needed refreshment. My exhausted missionary heart required an infilling only the Holy Spirit could give, a supernatural shot of encouragement from the throne room of Heaven. Unbeknownst to me at the time, a providential sequence of events arranged in the background.

In January 2016, John, one of our faithful donors at Within Reach Global, invited me to join him for a week-long trip to Pemba, Mozambique. For years, John and his wife, Fran, had been giving to Heidi Baker's ministry,

Iris Global. They received a hand-written note from Heidi, inviting them to visit Mozambique to see first-hand the fruit of their generous giving. Due to ill health, Fran could not make the long travel; John asked me to join him instead.

On June 17, 2016, our plane touched down in Pemba. We made our way north along the potholed boulevards, a short ten-minute drive from the airport to the shoreline and arrived at Village of Joy. The sprawling plot of land overlooking the Indian Sea hosted the many ministries of Rolland and Heidi Baker's organization. John and I were about to find out the scope of the Bakers' outreach.

Iris Global's Mercy Department supported five-hundred women and a small group of people with special needs. These widowed or single parent moms of three to eight kids received skill training, a solid meal, and weekly discipleship. The Kitchen outreach, staffed by forty Mozambicans, fed 2,000 underprivileged children daily. A health center, pre-school, and vocational school operated out of Village of Joy. The Bible School equipped men and women to become full-time pastors and leaders. Iris Harvest School of Missions offered international students a three-month, on-field internship with the goal of raising full-time global missionaries.

John and I made our way to the Visitors' Center where we joined over one hundred guests from around the world. "Iris Global oversees ten thousand churches, most of which planted in previously unreached areas," Heidi told us. "We feed over twenty thousand children every day, with over ten thousand in our full-time care in over thirteen nations." Her face beamed with delight; an air of adoration for her Savior accented her matter-of-fact account of God's goodness through her years of Kingdom work. "But truth be told," she continued, "I would like to see Iris Global take in one million children before I die." Heidi's eyes glinted. She paused as if caught in reverie; she contemplated the fantastic aspiration. The guests hushed in the humid heat under the outdoor bamboo thatch dome of the Visitors' Center. There was something heavenly about the simple quarters. The breath of God felt palpable; His presence permeated the atmosphere. "In my lifetime, I want to see that." Heidi's voice broke the silence. "Yes, one million homeless children brought into loving families."

Over the next week, John and I joined Heidi for meals and ministry outreach in the "bush-bush"—a term used to describe the poor, rural Mozambican communities. Heidi's demeanor imbued with exuberance. Whether in a beachfront restaurant or an impoverished village, her countenance diffused joy. She embraced Mozambican mamas; little children swarmed around her legs. She cupped infant cheeks with her hands, kissed their scabby foreheads, and shooed away the flies that flit around their faces. Her presence was magnetic; she exuded the fragrance of Heaven. "Heidi's life is infectious," said Bill Johnson, the senior pastor of Bethel Church. "It can't be described in three sentences. It's an ongoing experience with different nuances every single day." He stated that when people are in the same room with Heidi, they are drawn to a Presence greater than her own, and they will pay any price to have that. "They see in her the supreme call on a human being, and they want in."[1]

My time at Iris Global triggered a newfound simplicity in my relationship with Jesus. I experienced the counter-cultural characteristics of the Kingdom, or as Heidi likes to describe it, "the upside-down Kingdom."[2] Here, by going lower, we grow higher, by laying down, we stand up, and by becoming nothing, we become God's instruments of choice. I realized that for years, I misunderstood the goal of the missionary endeavor, namely humility. Jesus had the claims to everything in Heaven and on earth; but in humility, He gave it all up. He became nothing so that we might be called the sons and daughters of the Living God. He had the right to rebuke His accusers; instead, He stood mute before them, revealing meekness as a Kingdom value. He did not consider equality with God something to be grasped. Instead, He said that the meek and humble will inherit the whole earth; God hands the Kingdom of Heaven to the poor in spirit.[3]

On June 20, 2016, I sat on the cement slab under the thatched roof of the Iris Global prayer hut. Seagulls swirled in the distance, circling the coastline of the Indian Ocean one thousand feet to the East. The bony branches of a towering baobab tree obscured my view of the sea; its hundred-year-old roots settled deep in Mozambican soil; its enormous trunk rose from the heart of Village of Joy. A group of young men reclined in the adjacent hut, selling African trinkets outside the Visitors' Center. Giggling children chased a bicycle tire as it wheeled down the sloping terrain toward Iris Church; the warm breeze dispersed their laughter around the base. To my left, Rolland and Heidi Baker worshipped with 250 Harvest School of Missions interns.

I breathed deeply, inhaled the magical surroundings, and contemplated the Kingdom of God. The Bakers' ministry had impacted tens of thousands of people. The supernatural force of the Gospel transformed an entire environment. Christ the King sat enthroned on this plot of land in Pemba. Could transformation come to other parts of the world, too? I wondered. Might the ministry of Within Reach Global encounter a similar supernatural explosion among unreached people groups in China? What is required for the visible advent of God's Kingdom?

Suddenly, I sensed the Holy Spirit join me in the prayer hut. "Do not worry about tomorrow," He seemed to say.

> Look at the birds of the air; see the flowers of the field. All that you need to live a godly life will be added to you when you seek first My Kingdom and My righteousness. My ways are different than your ways. Lower yourself at My feet. That is the way you rise to new heights in My upside-down Kingdom.

All These Things Will Be Given

Today, 2.5 billion people (thirty-three percent of the world's population) profess Christianity. Yet, paradoxically, a staggering number of Christian adherents understand little about Jesus' central message. Throughout the four Gospels,[4] Jesus explicitly taught that the Kingdom of God[5] would be established on the earth. At times, He employed metaphors to contextualize His message to His listeners (as we read about in chapter eleven). More often, He spoke with crystal clarity about the Kingdom of God in terms of a real government—a structured, organized entity with the very authority of God behind it.[6] Thus, certain rulers viewed Jesus' explicit depiction of the Kingdom of God as a threat to their authority, which eventually led to His crucifixion.[7]

In teaching the message of the Kingdom, Jesus simply extended the central theme of the Old Testament. This Kingdom is the unifying reality of the scriptures. Referring to the Bible, John Bright wrote: "Had we to give that book a title, we might call it 'The Book of the Coming Kingdom of God.' That is, indeed, its central theme everywhere. Old Testament and New Testament thus stand together as the two acts of a single drama."[8]

What, then, *is* this Kingdom? What exactly do Jesus' teachings refer to and how do they impact our lives? What bearing does the Kingdom have on our missional efforts today? The "Kingdom of God" concept has triggered heated debates for centuries. The Hebrew prophets proclaimed that the advent of God's Kingdom on earth would bring global peace, physical abundance, and divine righteousness.[9] This has obviously not yet occurred. Much confusion still exists as to the timing of God's consummate global reign.

Jesus' teachings explicitly described God's kingly rule and pointed to His sovereign reign over Heaven and earth. The Kingdom of God—conceived as His gracious and saving rule in the lives of humankind—has always been a present reality. However, we exist in the tension of the "now" and "not yet" of the consummated Kingdom.[10] As ambassadors of Christ, we deal with this problem every single day; global Kingdom workers who seek to publish the name of Jesus Christ in foreign contexts wrestle with this reality. We live in the "already" and the "not yet" of God's Kingdom; it is both *present*, and it is still in *the future*. In Christ, God's rule entered historical life in a new way through the Person of Jesus Christ, for here was the King Himself coming "to announce the decisive redeeming act of God, and to perform it."[11]

Jesus repeatedly said that "the Kingdom of God is at hand." More explicitly, He said in Luke 11:20: "The Kingdom of God has come upon you;" and in Luke 17:21: "Behold, the Kingdom of God is in the midst of you." However, we clearly hear the future dimension in the Lord's Prayer: "Your Kingdom come."[12] We know that one day the kingdom of the world will become the Kingdom of our Lord;[13] the returning Christ will take His place as the Divine Ruler of the earth. He will "sit on the throne of His glory" and judge the nations according to their treatment of their fellow man.[14] There will be no confusion about His lordship at the second coming of Christ; the entire world will recognize the glorious and decisive consummation of His global reign on the earth.

Look around. Brokenness, war, poverty, and the presence of sin reveal itself in every culture and location on our planet. It is evident that we still live in the "already" and the "not yet" of God's total earthly dominion. Rolland and Heidi Baker understood this reality. And yet, they watched as the power of Heaven burst into earth with glorious signs and wonders. Missionaries the world over share similar experiences. "The Kingdom of God can be activated by faith," said Jeshua Ting, a Singaporean missionary in Chiang Mai, Thailand. He told me that "God's authority can be experienced on earth right now." He personally witnessed the "supernatural manifestations of healing that reveal God's glory to unbelievers today."[15]

A missionary friend of mine named Jacob Bennett told me, "We are a part of many small kingdoms." He referred to Dallas Willard's teaching that the ancient Israeli understanding of "kingdom" was your aegis of influence and where your will is made effective. Thus, a family is a kingdom, as is a country, a company, a group of friends, or a church. Bennett said, "All of these little kingdoms are constantly pulling for our allegiance. They tell us how to think, feel, believe, and behave." He admitted that we *should* be part of these little kingdoms and submit to their authorities. "But they often clash," he continued.

> Unfortunately, many Christians consider God's Kingdom to be just another kingdom among the many. They allow the kingdoms of politics, business, culture, and country to dethrone God's rightful authority in their lives. Some even mistakenly think that their little kingdoms are, in fact, synonymous with God's Kingdom.

He said that as Christians, all of these little realms should be subjected to the rule of God's Kingdom in our lives. "When Oprah's kingdom tells us to find 'our truth' or the kingdom of our politicians urge us to align our values with their agendas, we know to whom we bow. We exist in this conflicted state, but God's authority usurps every other little kingdom in our lives."[16]

I believe it is crucial that we understand Jesus' central message of the Kingdom of God; that we recognize the "now" and "not yet" realities of Heaven. Jesus said that "it is your Father's good pleasure to give you the Kingdom."[17] Though we have yet to experience the consummation of Christ's earthly rule, He gives us glimpses of His glory, graciously granting us access to the supernatural realm.

Peter, who had expected to see the Kingdom while he lived, wrote before he died that "an entrance will be supplied to you abundantly into the everlasting Kingdom of our Lord and Savior Jesus Christ."[18] He did not live to see God's Kingdom, but he did not lose heart. So must we continue to believe in the sure promise of the Kingdom. It has not yet broken into our dimension in the way we want to see it; the fullness of Christ's reign is yet to actualize. Confident that God's Divine narrative climaxes with His unmistakable global dominion, He calls us to imitate the mindset of His Son,

> who, although He existed in the form of God, did not regard equality with God a thing to be grasped, but emptied Himself, taking the form of a bond-servant, and being made in the likeness of men. Being found in appearance as a man, He humbled Himself by becoming obedient to the point of death, even death on a cross.[19]

Jesus moved from His place of Deity to His incarnation as the "God-man." In humility, He counted you and me more significant than Himself,[20] thus revealing the upside-down culture of His Kingdom.

As ambassadors of Christ, we must emulate our Master's meekness. As the advance emissaries of God's Kingdom, our missional efforts must mark with humility. This present-tense reality points to His glorious future reign. Unfortunately, "missions" history is tainted with a misconception of God's just objective, equating the term "missionary" with derogative connotations.

Over the last few centuries, a new twist of reasoning about God's Kingdom surfaced in Europe. "In the 1700s, European intellectuals revamped the millennium-old system for discerning truth: instead of grounding all knowledge in biblical revelation, they tried to build on the foundation of human reason."[21] What did they conclude about the Kingdom of God? They came to believe that "Western civilization was establishing Christ's earthly rule."[22] Thus ensued the often-bloody atrocities of colonialism in the name of Christendom. Three centuries later, global Kingdom workers are still trying to rid themselves of the negative implications of missionary work. Numerous books and articles allude to the notion that missionaries destroy culture and missions equates with nationalism and colonization. However, much more good than bad came from the efforts of global missionaries. (Consider Jim and Elisabeth Elliot's efforts among the Huaorani in Ecuador; Jackie Pullinger's outreach in the Walled City of Hong Kong; Amy Carmichael's ministry to the temple children of India; and Don Richardson's work among the Sawi of New Guinea.) Still, scores of modern-day Kingdom workers don't describe themselves as missionaries. One responder in Sarita Hartz' recent *Millennials on a Mission Survey* stated, "The millennials I work with are more apt to describe themselves by anything but as a 'missionary'—as a teacher, or as communications, etc. I think we are more conscious that the history of missions and being a missionary, especially in Africa, comes with a lot of baggage."[23]

The Kingdom of God "is not to be equated with any human state, race, or societal group," John Piper states, "but rather, it is made up of a humbled people who obey the will of God who rules over them as King."[24] The nature of His true Kingdom is unequivocally characterized by humility. It does not come with signs and portents and the overthrow of earthly kingdoms, but is instead revealed in an unobtrusive, seemingly weak Servant who willfully goes to the cross. The tables then turn; His upside-down Kingdom flips the world on end. The suffering and death Jesus encountered at Calvary accomplished the decisive victory of God's Kingdom. This Kingdom is now present at every corner of the earth; God's complete and total reign will consummate at the second coming of Christ.

Do you desire to thrive on mission today? By becoming nothing, you become God's instrument of choice to make His name known on the earth. Jesus reveals the secret to dispelling doubt and anxiety in your missional efforts through His well-known words: "But seek first His Kingdom and His righteousness, and all these things will be given to you as well."[25]

Rolland and Heidi Baker came to realize that the Kingdom of God is God's sovereign action in the world to redeem and deliver a people from the threat of death. At a future time, He would accomplish the work that He began; He would renew His people and the universe completely. In the meantime—in the "now" and "not yet" dimension of the Kingdom—the Bakers descended into African soil, believing for the supernatural to occur in Mozambique.

Compelled by Love

"Here I am, Lord, send me; send me to the ends of the earth; send me to the rough, the savage pagans of the wilderness; send me from all that is called comfort in earth, or earthly comfort; send me to death itself, if it be but in Thy service and to promote Thy Kingdom."[26]

David Brainerd, an American missionary to the Native Americans, wrote these words on May 22, 1746. Stationed at the time near the Susquehanna

River in Pennsylvania, his passionate obedience to the call of Christ took him 15,000 miles on horseback during his brief twenty-nine years on the earth. His diaries became a source of encouragement to Christians throughout history, inspiring the likes of William Carey and Jim Elliot, amongst many others. Two-hundred-thirty years after he penned these words, a teenage girl caught a glimpse of the same Kingdom he sought to promote.

One-thousand miles from Brainerd's stomping grounds, where the Susquehanna River and the Ohio River confluence and flows southwestwards towards the Mississippi, sixteen-year-old Heidi sat in a small church on a Choctaw Indian Reservation. It was there that Heidi met God.

On March 13, 1976, a Navajo preacher in full Indian dress stood on the church stage during a series of revival meetings. He spoke about the transformative love of Jesus that extends from the Kingdom of God into the earthly dimension. His testimony floored Heidi—literally. She sobbed and screamed, "I'm a sinner!" The thin veil between Heaven and earth ruptured, and a white light fell over her. She described the experience as a waterfall that cascaded over her entire body. Compelled by the love of God, she fell to her knees and raised her arms to Heaven. Heidi felt her spirit intertwine with the Spirit of God as she froze in that position for over three hours. The cry of her heart said, "Here I am, Lord, send me to the ends of the earth!" Suddenly, the audible voice of God said, "You're called to be a missionary to Africa, Asia, and England." This experience set the course for the rest of Heidi's life. From a humble posture of bowing in reverence to the King, Heidi went lower and lower until her life laid prostrate at the feet of Jesus.

She returned home to Laguna Beach, California, taking every opportunity to minister the love of Jesus to those around her. She joined many short-term mission trips, and her longing for the foreign field began to grow. So enamored by her Savior, her zeal for God's Kingdom drew the attention of a young man named Rolland Baker. The grandson of Harold Armstrong Baker, a missionary to Tibet from 1911 to 1919 and China from 1919 to 1950, Rolland's worldview was shaped by his family's missionary legacy.

Shortly after the turn of the 20th-century, the Spirit of God fell upon a handful of beggar children and street kids in Southwest China. Rolland's grandfather witnessed this miraculous outpouring at Adullam Rescue Mission, his humble orphanage in Yunnan Province in Southwest China. The children—untrained and ignorant about spiritual truths—spent days in powerful meetings, praying and praising God. Under the anointing of the Holy Spirit, they saw visions of the realm beyond our earthly dimension. The children saw angels and demons and prophesied about our future heavenly occupations. H. A. Baker recounted the revival in his book *Visions Beyond the Veil*.

"Nobody was talking about the Christian life like my grandfather," Rolland said of the 1970s. "Nobody was talking about being caught up into Heaven, giving up all that you possess, and losing your life so that you could gain it." But there *was* one such a girl in Southern California. "She was such a friend of Jesus," Rolland said. He paused, exhaled, and reminisced about Heidi's affection for God. "She caught my attention. Hers was a relationship with Jesus I hadn't seen before."[27]

Their hearts collided. On May 24, 1980, Rolland and Heidi married; they set out on an adventure to find Jesus in the face of the most desperate people in the world. Two weeks after their wedding, with thirty dollars in their pockets, Rolland and Heidi bought a one-way ticket to Indonesia. "I *did* leap off into the unknown," Heidi admitted. Rolland agreed: "There are no words to describe how rough those first six months were."

For years, they ministered to the desperate and destitute. They found among the poor a striking hunger for the Kingdom of God. It was during this time that Matthew 5:3 came alive to them: "Blessed are the poor in spirit, for theirs is the Kingdom of Heaven." Determined to become all things to all men, the Bakers took a counter-cultural missionary stance and lived among the people. Their Indonesian home did not have indoor plumbing; they slept in the dirt; their only toilet was a single hole in the ground. Their missionary service in Indonesia marked with suffering then came to a sudden halt when the government gave them forty-eight hours to leave the country. They then utilized their appreciation of the arts by leading Christian dance and drama crusades in the Philippines, Taiwan, and Hong Kong.

In the mid-1980s, Heidi found out about Jackie Pullinger's work among the forgotten street-sleepers and drug addicts in the Walled City of Hong Kong. Pullinger's ministry to the poor left a lifelong imprint on the Bakers' missional endeavors. They saw that light belongs in the darkness. Thus, they followed the Holy Spirit into the shadowlands of Southeast Asia's seemingly impenetrable places, some of the most poverty-stricken and challenging mission fields in the world.

Countless numbers of people throughout history made the same decision to give their lives away on the foreign mission field. But when faced with the many trials of cross-cultural work, countless missionaries did not know how to follow through. After years on the mission field, Rolland and Heidi had just begun to get their feet wet. They were unique in that they consistently said, "Everything for You, God." But a new season came to the Bakers; God had different plans in mind for the next three years of their lives.

After twelve years in Asia, God called the Bakers back to the Western world for Heidi to get her Ph.D. in systematic theology at King's College, University of London. During her studies, Heidi's heart grew for the poor.

One day, Rolland read about the war raging in Mozambique in *TIME Magazine*. Flipping through the issue, he shocked to see images of kids' bodies scattered and lifeless in the African dirt. Their corpses laid silent; flies alighted on their soft eyelashes. He saw scores of women and children scavenging through mountains of garbage in search for their next meal. White smoke billowed up from bombed-out refugee camps and ramshackle huts. Military vehicles parked on distant plains while emaciated mothers skirted live landmines. He set the magazine on the table and said, "Heidi, do you want a *real* mission field?" She scanned the images and immediately responded, "Let's go there!"

Eager to prove the power of God's ever-present Kingdom, in January 1995, Rolland traveled to Maputo. In Mozambique's capital, Rolland explored opportunities for ministry. Then, in August 1995, Heidi went to Mozambique while Rolland finished his research in England. Heidi said they went, compelled by love, "to be Jesus' hands extended among the poor" and "to see righteousness, peace, and joy established." They went to "some of the most grief-stricken, suffering people we could find in the world—a population that had suffered decades of war, disease, and oppression." They obeyed the commands of Christ to go, not as daredevils with a death wish, but as humble servants of the Kingdom. "We came to learn from them," Heidi continued, "to learn about the Kingdom of God."[28]

One Smiling Child at a Time

Situated on the southeastern coast of the African Continent, Mozambique is presently home to nearly 30,000,000 people. After over four centuries of Portuguese rule, Mozambique gained independence in 1975. Two years later, the country descended into an intense and protracted civil war that lasted from 1977 to 1992. The scale of human suffering was immense. Guerrilla insurgents forcibly recruited child soldiers to salt a significant percentage of the countryside indiscriminately with land mines. Mozambique's rural infrastructure lay in ruins; dilapidated homes bombed out on nearly every street corner. The severe fighting killed many of the 1,000,000 Mozambicans lost to the civil war; the remainder starved due to interrupted food supplies. An additional 5,000,000 were displaced.

The conflict's downward spiral gradually tapered in the early 1990s, but by then, Mozambique's citizens were characterized by desperation and abject poverty. HIV peaked at sixteen percent in the wake of violent rape and other horrific human rights abuses. Hopelessness filled millions of hearts. By 1995, Mozambique rated as the poorest country in the world. It was the perfect place for Rolland and Heidi to land.

Two days after their arrival in 1995, the Bakers accepted charge of a dilapidated orphanage with eighty children. Food was scarce, living quarters stark, and medical care all but absent. Physical and sexual abuse were common; a significant proportion of the children were infected with STDs.[29] The situation seemed impossible if not for God's Divine intervention.

Surrounded by such overwhelming need, Heidi daily sought help from the Lord. Naturally speaking, she had little to offer. The Spirit of God alone could reveal the Heavenly glory required to penetrate a nation. "The Kingdom looks like one smiling child at a time until nations are full of people who are passionate lovers of God,"[30] she said. "The love of God manifested through you is what people really need. You must become so close to His very heartbeat that you can feel what others feel. This is how we will reach the world."[31] Despite story after story of extreme neglect, Heidi noticed Jesus in the faces of the orphaned children. The ministry took in more street kids; after one year, the orphanage grew to three-hundred-twenty.

Conditions quickly improved. The children and many people in the nearby community responded enthusiastically to the Gospel. After years of horrific conflict, people hungered for unconditional love. Supernatural signs and wonders occurred; Heavenly visions and healings manifested, and many became filled with the Holy Spirit.

However, Kingdom breakthrough did not come without opposition. The roots of ancestral religion sunk deep in Mozambican soil, marred by violence and hatred. Witch doctors camped around bonfires at the property's edge. Their curses and incantations merged with the sounds of AK-47 gunfire from nearby street gangs. Burglars broke into the property repeatedly; Iris staff underwent many muggings. Corrupt police and displaced ex-soldiers extorted bribes for trivial or invented violations. Sporadic electricity and inaccessibility to clean water augmented the ongoing trials. But these difficulties were relatively minor compared to what was coming.

Explicit anti-religious sentiment still survived among some officials of Mozambique's former Marxist government. One day, they entered the center with legal documents, mandating that Iris cease all religious activities, as well as any "unauthorized" distributions of food, clothing, and medicine.[32] Two days were given to vacate the premises. The Bakers also learned that there was a twenty-dollar bounty for Heidi's head.

Exhausted and with considerable anguish, the Bakers and Iris staff moved out immediately. Ruthless officials forbade the children from praying and singing the worship songs they had learned; those who continued to do so received beatings. After more than a year of earnest toil for the Kingdom, everything seemed in jeopardy. But the Gospel of the Kingdom is good news, not just good history. The Heavenly realm is meant to be administered in the present-tense, signaling God's irrefutable future reign.

The Holy Spirit moved in the hearts of the young Mozambican children. They hitchhiked and walked many hot miles to the Bakers' small home, longing to worship the One who accepted them unconditionally. Heidi said, "I am finally beginning to understand God's Kingdom from the children and the poor." Heaven unveiled through unpretentious spiritual hunger. She saw the unearthly domain express through unassuming instruments. "They teach us about dependence, humility, and being emptied of all else so that God can fill us. They simply have nothing else."[33]

There was no space for so many, but Rolland and Heidi could not turn them away. A swelling crowd of kids camped cheek by jowl in the small quarters. The Bakers' home housed more than fifty children. Reminiscent of their early ministry years, superfluous need set the stage for the miraculous. At one point, when food supplies ran low, a single pot of chili gifted by an employee from the United States embassy multiplied before Heidi's eyes. One by one, she served every child a heaping bowl of food. Heidi marveled at the miracle as over fifty people feasted on Heaven's bounty.

After three months of miraculous provision, sympathetic officials donated undeveloped land to Iris Ministries. Only ninety days earlier, the Mozambican government forced the missionaries off their land. But tragedy gave way to a new and glorious season. Overnight, a village sprung up where there had only been grass and trees. Old army tents (and one big circus tent) now housed the overjoyed children. They witnessed the Kingdom of God break through to the earthly realm. The beginnings of a vast and tangible transformation began to materialize.

God lavishly poured out His Spirit. Mozambican boys and girls prophesied, young men saw visions, and old folks dreamt of God's Kingdom coming to Africa. Heidi daily made her way to some of the most miserable spots in the city in search of the unloved and overlooked. Her counter-cultural outreach led her to a massive dump on the outskirts of the town where crowds of people scavenged mountains of trash for a meager living. Here she witnessed blind eyes receive sight and deaf ears hear. Throngs of people found freedom from mental illness, leprosy, and sicknesses of every sort. It seemed that God had reserved the supernatural for the physically famished and the spiritually starved.

Heaven opened, and souls came rushing in. The ministry echoed the miraculous outpouring that Rolland's grandfather experienced over eighty years earlier in Southwest China. In the late 1990s and 2000s, the Bakers experienced explosive growth in their ministry. One by one, hundreds of smiling children found a home at Iris. Further outreach brought multitudes to the Lord. Pastors long isolated in the Mozambican countryside recognized God at work, and they requested pastoral training. Some walked for days to attend the conferences Rolland and Heidi hosted. Hundreds, then thousands of new churches sprang up. The people of Mozambique experienced Gospel presence like never before in the history of their country.

Global Kingdom workers throughout history longed to see the Kingdom of God come to earth in a similarly powerful way. So, too, do modern-day missionaries yearn for God's manifest presence. An intrinsic sense of belief drives their missional efforts; a passion for God's glory prompts compassion for the lost. They posture expectantly, hoping to see the fruits of their efforts; they long to hear God say, "Well done, My good and faithful servant."

Missionaries are risk-takers. They responded to the Great Commission with a resounding "Yes!" They crossed cultural, geographical, and linguistic boundaries to publicize the name of Jesus. However, the truth is that many missionaries are unsatisfied by the seemingly marginal yield for all their labors. *What is the catalyst that rents the veil between Heaven's dimension and ours?* they wonder. What prompts the Kingdom of God to manifest on the earth? Are hard work and missionary toil reason enough for God to reveal Himself? Or is there another stimulus that incites the advent of the Kingdom in tangible forms?

"Where can I go from Your Spirit?" the psalmist questioned. "Where can I flee from Your presence?"[34] Neither the heavens nor the depths can hide you from God. The far side of the sea and the darkness itself cannot sequester you from your Maker. The dimensions of space and time notwithstanding, God is. Period. He reigns supreme both now and forever. And if He is, indeed, omniscient, it follows that He has been at work in your mission field long before your arrival. His presence is accessible to people at every geographical point on the earth.

In our experience of the "now" and "not yet" Kingdom, God's tangible presence on the earth is the ultimate Christian aim. He sits on the throne of our hearts, establishing His reign wherever our feet may tread. And when we give God permission to light our lives like candles in the dark, the world cannot help but recognize the Presence that we so evidently value.

The Value of the Presence

The explosive Kingdom growth in Mozambique through the ministry of Iris Global can only be accredited to God's presence. "For me, it's not about saving Africa," Rolland Baker explained. "It's about getting as close to Jesus as possible. That's the only job I really have."[35] Today, the network of Iris Global comprises of 10,000 churches, five Bible schools, three primary schools, and an international missionary training school. Every day, the ministry feeds over 20,000 children in a place only recently named the poorest country in the world. "I need my four or five or six hours alone with God, and I can't always find that place now," Heidi admitted of her busy ministry schedule. Knowing that all fruitfulness flows from intimacy, she said, "If I'm not full of joy and full of love, I have nothing to offer. I have to stay filled. That's why I will fight for my secret place alone with God."[36]

The Bakers are made of the same stuff that you and I are made from. Their secret to thriving on mission stems from anchoring to the manifest presence of the Spirit of God. That is the heart and soul of who they are; it is why God has entrusted to them such great responsibility and favor. Bill Johnson believes that

> they have been faithful to the Greatest Treasure: the Person of the Holy Spirit. Because of that, all the other things that everybody works and fights for has been added to them—the miracles, the favor, and the open doors. It has all come because of the value of the Presence.[37]

Some people have a tendency to place the "successful" Christian minister on a pedestal. They applaud the person whom God uses, overlooking the fact that they can do nothing apart from God's providential design. To their own detriment, many ministers relish the accolades of man. Not so with Heidi. She is quick to dispel of this notion, saying, "There's absolutely nothing extraordinary about me." Her view of the spiritual realm is notably childlike. She imagines herself standing on her Heavenly Father's feet, clasping His legs as He walks. He does the hard work and the heavy lifting; "I'm just along for the ride,"[38] she smiles.

Still, when the Kingdom of God displays on the earth, people take notice. The Western world heard rumors of God's outpouring in Africa and leaders around the globe invited Rolland and Heidi to speak at their churches and conferences.

In January 1998, the Bakers traveled to North America to join the Toronto Blessing revival. It was their third year to attend the Catch the Fire Conference since moving to Mozambique in 1995. Their ministry continued its steady expansion, but the Bakers hungered for more of God's presence. He came. Heaven fell "like a heavy blanket of liquid love,"[39] Heidi recounted. In one session, Randy Clark, the founder of Global Awakening, preached with great conviction about the anointing, power, and destiny of God. Heidi could not contain herself. In front of thousands of people, she ran to the front, knelt at the altar, and started screaming. Clark stopped his message, looked at Heidi's tear-streaked face, grabbed her hand, and confirmed the apostolic anointing on her life. "God wants to know," he began, "do you want the nation of Mozambique?" Nationwide impact seemed implausible. By that time, the

Bakers had toiled for years in Africa; they planted four churches, two of which were fairly weak. But engulfed in God's presence, Heidi saw beyond the tangible and responded with a resounding "Yes!" Clark continued: "The blind will see, the deaf will hear, the crippled will walk, the dead will be raised, and the poor will hear the good news."[40] Heidi's vision to see one-million kids rescued and brought into loving families mushroomed in her heart. The God of the impossible promised His Kingdom on the earth and Heidi believed Him.

But the heavenly promise did not come immediately. In fact, things grew worse for the Bakers. Doctors diagnosed Heidi with multiple sclerosis, saying that she would likely die if she returned to Africa. She went back anyway, trusting the prophetic word spoken over her. Rolland fell ill with cerebral malaria; their daughter, Crystalyn, also contracted malaria several times. Heidi was in a car crash; riots broke out at the dump, where Heidi got hit in the face; and the well pump at Iris center broke, leaving hundreds without water.[41]

The constraints of space and time do not bind the Kingdom of God; He accomplishes His will on His terms. Questioning God's timeline is a futile endeavor. He allows the answer to tarry that we might come to value His presence more than the desired results of our missional efforts. Oftentimes, the answer God gives looks nothing like the solution we expected.

Beginning on February 8, 2000, five weeks of heavy rainfall drenched southern Africa. Three days into the catastrophic storm, the banks of the Limpopo River burst, submerging large portions of Mozambique. Then, on February 22, Cyclone Eline battered the country, flooding miles of farmland. Seven hundred people died; forty-four thousand lost their homes; the displaced totaled 463,000.[42] The colossal damages estimated at five-hundred-million dollars.[43] The floods disrupted clean water supply and covered roads; malaria and diarrhea affected countless families; hundreds died of starvation. The floods caused more damage than Mozambique's many years of civil war.

God placed Rolland and Heidi in the midst of catastrophe to exhibit His Kingdom on the earth. The Bakers' far-reaching network of rural churches thus became an effective arm of relief. Working in temporary refugee camps, Iris fed many thousands beyond its usual numbers. A deep spiritual hunger arose among battered Mozambican survivors, and a great outpouring of the Spirit fell upon them. Desperation caused by the horrific flooding fueled a revival that spread across the land at an accelerated rate. By December 2000, over five hundred churches planted through Iris Global. [44]

People began to call Heidi Baker "a modern-day Mother Teresa." [45] "I don't know what love is if it doesn't look like something," Heidi said. She echoed Mother Teresa's sentiments that "love has no meaning if it isn't shared. Love has to be put into action." [46] The modern-day Mother Teresa urged Christians to go to the brothels and drug dens, the streets, villages, and universities. "It's not complicated," she said. "God places people in your path so you can stop for the one and spread His love abroad."

Her words did not fall on deaf ears. "The first time I heard Heidi speak, an indescribable hunger for the presence of God stirred inside me," Samantha Gordon told me. Heidi's life and message impacted the American's twenty-year missionary service in China and Thailand. The pursuit of God's presence became Samantha's primary focus; love for others flowed from her adoration for her Savior. "Heidi's exhortation to 'stop for the one' and sacrificially lavish love on people shaped my view of ministry. In her life I recognized God's utmost concern for humankind." [47]

Iris Global Family Care member, Brian Britton, told me that he learned the most from Heidi by simply watching her go about her daily business. "Whatever situation she enters, she is confident that she has an answer," he said. "That answer is love, and it always looks like something." Each situation calls for a distinct response, Brian told me. "Sometimes love looks like mourning with those who mourn. At other times, it exhibits as food or water shared with those who have none. God's presence compels her to release the Treasure of Himself to everyone around her." [48]

People recognized Heidi's value for the Presence; through her example, they began to find out why God created them. Contagious love flowed from Mozambique, triggering an array of Gospel-centered outreaches. God picked Heidi up like a paintbrush and, stroke by stroke, applied an assortment of colors to His canvas. His masterpiece began to take shape around the world.

Pick Me Up Like a Paintbrush

"When I heard about 1.2 million child prostitutes in the nation of India, [49] I just wasn't cool with that happening on my watch." In January 2009, Lyle

Phillips returned home from Iris Global's Harvest School of Missions in Mozambique. His intense internship at the Bakers' ministry marked him with a mandate to help Heidi accomplish her "million-kid vision." He believes God gave him the task to rescue one hundred thousand children in his lifetime. "That's my vision and my purpose," he said, "and I intend to get those one hundred thousand kids, or spill my blood trying."[50]

Two days after he arrived in southern India, God led Lyle to a granite quarry where over eight-hundred children labored as slaves. Day after day, the kids gathered stone shards into wicker baskets under the scorching sun. There he met Anetha, a twelve-year-old girl who had been working in the mine longer than she could remember. Every night, the slave owner sexually abused her. All three of her older sisters committed suicide due to the similar abuses they suffered. Anetha was caught in a web of mental, emotional, and sexual suffering; little hope remained for the young Indian girl.

In many ways, Lyle picked up the baton passed from Amy Carmichael's ministry in southern India. "I don't consider myself an expert abolitionist," Lyle said, "but I promised Anetha I would get her out of her horrible situation." He approached the slave owner to negotiate for the girl's life; his appeals met with a vehement response. The slave owner threatened Lyle's life and forbade any form of Christian outreach at his quarry. But Lyle remained adamant. Regardless of the cost, his mind fixed on Anetha's rescue.

Christian missions is essentially a relocation plan to a realm outside our own.[51] God rescued us from the domain of darkness and transferred us into the Kingdom of His beloved Son.[52] Our primary task is to populate Heaven, not by might nor by power, but through the influence of His Spirit.[53] Lyle's uncompromising commitment moved Anetha from the mine and brought her physical and spiritual freedom. God wrote her name on Heaven's roll call. She became the catalyst that led to the rescue of four-hundred children. Eventually, the slave owner's heart transformed by the power of the Gospel and the ministry of Mercy29 established in southern India. "This ministry was born out of brokenness," Lyle said. "Time spent in the secret place of God's presence led to mass abolition and breakthrough."[54]

Intimacy with God is the means through which God's upside-down Kingdom comes to the earth. "We must all be pliable in the Master's hands," Heidi Baker said. "For He wants to turn you upside down in order to turn the world upside down."[55]

Power is perfected in weakness. There is only one direction in ministry: lower then lower still. God, then, picks you up like a paintbrush and paints a picture for the world to see. The angels gather round in awe and wonder; the nations bow in His presence. His masterpiece is on display for all eternity. He is the Artist; you are His instrument of choice. Your unique tints and hues merge with the colored strokes from other brushes. A portrait of His Kingdom emerges glorious and divine—a striking reminder of His great love for humankind.

The Mind of Christ

In *The Mind of a Missionary*, we journeyed throughout history and met some of the unique people God used to build His Kingdom on the earth. The voices of the past showed us keys to thriving on mission today. Their words coupled with the views of modern-day missionaries serving around the world show us that God's Kingdom still advances in our era. The manifestations of Heaven have no end; there is no expiration to the supernatural workings of the Holy Spirit. The Kingdom of God is "a present and victorious reality"[56] and all who obey the call of Christ are citizens of that Kingdom.[57] Heidi Baker's life reveals this reality as do the other missionary "guides" in the pages of this book. God still uses ordinary, run-of-the-mill individuals—men and women who abandon their lives to His will and make themselves available to His maneuvering.

Jesus commanded every believer to join the Great Commission by making disciples of all nations. Some may enroll in this missional endeavor at home; others will go abroad. The location you serve at is not as important as your joyful obedience to God's global mandate. I will spend my life serving unreached people groups as a foreign missionary. With William Carey's admonition in mind, I will ask you to lower me down into the goldmine of souls. Some of you will go with me as global Kingdom workers; others will stand on the ridge and hold the ropes while you lower us down. You and I are "sent ones" called to live and thrive on mission today.

God created you for eternity; He purposed you to take part in His Kingdom narrative. How thoughtless it is, then, to downplay the unique giftings and roles in the body of Christ! John Piper's encouragement to "go, send, or disobey" holds true today. Somehow, in some way, play your part in God's master plan. Don't be foolish by collecting the stuff that moth and rust destroy. Don't cling to the things of the world; busy yourself with the Father's business. Be wise and win souls. Make disciples. Raise up a generation to serve the Lord.

Each of us must examine our motives. Does God's glory compel you to deep-seated compassion for people? Do you obey the commands of Christ because you long for His Kingdom to manifest on the earth? And what can be said about the basis of your expectations? Do you easily succumb to your negative internal monologue or sway to the chatter of the masses? As you posture expectantly on the promises of God, you effectively drown out the world's droning murmur. Are you a risk-taker? What are you willing to do to proclaim the name of Jesus? Will the physical, emotional, and spiritual uncertainties of life disrupt your passionate pursuit of Christ? He promises joy for the journey and calls forth revival through your missional efforts. Do you value the presence of the Holy Spirit? If so, the advent of His Kingdom is near to you now, ready to invade the earth and reveal the secrets of Heaven.

Henry Martyn, an early 19th-century missionary to India and Persia said, "The spirit of Christ is the spirit of missions. The nearer we get to Him, the more intensely missionary we become."[58] God's presence is the springboard to living the victorious Christian life. All fruitfulness in ministry flows from intimacy with Christ.

If you have read to this point in *The Mind of a Missionary*, you undoubtedly desire to thrive on mission today. Though the thoughts and concerns of your busy life tug for your attention at every turn, allow me to remind you to keep the main thing the main thing. Don't complicate your missional calling. Jesus clarified your life's objective with two key commands: "Love the Lord your God with all your heart and with all your soul and with all your mind" and "love your neighbor as yourself."[59] It indeed is that simple.

Your mind, however, is a complicated entity. It is the control center of your entire being. Your pervading values, beliefs, underlying assumptions, attitudes, and behaviors emanate from your mind. Neuroscientist Dr. Caroline Leaf says that "what we say and do is based on what we have already built into our minds."[60] Experiential life fills with nuance and ambiguity. We do not reside in a black and white world. But because "your mind (soul) has one foot in the door of the spirit and one foot in the door of the body, you can... essentially renew your mind."[61] Only then can we "test and approve what God's will is—His good, pleasing, and perfect will."[62]

The global Kingdom workers represented in *The Mind of a Missionary* help guide us to understand our role in God's global plan. Their examples inspire and propel us to thrive on mission today. In many ways, their heroic lives are worth emulating. But the mind of a missionary, noble as it may be, is but a shadow of the posture we ought to assume. David Livingstone understood this truth. "I am a missionary, heart and soul," he said. Yet, he directed our attention to a Model with following: "God had an only Son, and He was a missionary and a physician. A poor, poor imitation of Him I am or wish to be."[63]

You may be tempted to imitate Jim and Elisabeth Elliot's compassion for the lost, C. T. Studd's willing obedience, or Nikolaus Zinzendorf's passion for God's glory. However, these men and women are imperfect models. Perhaps you are drawn to follow Robert Moffat's internal thought process, Jackie Pullinger's intrepid valor, or David Eubank's expectant posture. But they are rough prototypes. Nik and Ruth Ripken faced physical challenges head-on, William Carey overcame emotional struggles, and Hudson Taylor leaped over the spiritual hurdles he encountered. Still, their lives are not the ideal standard. Amy Carmichael's joyful attitude stirs your soul, Don Richardson's discoveries rouses hope, and Heidi Baker's longing for God's Kingdom fires your spirit. God graciously used these men and women—both past and present—to paint a portrait of the missionary mind. And yet, their laid-down lives point to one single Person worth following: Jesus Christ, the perfect version of a missionary.

Heidi Baker's following words call us to a higher Kingdom mindset:

> The Lord is inviting us into a place we have been afraid to live in— the supernatural realm of His Kingdom, where His man-ifest presence surrounds and holds us like water in the ocean's depths. We were created to breathe in this realm... No matter how deep we have gone, there is more. We need to go deeper and lower until all we have is the mind of Christ. We are called to be more than a people who can dive for brief periods but have to keep popping up our heads, trying to figure it all out. We have to be able to breathe in His atmosphere without coming up for the world's air.[64]

Do you want to experience the fullness of God's Kingdom in and through your life? The mind of Christ is the ultimate key to unlocking the power of Heaven on the earth. Countless souls wait in the balance. God cheers you on, daily seeking to conform you to the image of His Son. So walk in this transformative attitude and orientation toward life. The promise of God's presence goes with you, for you have the mind of Christ.[65]

REFERENCES

Books

Aenkaedi, Menkaye. *Gentle Savage Still Seeking the End of the Spear: The Autobiography of a Killer and the Oral History of the Waorani*. Xulon Press, 2013.

Baker, Heidi and Baker, Rolland. *There Is Always Enough: The Miraculous Move of God in Mozambique*. England: Sovereign Publishing, 2003.

Baker, Heidi. *Birthing the Miraculous: The Power of Personal Encounters with God to Change Your Life and the World*. Florida: Charisma House, 2014.

Baker, Heidi. *Compelled By Love: How to Change the World Through the Simple Power of Love in Action*. Florida: Charisma House, 2008.

Beck, James R. *Dorothy Carey: The Tragic and Untold Story of Mrs. William Carey*. Baker, 1992.

Birkel, Michael Lawrence. *Silence and Witness: The Quaker Tradition*. Orbis Books, 2004.

Bounds, Edward M. *Power Through Prayer*. Michigan: Baker, 2007.

Brainerd, David. *Jonathan Edwards, An Account of the Life of the Late Reverend Mr. David Brainerd*. Boston: D. Henchman, 1749.

Bright, John. *The Kingdom of God: The Biblical Concept & Its Meaning for the Church*. Tennessee: Abingdon-Cokesbury Press, 1953.

Broomhall, A.J. *Hudson Taylor and China's Open Century*. London: Hodder and Stoughton and Overseas Missionary Fellowship, 1988.

Buckley, Peter J. and Brooke, Michael Z, eds. *International Business Studies: An Overview*. Blackwell Publishing, 1992.

Campbell, Joseph. *The Hero with a Thousand Faces*. New York: Princeton University Press, 1949.

Carmichael, Amy and Hazard, David. *I Come Quietly to Meet You: An Intimate Journey in God's Presence*. Minnesota: Bethany House Publishers, 2005.

Carmichael, Amy. *Amma's Book: Amy's Autobiography*. Unpublished, in the Dohnavur library.

Carmichael, Amy. *Candles in the Dark: Letters of Amy Carmichael*. Christian Literature Crusade, 1981.

Carmichael, Amy. *Fragments That Remain*. Christian Literature Crusade, 1964.

Carmichael, Amy. *From Sunrise Land: Letters from Japan*. London: Marshall Brothers, 1895.

Carmichael, Amy. *Gold Cord: The Story of a Fellowship*. London: Society for Promoting Christian Knowledge, 1932.

Carmichael, Amy. *Lotus Buds*. London: Morgan & Scott Ld., 1909.

Carmichael, Amy. *Overweights of Joy*. London: Morgan & Scott, 1906.

Carmichael, Amy. *Ploughed Under: The Story of a Little Lover*. London: S.P.C.K., 1934.

Carmichael, Amy. *Ponnammal, Her Story*. London: Society for Promoting Christian Knowledge, 1918.

Carmichael, Amy. *Ragland, Pioneer*. Madras: S.P.C.K. Depository, 1922.

Carmichael, Amy. *Raj, Brigand Chief: The True Story of an Indian Robin Hood Driven by Persecution to Dacoity; An Account of His Life of Daring Feats of Strength, Escapes & Tortures, His Robbery of the Rich & Generosity to the Poor, His Sincere Conversion to Christianity & His Tragic End*. London: Seeley, Service & Co. Ltd., 1927.

Carmichael, Amy. *The Continuation of a Story*. London: Dohnavur Fellowship, 1914.

Carmichael, Amy. *Things As They Are: Missionary Work in South India*. London: Morgan & Scott, 1903.

Carmichael, Amy. *Thou Givest They Gather*. Pennsylvania: CLC Publications, 1982.

Chambliss, J. E. *The Life and Labors of David Livingstone*. Philadelphia: Hubbard Bros., 1876.

Clark, Randy. *There Is More!: The Secret to Experiencing God's Power to Change Your Life*. Minnesota: Chosen Books, 2013.

Clark, Robert. *The Missions of the Church Missionary Society and the Church of England Zenana Missionary Society in the Punjab and Sindh*. Wisconsin: Church Missionary Society, 1904.

Covey, Stephen. *Living the 7 Habits: Stories of Courage and Inspiration*. New York: Simon & Schuster, 1999.

Cunningham, Loren and Rogers, Janice. *Is That Really You, God?: Hearing the Voice of God*. YWAM Publishing, 2001.

Elliot, Elisabeth. *A Chance to Die: The Life and Legacy of Amy Carmichael*. Michigan: Fleming H. Revell Company, 1987.

Elliot, Elisabeth. *Amy Carmichael, God's Missionary*. Pennsylvania: Christian Literature Crusade, 1997.

Elliot, Elisabeth. *Passion and Purity*. Grand Rapids: Fleming H. Revell Co., 1984.

Elliot, Elisabeth. *Shadow of the Almighty: The Life and Testament of Jim Elliot*. New York: HarperOne, 2009.

Elliot, Elisabeth. *Through Gates of Splendor*. New England: Tyndale House Publishers, 1957.

Ellison, Matthew and Spitters, Denny. *When Everything Is Missions*. Pioneers-USA & Sixteen: Fifteen, 2017.

Finney, Charles. *What A Revival of Religion Is*. New York: Lectures on the Revivals of Religion, 1834.

Frazier, David. *Mission Smart: 15 Critical Questions to Ask Before Launching Overseas*. Tennessee: Equipping Servants International, 2014.

Furey, Robert J. *The Joy of Kindness*. New York: Crossroad, 1993.

Furtick, Steven. *Crash the Chatterbox: Hearing God's Voice Above All Others*. Colorado: Multnomah Books, 2014.

Gilmour, James and Lovett, Richard. *James Gilmour of Mongolia: His Diaries, Letters, and Reports*. London: The Religious Tract Society, 1892.

Goddard, Charles. *City of Darkness: Life in Kowloon Walled City*. Hong Kong: Watermark, 1999.

González-Balado, José Luis. *Mother Teresa: In My Own Words*. Missouri: Liguori Publications, 1997.

Grubb, Norman P. *C. T. Studd: Athlete and Pioneer*. World-Wide Revival Prayer Movement, 1947.

Guinness, M. Geraldine. *The Story of the China Inland Mission.* London: Morgan and Scott, 1893.

Hamilton, J. Taylor. *A History of the Missions of the Moravian Church During the Eighteenth and Nineteenth Centuries.* Pennsylvania: Times Publishing Company, 1901.

Harford, Charles F. *The Keswick Convention: Its Message, Its Message and Its Men.* London: Marshall Brothers, 1907.

Hogan, Brian P. *There's a Sheep in my Bathtub: Birth of a Mongolian Church Planting Movement.* California: Asteroidea Books, 2008.

Houghton, Frank L. *Amy Carmichael of Dohnavur.* Pennsylvania: Christian Literature Crusade, 1988.

Howe, Neil and Strauss, William. *The Fourth Turning: What the Cycles of History Tell Us About America's Next Rendezvous with Destiny.* New York: Broadway Books, 1997.

Hutton, J. E. *History of the Moravian Church.* Kessinger Publishing, 2004.

Irenaeus of Lyons. *Saint Irenaus of Lyons: Against Heresies.* Translated by Alexander Roberts. Ex Fontibus Co., 2015.

Jacobsen, Douglas and Jacobsen, Rhonda. *The American University in a Postsecular Age.* New York: Oxford University Press, 2008.

Jayawardena, Kumari. *The White Woman's Other Burden: Western Women and South Asia During British Colonial Rule.* New York: Routledge, 1995.

Joannes, David. *The Space Between Memories: Recollections from a 21st Century Missionary.* Arizona: Within Reach Global Inc., 2016.

Johnson, Bill. *Defining Moments: God-Encounters with Ordinary People Who Changed the World.* Pennsylvania: Whitaker House, 2016.

Kane, J. Herbert. *Christian Missions in Biblical Perspective.* Baker Book House, 1976.

Kent, Eliza F. *Converting Women: Gender and Protestant Christianity in Colonial South India.* New York: Oxford University Press, 2004.

Kolodiejchuk, Brian. *Mother Teresa: Come Be My Light: The Private Writings of the Saint of Calcutta.* New York: The Doubleday, 2007.

Kommers, J. (Hans). *Triumphant Love: The Contextual, Creative, and Strategic Missionary Work of Amy Beatrice Carmichael in South India.* Cape Town: AOSIS, 2017.

Kumm, H. K. W. *African Missionary Heroes and Heroines.* New York: The MacMillan Company, 1917.

Lakoff, George and Johnson, Mark. *Metaphors We Live By.* Illinois: University of Chicago Press, 1980.

Leaf, Caroline. *Switch On Your Brain: The Key to Peak Happiness, Thinking, and Health.* Michigan, Baker Books, 2013.

Lewis, A. J. *Zinzendorf, The Ecumenical Pioneer: A Study in the Moravian Contribution to Christian Mission and Unity.* SCM Press, 1962.

Lewis, C. S. *Mere Christianity.* San Francisco: Harper San Francisco, 1952.

Lewis, C. S. *The Screwtape Letters.* New York: HarperOne, 1996.

Lyall, Leslie T. *A Passion for the Impossible: The Continuing Story of the Mission Hudson Taylor Began.* London: OMF Books, 1965.

Mangalwadi, Vishal. *The Legacy of William Carey: A Model for the Transformation of a Culture*. Crossway Books, 1999.

Marshall, Andrew. *The Trouser People: Burma in the Shadows of the Empire*. New York: Counterpoint, 2002.

Mayo, Katherine. *Mother India*. London: Jonathan Cape Ltd., 1927.

McConnell, Alexander and Moody, William Revell and Fitt, Arthur Percy. *Record of Christian Work*. New York: F.H. Revell Company, 1912.

McDermott, Timothy. *Aquinas: Selected Philosophical Writings*. New York: Oxford University Press, 2008.

Medhurst, Walter Henry. *China: It's State and Prospects, with Special Reference to the Spread of the Gospel, Containing Allusions to the Antiquity, Extent, Population, Civilization, Literature, and Religion of the Chinese*. Crocker & Brewster, 1838.

Miller, Basil. *William Carey: The Father of Modern Missions*. India: Bethany House Publishers, 1985.

Moffat, John S. *The Lives of Robert and Mary Moffat*. London: T. Fisher Unwin, 1886.

Moffat, Robert and Snow, John. *Missionary Labours and Scenes in Southern Africa*. London: Paternoster-Row, 1842.

Morden, Peter. *Offering Christ to the World: Andrew Fuller (1754–1815) and the Revival of Eighteenth Century Particular Baptist Life (Studies in Baptist History and Thought)*. Carlisle: Paternoster, 2003.

Moreau, A. Scott, ed. *The Evangelical Dictionary of Missions*. Baker Academic, 2000.

Morrison, J. H. *The Missionary Heroes of Africa*. New York: George H. Doran Co., 1922.

Mott, John R. et el. *Student Mission Power: Report of the First International Convention of the Student Volunteer Movement for Foreign Missions*. California: William Carey Library, 1979.

Muggeridge, Malcolm. *Something Beautiful for God*. New York: Harper & Row, 1971.

Murray, Andrew. *Andrew Murray at Keswick: Three Unrevised Talks Given in 1895*. Australia: Clairview House, 2014.

Murray, Andrew. *That God May Be All In All*. Florida: Bridge-Logos, 2012.

Murray, Andrew. *The Ministry of Intercession: A Plea For More Prayer*. London: James Nisbet & Co. Limited, 1898.

Murray, Iain H. *Amy Carmichael: Beauty for Ashes, A Biography*. Edinburgh: The Banner of Truth Trust, 2015.

Murray, Iain H. *The Puritan Hope: A Study in Revival and the Interpretation of Prophecy*. Edinburgh: The Banner of Truth, 1971.

Myers, J. B. *William Carey: The Shoemaker Who Became the Father and Founder of Modern Missions*. London: Fleming D. Rebell Company, 1887.

Neill, Stephen. *A History of Christian Missions*. New York: Penguin, 1964.

Niebuhr, H. Richard. *Christ and Culture*. Harper Collins, 1956.

Olson, C. Gordon. *What in the World Is God Doing: The Essentials of Global Missions: An Introductory Guide*. Branches Publications, 1989.

Outler, Albert. *Augustine: Confessions*. Massachusetts: Gordon College. https://faculty.gordon.edu/hu/bi/ted_hildebrandt/spiritualformation/texts/augustine_confessions.pdf.

Payne, Tom. *The Template of Time: Our Destiny Decoded*. Indiana: iUniverse, 2013.

Peterson, Eugene. *A Long Obedience in the Same Direction*. Illinois: InterVarsity, 1980.

Pierson, Delavan L. *The Missionary Review of the World*. Funk and Wagnalls Company, 1915.

Pigott, Blanche A. F. I. *Lilias Trotter: Founder of the Algiers Mission Band*. London: Marshall, Morgan & Scott Ltd., 1930.

Pink, Daniel H. *Drive: The Surprising Truth About What Motivates Us*. New York, Penguin Publishing Group, 2011.

Piper, John. *Andrew Fuller: Holy Faith, Worthy Gospel*. Illinois: Crossway, 2016.

Piper, John. *Desiring God: Meditations of a Christian Hedonist*. Colorado: Multnomah Books, 2011.

Piper, John. *Let the Nations Be Glad!: The Supremacy of God in Missions*. Michigan: Baker Academic, 1999.

Platt, David. *Radical: Taking Back Your Faith from the American Dream*. Colorado: Multnomah Books, 2010.

Pollack, John Charles. *A Cambridge Movement*. Cambridge: Murray, 1953.

Pollock, John Charles. *The Cambridge Seven: The True Story of Ordinary Men Used in no Ordinary Way*. London: InterVarsity Fellowship, 1956.

Preston, Diana. *The Boxer Rebellion: The Dramatic Story of China's War on Foreigners that Shook the World in the Summer of 1900*. USA: Bloomsbury Publishing, 2000.

Pullinger, Jackie. *Chasing the Dragon: One Woman's Struggle Against the Darkness of Hong Kong's Drug Dens*. London: Hodder and Stoughton, 1980.

Pullinger, Jackie. *Crack In the Wall: Life and Death in Kowloon Walled City*. London: Hodder & Stoughton, 1989.

Rath, Tom. *Strengths Finder 2.0*. New York: Gallup Press, 2007.

Reichel, Levin Theodore. *The Early History of the Church of the United Brethren, Commonly Called Moravians, in North America, A. D. 1734-1748*. The Moravian Historical Society, 1888.

Richardson, Don. *Peace Child: An Unforgettable Story of Primitive Jungle Treachery in the 20th Century*. California: Regal Books, 1976.

Riley, Naomi Schaefer. *God on the Quad: How Religious Colleges and the Missionary Generation are Changing America*. Chicago: Ivan R. Dee, 2006.

Ripken, Nik and Lewis, Gregg. *The Insanity of God: A True Story of Faith Resurrected*. Tennessee: B&H Publishing Group, 2013.

Shuey, T. F. *Official Report of the Debates and Proceedings of the Twenty-First General Conference of the United Brethren in Christ Held in Dayton, OH, May 11, 1893*. Ohio: United Brethren Printing, 1893.

Shuji, Cao. *Zhongguo Renkou Shi [A History of China's Population]*. Shanghai: Fudan Daxue Chubanshe, 2001.

Smith, George. *The Life of William Carey, D.D.: Shoemaker and Missionary, Professor*. Edinburgh: R&R Clark, 1885.

Stott, John R. W. *The Incomparable Christ*. Illinois: InterVarsity Press, 2004.

Taylor, Geraldine. *Behind the Ranges: The Story of J. O. Fraser of Lisuland*. Moody Press, 1964.

Taylor, Howard. *Hudson Taylor and the China Inland Mission: The Growth of a Work of God*. London: The Religious Tract Society, 1913.

Taylor, J. Hudson. *A Retrospect: The Story Behind My Zeal for Missions*. Toronto: China Inland Mission, 1902.

Taylor, J. Hudson. *China's Millions*. London: China Inland Mission, 1950.

Taylor, J. Hudson. *Hudson Taylor's Choice Sayings: A Compilation from His Writings and Addresses*. London: China Inland Mission, 1905.

Taylor, William. *Too Valuable to Lose: Exploring the Causes and Cures of Missionary Attrition*. California: William Carey Library, 1997.

Teresa, Mother. *One Heart Full of Love*. Michigan: Servant Publications, 1988.

Timms, Moira. *Beyond Prophecies and Predictions: Everyone's Guide To The Coming Changes*. Ballantine Books, 1996.

Tozer, A. W. *The Knowledge of the Holy*. New York: 1961.

Trotter, Isabella Lilias. *A Life on Fire*. London: Marshall Brothers, 1888.

Weinlick, John. *Count Zinzendorf: The Story of His Life and Leadership*. Interprovincial Board of Comm., 1989.

Wellman, Sam. *Amy Carmichael: Selfless Servant of India*. Barbour Publishing Inc., 2012.

Wesley-Smith, Peter. *Unequal Treaty 1898-1997: China, Great Britain, and Hong Kong's New Territories*. Hong Kong: Oxford University Press, 1998.

Wilder, Robert P. *The Great Commission: The Missionary Response to the Student Volunteer Movements in North America and Europe*. London: Oliphants Ltd., 1936.

Wilkinson, Margaret. *At BBC Corner I Remember Amy Carmichael*. Belfast: Impact Printing, 1996.

Winter, Ralph D. and Hawthorne, Steven C. *Perspectives on the World Christian Movement: A Reader*. California: William Carey Library, 1999.

Wright, Jamie. *The Very Worst Missionary: A Memoir or Whatever*. New York: Convergent Books, 2018.

Zwemer, Samuel M. *The Unoccupied Mission Fields of Africa and Asia*. Cornell University Library, 1918.

Hymns and Archives

Elliott, Charlotte. "O Holy Savior, Friend Unseen." 1836. *The Christian Life: Faith and Trust*. Publication date: 1929.

KCMMB. Annual Mission Report (August 5, 1896).

"SVM Prepares for Reconversion of Missionary Enterprise," SVM Archives, series V (1945).

The Church Missionary Review. Vol. 52, 1901.

Zinzendorf, Nikolaus. "The Servants of Christ." *The Liturgy and Hymns of the American Province of the Unitas Fratrum* no. 725, 1876.

Journals and Magazines

Asch, Solomon E. "Opinions and Social Pressure." *Scientific American* 193, no. 5 (November 1955). https://www.scribd.com/doc/249982831/Asch-1955.

Brigard, Felipe de and Sarkissian, Hagop and Chatterjee, Amita and Knobe, Joshua and Nichols, Shaun and Sirker, Smita. "Is Belief in Free Will a Cultural Universal?" *Mind and Language* 25, issue 3 (June 2010). https://doi.org/10.1111/j.1468-0017.2010.01393.x.

Carl, Harold. "User-Friendly Faith." *Christian History* 55: The Monkey Trial and the Rise of Fundamentalism (1997). https://christianhistoryinstitute.org/magazine/issues.

Carter, Joan. "Missionary Stressors and Implications for Care." *Journal of Psychology and Theology* 27, no. 2 (June 1, 1999): 171-180.

Deci, Edward L. "Effects of Externally Mediated Rewards On Intrinsic Motivation." *Journal of Personality and Social Psychology* 18, no. 1 (1971): 105-115. https://selfdeterminationtheory.org/SDT/documents/1971_Deci.pdf.

Gannon, Martin J. "Cultural Metaphors: Their Use in Management Practice as a Method for Understanding Cultures." *Online Readings in Psychology and Culture* 7, no. 1 (November 1, 2011). https://scholarworks.gvsu.edu/cgi/viewcontent.cgi?article=1065&context=orpc.

Hart, D. G. "Right Jabs and Left Hooks." *Christian History* 55: The Monkey Trial and the Rise of Fundamentalism (1997). https://christianhistoryinstitute.org/magazine/issues.

Hoover, Eric. "The Millennial Muddle: How Stereotyping Students Became a Thriving Industry and a Bundle of Contradictions." *The Chronicle of Higher Education*, October 11, 2009. https://www.chronicle.com/article/The-Millennial-Muddle-How/48772.

Hornor, Noel. "Why Don't People Understand the Kingdom of God?" *Good News Magazine*, September 23, 1998. https://www.ucg.org/the-good-news/why-dont-people-understand-the-kingdom-of-god.

Howell, Brian. "Roots of the Short-Term Missionary 1960-1985: A brief History of Short-Term Mission in America (Part 1)." *Christianity Today*, March, 2006. http://www.christianitytoday.com/pastors/2006/march-online-only/rootsmissionary.html.

Shames, Germaine W. United Airlines Hemispheres, February, 1995.

Sinn, Elizabeth. "Kowloon Walled City: Its Origin and Early History." *Journal of the Royal Asiatic Society Hong Kong Branch*, vol. 27 (1987): 30-45.

Taylor, William D. "Mission Frontiers' Missionary Attrition Series, Part 1." *Mission Frontiers*, July 1, 1999. http://www.missionfrontiers.org/issue/article/mission-frontiers-missionary-attrition-series-part-1.

Verwer, George. "Ten Reasons Why Missionaries Leave the Field and Don't Return." *Mobilizer's Forum*, January 22, 2003. https://www.mrnet.org/system/files/library/ten_reasons_why_missionaries_leave_the_field.pdf.

Sermons, Speeches, and Films

Baker, Heidi. "Lay Down and Let Him Love You." Sermon: Show Me Your Glory Conference. Toronto Airport Christian Fellowship, March 5, 2004 recording transcribed by Jennifer A. Miskov.

Carey, William. "The Deathless Sermon." Sermon: Friar Lane Baptist Chapel, Nottingham, England, May 30, 1792.

Platt, David. "Matthew 26:1-16 – Urbana 15." Posted by InterVarsity TwentyOneHundred on Vimeo, December 30, 2015. Video, 34:31. https://vimeo.com/150364821.

Platt, David. "The Gospel Demands Radical Sacrifice." Posted by David Platt Radical on YouTube, March 15, 2010. Video, 9:16. https://youtu.be/XcdCPzXsI5Y.

Platt, David. "Urgency of Missions." Posted December 23, 2010 at YouTube. Video, 8:05. https://youtu.be/01QnPDZ7Ab4.

Pioneers-USA. "Never The Same." Accessed May 29, 2018. https://www.pioneers.org/connect/connect-full-view/never-the-same.

Pradhan, Shara. *Compelled by Love*. Documentary Film. California: Iris Global Films, 2014.

Pullinger, Jackie. "Dying." Posted by Church of Our Saviour, Singapore, April 23, 2017 at YouTube, audio, 37:36. https://youtu.be/fKFq_RS6bdw.

Reidhead, Paris. "Ten Shekels and a Shirt." Sermon: Bethany Fellowship, Bloomington, Minnesota, 1965. http://www.parisreidheadbibleteachingministries.org/pdf/Ten_Shekels.pdf.

Richardson, Don. "Cultural Compasses – Guest Speaker Don Richardson." Posted by Stonebridge Church, January 18, 2014. Video, 44:05. https://youtu.be/GDf3HpC9yms.

Roosevelt, Franklin D. "Acceptance Speech for the Renomination for the Presidency," Speech, Philadelphia, PA, June 27, 1936. http://www.presidency.ucsb.edu/ws/?pid=15314.

Spurgeon, Charles H. "A Sermon and a Reminiscence." Sermon: Metropolitan Tabernacle, Newington, early in the year 1873. Metropolitan Tabernacle Pulpit, sermon #3112. Published October 1, 1908. http://www.spurgeongems.org./vols52-54/chs3112.pdf.

Spurgeon, Charles H. "Daniel: A Pattern For Pleaders." Sermon: Metropolitan Tabernacle, Newington, September 25, 1870. Blue Letter Bible, no. 3484. Published November 4, 1915. https://www.blueletterbible.org/Comm/spurgeon_charles/sermons/3484.cfm.

Taylor, Hudson. "The Source of Power." Speech: Ecumenical Missionary Conference, New York City, 1900.

Websites and Articles

"Your Amazing Brain," accessed March 3, 2018, http://www.youramazingbrain.org/brain-changes/stressbrain.htm.

Bangor Worldwide Missionary Convention. "Bangor Welcomes New Sculpture of Amy Carmichael." https://www.worldwidemission.org/year/2017/news/bangor-welcomes-new-sculpture-of-amy-carmichael.

Barna Group. "51% of Churchgoers Don't Know of the Great Commission." *Barna*, March 27, 2018. https://www.barna.com/research/half-churchgoers-not-heard-great-commission.

Barna Group. "Is Evangelism Going Out of Style?" *Faith and Christianity*, December 17, 2013. https://www.barna.com/research/is-evangelism-going-out-of-style.

Barnes, Rebecca. "The Rest of the Story." *Christianity Today*, January 1, 2006. http://www.christianitytoday.com/ct/2006/january/30.38.html.

Bassham, Philip. "John 3:16 from a Thai Buddhist Worldview - Total Opposite!" *Project Thailand*, January 4, 2011. https://projectthailand.net/2011/01/04/john-316-from-a-thai-buddhist-worldview-total-opposite.

Baynham, Jacob. "Hong Kong Missionary Uses Intensive Prayer to Help Heroin Addicts." *SFGate*, December 14, 2007. https://www.sfgate.com/news/article/Hong-Kong-missionary-uses-intensive-prayer-to-3235012.php.

BBC World Service. "I Brought My Family With Me to Mosul." Posted July 16, 2017 at BBC World Service. Audio Clip, 1:57. http://www.bbc.co.uk/programmes/p058vpw5.

Bell, Bradley. "Expectations vs. Expectancy: The Fine Line of Missionary Attrition." *International Mission Board*, September 20, 2017. https://www.imb.org/2017/09/20/expectations-vs-expectancy-fine-line-missionary-attrition.

Bruce, Clare. "What Aussie Christians Can Learn from Persecuted Believers." *Hope 103.2*, November 22, 2016. https://hope1032.com.au/stories/faith/2016/aussie-christians-can-learn-persecuted-church.

Cassandra Soars. "Heidi Baker: 'A Modern-Day Mother Teresa.'" *Charisma Magazine*, May 11, 2016. https://www.charismamag.com/spirit/evangelism-missions/26027-heidi-baker-love-like-fire.

Cherry, Kendra. "Extrinsic vs. Intrinsic Motivation: What's the Difference?" *Very Well Mind*, May 23, 2018. https://www.verywellmind.com/differences-between-extrinsic-and-intrinsic-motivation-2795384.

Christian Focus Publications. "Trailblazers Series." https://www.christianfocus.com.

Christian History Magazine. "The Rich Young Ruler Who Said Yes," *Christianity History Institute*, December 1, 1989. https://www.christianitytoday.com/history/issues/issue-1/rich-young-ruler-who-said-yes.html.

CNN. "Official: More Than 1M Child Prostitutes in India." Posted on May 11, 2009. http://edition.cnn.com/2009/WORLD/asiapcf/05/11/india.prostitution.children/index.html.

Crash Course. "Social Influence: Crash Course Psychology #38." *Psychology Crash Course*, November 11, 2014. https://thecrashcourse.com/courses/psychology.

Crist, John. "The Millennial Missionaries." Posted June 27, 2017 at YouTube. Video, 2:49. https://youtu.be/XqFZVajMycI.

Deidox. "Free Burma Rangers, A Feature Documentary Film." *Deidox*, accessed May 24, 2018. https://deidox.org/fbr.

Dow, Thomas. "The Tragic and Untold Story of Mrs. William Carey – Bethel College." Review of *Dorothy Carey: The Tragic and Untold Story of Mrs. William Carey*, by James R. Beck. https://mafiadoc.com/the-tragic-and-untold-story-of-mrs-william-carey-bethel-college_5a13e7e71723ddb7810a8a9d.html.

Elliot, Elisabeth. "Amy Carmichael, God's Missionary." *The Elisabeth Elliot Newsletter* (May/June 2002). http://www.elisabethelliot.org/newsletters/2002-05-06.pdf.

Ellison, Matthew and Spitters, Denny. "When Everything is Missions, Episode One." *When Everything is Missions*, Podcast Episode One, December 3, 2017. Audio, 28:03. https://www.wheneverythingismissions.com/podcast/2017/12/3/when-everything-is-missions-episode-one.

Free Burma Rangers. "Global Day of Prayer for Burma 2017." http://www.freeburmarangers.org/wp-content/uploads/2017/01/2017-DOP-LowRes.pdf.

Free Burma Rangers. "Vision, Mission." Who We Are, *Free Burma Rangers*, accessed May 24,2018. http://www.freeburmarangers.org/who-we-are.

Fuller Studio. "David Eubank on War Zone Ministry." *Fuller Studio*, January 22, 2018. http://www.freeburmarangers.org/2018/01/22/fuller-studio-david-eubank-war-zone-ministry.

Gallup. "Clifton Strengths." Gallup, accessed March 17, 2018. https://www.gallupstrengthscenter.com.

Goodreads. "John R. W. Stott quotes." Goodreads, accessed March 17, 2018. https://www.goodreads.com/author/quotes/14919141.John_R_W_Stott.

Hartz, Sarita. "A Missionary's Story of PTSD and Healing." *Sarita Hartz*, June 29, 2017. http://www.saritahartz.com/a-missionarys-story-of-ptsd-and-healing.

Hartz, Sarita. "The Danger of Being a Barbie Savior," *Sarita Hartz*, July 6, 2016. http://www.saritahartz.com/the-danger-of-being-a-barbie-savior.

Hartz, Sarita. "The Need for a New Missions Paradigm," *Sarita Hartz*, September 29, 2015. http://www.saritahartz.com/the-need-for-a-new-missions-paradigm.

Hartz, Sarita. "The Surprising Ways the Church is Failing Millennial Missionaries." *Sarita Hartz*, May 10, 2018. http://www.saritahartz.com/the-surprising-ways-the-church-is-failing-millennial-missionaries.

Imtiaz, Saba. "A New Generation Redefines What It Means to Be a Missionary." *The Atlantic*, March 8, 2018. https://www.theatlantic.com/amp/article/551585/.

Iris Global. "History." About. Accessed June 13, 2018. https://www.irisglobal.org/about/history.

JIBC. "The Holmes and Rahe Stress Scale." http://www-files.jibc.ca/community_social_justice/pdf/cl/Life_Stress_Self_Assessment_(Holmes_and_Rahe).pdf.

Joshua Project. "Global Statistics." Accessed May 29, 2018. https://joshuaproject.net/people_groups/statistics.

Joshua Project. "Sawi Progress Report." Accessed May 29, 2018. https://joshuaproject.net/people_groups/18881/ID.

Koteskey, Ronald. "What Missionaries Ought to Know About Burnout." Missionary Care. http://www.missionarycare.com/burnout.html.

Le Blanc, Annie. "Chinese Triads Cont. Page 2." *WebCite*, cached October 19, 2009. https://www.webcitation.org/5keWc8Z47?url=http://www.geocities.com/leixiaojie/Triads2.

Li, Jane. "Who and What Are Behind Myanmar's Long-Running Civil War on China's Doorstep?" *South China Morning Post*, November 21, 2016. http://www.scmp.com/news/china/diplomacy-defence/article/2047966/who-and-what-are-behind-myanmars-long-running-civil-war.

LIFE Magazine. "Go Ye and Preach the Gospel: Five Do and Die." January 30, 1956.

Mathis, David. "Let's Revise the Popular Phrase 'In, But Not Of.'" *Desiring God*, August 29, 2012. https://www.desiringgod.org/articles/lets-revise-the-popular-phrase-in-but-not-of.

Moessner, Jeanne Stevenson. "Missionary Motivation." *Sociology of Religion* 53, issue 2 (July 1, 1992): 189–200. https://doi.org/10.2307/3711123.

Necrometrics. "Somalia." Secondary Wars and Atrocities of the Twentieth Century. Last modified February 2012. http://necrometrics.com/20c300k.htm#Somalia.

Ng, Edmond. "Reaching Across Cultures." *Living Water*, April 15, 2011. http://livwater.blogspot.com/2011/04/reaching-across-cultures.html.

Nik Ripken Ministries. "About." Accessed March 5, 2018. http://www.nikripken.com/about.

Nosowitz, Dan. "Life Inside The Most Densely Populated Place On Earth [Infographic]." *Popular Science*, April 19, 2013. https://www.popsci.com/technology/article/2013-04/life-inside-most-densely-populated-place-earth-infographic.

OMF International. "OMF and China Inland Mission (CIM) History." *OMF International*, accessed June 17, 2018. https://omf.org/about-omf/history.

Open Doors. "World Watch List 2018." *Open Doors*, accessed May 12, 2018. https://www.opendoorsusa.org/christian-persecution/world-watch-list.

Paracletos. "The Sad Facts About Missionary Attrition." *Paracletos*, March 25, 2015. https://paracletos.org/the-sad-facts-about-missionary-attrition.

Peterson, Amy "Farewell to the Missionary Hero." *Christianity Today*, September 14, 2015. http://www.christianitytoday.com/ct/2015/september/farewell-to-the-missionary-hero.html.

Piper, John. "Book Review of 'The Kingdom of God' by John Bright." Review of *The Kingdom of God*, by John Bright. Desiring God, February 1, 1975. https://www.desiringgod.org/articles/book-review-of-the-kingdom-of-god-by-john-bright.

Platt, David. "Mission Precision: Defining Missionary." *Radical*, June 12, 2017. http://www.radical.net/resources/sermons/defining-missionary-missionary-team.

Richardson, Jill. "Millennials, Missions, and Making Them Mix," *Theology Mix*, October 6, 2016. https://theologymix.com/missions/millennials-missions-mix.

Roberts, Sam. "Elisabeth Elliot, Tenacious Missionary in Face of Tragedy, Dies at 88." *The New York Times*, June 18, 2015. https://www.nytimes.com/2015/06/18/us/elisabeth-elliot-tenacious-missionary-to-ecuador-dies-at-88.html.

Rough Rider, Asian. "10 Reasons Why Mission Matters in a Post Millennial World." *Asian Rough Rider*, June 1, 2017. https://asianroughrider.com/2017/06/01/10-reasons-why-mission-matters-in-a-post-missional-world/.

Rowe, Katie. "Closer to the Truth about Current Missionary Attrition: An Initial Analysis of Results." *A Life Overseas*, April 16, 2018. http://www.alifeoverseas.com/closer-to-the-truth-about-current-missionary-attrition-an-initial-analysis-of-results.

RSMC La Reunion. Report: "Cyclone Season 1999–2000." *Meteo-France*. Retrieved July 15, 2014. http://www.meteo.fr/temps/domtom/La_Reunion/webcmrs9.0/anglais/archives/publications/saisons_cycloniques/index19992000.html.

Serithai, Jiraphon. "God of the Thai: How One Movement Overcomes the Perception of a Foreign God." *Mission Frontiers*, November 1, 2014. http://www.missionfrontiers.org/issue/article/god-of-the-thai.

Sitton, David. "Don't Complicate the 'Missionary Call.'" *Desiring God*, July 27, 2011. https://www.desiringgod.org/articles/don-t-complicate-the-missionary-call.

South China Morning Post. "Walled City's Transformation Sparks Hopes for Other Sites," *South China Morning Post*, December 23, 1995. http://www.scmp.com/article/143914/walled-citys-transformation-sparks-hopes-other-sites.

South China Morning Post. "Work to Start on Slum Area," *South China Morning Post*, March 19, 1993. http://www.scmp.com/article/22682/work-start-slum-area.

St. Stephen's Society. "Our Story." *St. Stephen's Society*, accessed June 10, 2018. http://www.ststephenssociety.com/en/story.php.

Stetzer, Ed. "Involving All of God's People in All of God's Mission, Part 2." *Christianity Today*, June 1, 2010. http://www.christianitytoday.com/edstetzer/2010/june/involving-all-of-gods-people-in-all-of-gods-mission-part-2.html.

Taylor, Tegan. "The Man Who Willingly Takes His Family to War." *ABC Australia*, September 4, 2017. http://www.abc.net.au/news/2017-09-04/david-eubank-man-who-willingly-takes-his-family-to-war/8867792.

The Irish News. "Amy Carmichael's 'Giving Heart' Continues to Inspire." Posted on December 21, 2017. https://www.irishnews.com/lifestyle/faithmatters/2017/12/21/news/amy-carmichael-s-giving-heart-continues-to-inspire-1214155.

Thompson, Craig. "Is Conflict with Teammates Really the Top Reason for Missionaries Leaving the Field?" *A Life Overseas*, July 28, 2017. http://www.alifeoverseas.com/is-conflict-with-teammates-really-the-top-reason-for-missionaries-leaving-the-field.

Trotter, Jonathan. "The Idolatry of Mission. *A Life Overseas*, November 9, 2014. http://www.alifeoverseas.com/the-idolatry-of-missions.

UN Office for the Coordination of Humanitarian Affairs. "Mozambique: Ross Mountain Praised Media's Role and International Solidarity." *Reliefweb*, March 17, 2000. https://reliefweb.int/report/mozambique/mozambique-ross-mountain-praised-medias-role-and-international-solidarity.

United Nations. "Somalia - United Nations Operation in Somalia 1." Last modified March 21, 1997. https://www.un.org/Depts/DPKO/Missions/unosomi.htm.

Watson, Ivan and Iqbal, Javed and Maung, Manny. "Myanmar's Hidden War." *CNN*, November 11, 2015. https://edition.cnn.com/2015/11/11/asia/myanmar-shan-rebels-civil-war/index.html.

Wikipedia. "Free Burma Rangers." *Wikipedia*, accessed May 24, 2018. https://en.wikipedia.org/wiki/Free_Burma_Rangers.

Wilson, David J. "Selfless Or Selfish: A Missionary's Motivation, Discovering My Own Motivation." *The Odyssey Online*, June 6, 2016. https://www.theodysseyonline.com/selfless-selfish-missionarys-motivation.

Winn, Patrick. "Myanmar: Ending the World's Longest-Running Civil War." *Pittsburgh Post-Gazette*, May 13, 2012. http://www.post-gazette.com/world/2012/05/13/Myanmar-ending-the-world-s-longest-running-civil-war.

Youth With A Mission. "About Us." Accessed March 4, 2018. https://www.ywam.org/about-us.

NOTES

Introduction

1 Robert Clark, *The Missions of the Church Missionary Society and the Church of England Zenana Missionary Society in the Punjab and Sindh* (Wisconsin: Church Missionary Society, 1904), 71.

Chapter One: Compassion for the Lost

1 Last letter written by Jim Elliot on December 28, 1955, to his parents before being killed by the Auca of Ecuador.

2 Elisabeth Elliot, *Through Gates of Splendor* (Tyndale House Publishers, 1957), 172.

3 Elliot, *Through Gates of Splendor*, 184.

4 Ibid., 182-83.

5 Ibid., 183.

6 Ibid., "Success on Friday," 172.

7 Amy Carmichael, *Things As They Are: Missionary Work in South India* (London: Morgan & Scott, 1903), 158.

8 "Go Ye and Preach the Gospel: Five Do and Die," *LIFE Magazine*, January 30, 1956, 15.

9 Elliot, *Through Gates of Splendor*, 253.

10 Dr. Caroline Leaf, *Switch On Your Brain: The Key to Peak Happiness, Thinking, and Health* (Baker Books, 2013), 53.

11 Hagop Sarkissian et al., "Is Belief in Free Will a Cultural Universal?" *Mind and Language* 25, issue 3 (June 2010): 346– 58, https://doi.org/10.1111/j.1468-0017.2010.01393.x.

12 Leaf, *Switch On Your Brain*, 42.

13 Kendra Cherry, "Extrinsic vs. Intrinsic Motivation: What's the Difference?" *Verywell Mind*, May 23, 2018, https://www.verywellmind.com/differences-between-extrinsic-and-intrinsic-motivation-2795384.

14 Daniel H. Pink, *Drive: The Surprising Truth About What Motivates Us* (Penguin Publishing Group, 2011), 133.

15 Pink, *Drive*, 8.

16 Edward L. Deci, "Effects of Externally Mediated Rewards On Intrinsic Motivation," *Journal of Personality and Social Psychology*, 18, no. 1 (1971), 105-115 https://selfdeterminationtheory.org/SDT/documents/1971_Deci.pdf.

17 Proverbs 20:27 (New Living Translation).

18 Galatians 5:25 (New Living Translation).

19 1 Timothy 6:11 (New International Version).

20 Romans 8:5-6 (The Passion Translation).

21 Saba Imtiaz, "A New Generation Redefines What It Means to Be a Missionary," *The Atlantic*, March 8, 2018, https://www.theatlantic.com/amp/article/551585/

22 Imtiaz, "New Generation."

23 John R. W. Stott, "Introduction: The Centrality of Jesus" in *The Incomparable Christ* (IVP Books, 2004).

24 Leaf, *Switch On Your Brain*, 53.

25 Matthew 9:38 (New Living Translation).

26 Twenty-year-old Amy Carmichael in *Scraps*, a Carmichael family magazine, beautifully handwritten, illustrated, and published monthly for family and friends; It was Amy who proposed a family journal. The object of Scraps was "for the improvement and amusement of the members" (*Scraps*, March 18, 1887 onwards). Amy signed all her

contributions with the pseudonym "Nobody." This quote is also found in *Amy Carmichael (Heroes of the Faith)* by Sam Wellman (Barbour Publishing, Inc., 2012), 32.

[27] Galatians 2:20 (The Passion Translation).

[28] David J. Wilson, "Selfless Or Selfish: A Missionary's Motivation, Discovering My Own Motivation," *Odyssey*, June 6, 2016, https://www.theodysseyonline.com/selfless-selfish-missionarys-motivation

[29] David Frazier, *Mission Smart: 15 Critical Questions to Ask Before Launching Overseas* (2014), 22-23.

[30] Elisabeth Elliot, *Shadow of the Almighty: The Life and Testament of Jim Elliot* (HarperOne, 2009), 237.

[31] Ephesians 2:10 (English Standard Version).

[32] Ephesians 2:10 (The Passion Translation).

[33] 2 Peter 2:9 (New American Standard Bible).

[34] The author's interview with Deanna Fraser, March 13, 2018.

[35] Elliot, *Through Gates of Splendor*, 151.

[36] Ibid., 152.

[37] Ibid., 154.

[38] Ibid., 155.

[39] Ibid., 252.

[40] Ibid., 250.

[41] Ibid., 252.

[42] Ibid., 253.

[43] Sam Roberts, "Elisabeth Elliot, Tenacious Missionary in Face of Tragedy, Dies at 88," *The New York Times*, June 18, 2015, https://www.nytimes.com/2015/06/18/us/elisabeth-elliot-tenacious-missionary-to-ecuador-dies-at-88.html.

[44] Elliot, *Through Gates of Splendor*, 257.

[45] Elisabeth Elliot, *Passion and Purity* (Grand Rapids: Fleming H. Revell, 1984), 162-165.

[46] Menkaye Aenkaedi, *Gentle Savage Still Seeking the End of the Spear: The Autobiography of a Killer and the Oral History of the Waorani* (Xulon Press, 2013), 231.

[46] Rebecca Barnes, "The Rest of the Story," *Christianity Today*, January 1, 2006, http://www.christianitytoday.com/ct/2006/january/30.38.html.

[47] Barnes, "The Rest of the Story."

[48] Elliot, *Through Gates of Splendor*, 175.

Chapter Two: Obedience to the Commands of Christ

[1] M. Geraldine Guinness, *The Story of the China Inland Mission* (Morgan and Scott, 1900), 444.

[2] John Charles Pollack, *A Cambridge Movement* (Cambridge: Murray, 1953), 77.

[3] T. F. Shuey, *Official Report of the Debates and Proceedings of the Twenty-First General Conference of the United Brethren in Christ Held in Dayton, OH, May 11, 1893* (United Brethren Printing, 1893), 63.

[4] Delavan L. Pierson, *The Missionary Review of the World* (Funk and Wagnalls Company, 1915), 540.

[5] Guinness, *The Story of the China Inland Mission*, 445.

[6] Daniel 9:23.

[7] Guinness, *The Story of the China Inland Mission*, 431.

[8] Geraldine Taylor, *Behind the Ranges: The Story of J. O. Fraser of Lisuland* (Moody Press, 1964).

[9] Guinness, *The Story of the China Inland Mission*, 441.

[10] Ibid., 445-446.

[11] John Charles Pollock, *The Cambridge Seven: The True Story of Ordinary Men Used in no Ordinary Way* (London: InterVarsity Fellowship, 1956).

[12] Charles Finney, *What A Revival of Religion Is* (New York: Evangelist, 1834), 194.

[13] Andrew Murray, *The Ministry of Intercession: A Plea For More Prayer* (James Nisbet & CO. Limited, 1898), 185.

[14] Pollock, *A Cambridge Movement.*

[15] David Joannes, *The Space Between Memories: Recollections from a 21st Century Missionary* (Within Reach Global, 2016), 11.

[16] Joannes, *The Space Between Memories*, 13.

[17] Asian Rough Rider, "10 Reasons Why Mission Matters in a Post Millennial World," June 1, 2017, https://asianroughrider.com/2017/06/01/10-reasons-why-mission-matters-in-a-post-missional-world/.

[18] Rough Rider, "10 Reasons."

[19] Alexander McConnell, William Revell Moody, Arthur Percy Fitt, *Record of Christian Work* (F.H. Revell Company, 1912), 474.

[20] "The Church Missionary Review," vo. 52 (1901): 875.

[21] Nik Ripken, Gregg Lewis, *The Insanity of God: A True Story of Faith Resurrected* (B&H Publishing Group, 2013), 78.

[22] James Gilmour, Richard Lovett, *James Gilmour of Mongolia: His Diaries, Letters, and Reports* (London: The Religious Tract Society, 1892), 42.

[23] Psalm 16:11.

[24] Guinness, *The Story of the China Inland Mission*, 442.

[25] Robert P. Wilder, *The Great Commission: The Missionary Response to the Student Volunteer Movements in North America and Europe* (London: Oliphants Ltd., 1936), 13; material related to the Princeton band is also found in the SVM archives, particularly in Series V, Organization and Policy Records.

[26] "SVM Prepares for Reconversion of Missionary Enterprise," *SVM Archives*, series V (1945): 3.

[27] "Board of Directors," *SVM Archives*, series V (1949).

[28] William Strauss, Neil Howe, *The Fourth Turning: What the Cycles of History Tell Us About America's Next Rendezvous with Destiny* (Broadway Books, 1997), 55.

[29] Franklin D. Roosevelt, "Acceptance Speech for the Renomination for the Presidency," *The American Presidency Project*, June 27, 1936, Philadelphia, PA, USA, http://www.presidency.ucsb.edu/ws/?pid=15314.

[30] Strauss, Howe, *The Fourth Turning*, 2-3.

[31] Ibid.,14-15.

[32] New Silent Generation was a proposed holding name used by Howe and Strauss in their demographic history of America, *Generations*, to describe the generation whose birth years began somewhere in the mid-2000s and the ending point will be around the mid-2020s. Howe now refers to this generation (most likely currently being born) as the Homeland Generation. (Eric Hoover, "The Millennial Muddle: How Stereotyping Students Became a Thriving Industry and a Bundle of Contradictions," *The Chronicle of Higher Education* (October 11, 2009), https://www.chronicle.com/article/The-Millennial-Muddle-How/48772.)

[33] Pollock, *The Cambridge Seven.*

[34] Douglas Jacobsen, Rhonda Jacobsen, *The American University in a Postsecular Age* (Oxford University Press, 2008).

[35] Naomi Schaefer Riley, *God on the Quad: How Religious Colleges and the Missionary Generation are Changing America* (Ivan R. Dee, 2006).

[36] Jill Richardson, "Millennials, Missions, and Making Them Mix," *Theology Mix*, October 6, 2016, https://theologymix.com/missions/millennials-missions-mix/.

[37] "Is Evangelism Going Out of Style?" *Barna Group*, December 17, 2013, https://www.barna.com/research/is-evangelism-going-out-of-style/.

[38] Sarita Hartz, "The Surprising Ways the Church is Failing Millennial Missionaries," *Sarita Hartz*, Millennials on a Mission Survey, May 10, 2018, http://www.saritahartz.com/the-surprising-ways-the-church-is-failing-millennial-missionaries/.

[39] Hartz, "The Surprising Ways."

[40] Matthew 16:24.

[41] Rough Rider, "10 Reasons."

[42] John Crist, "The Millennial Missionaries," YouTube, June 27, 2017, https://youtu.be/XqFZVajMycI.

[43] Sarita Hartz, "The Danger of Being a Barbie Savior," *Sarita Hartz*, July 6, 2016, http://www.saritahartz.com/the-danger-of-being-a-barbie-savior/ See striking images of this mentality on Barbie Savior (@barbiesavior), Instagram.

[44] Jamie Wright, *The Very Worst Missionary: A Memoir or Whatever* (Convergent Books, 2018).

[45] Hartz, "The Surprising Ways."

[46] Similar quotes have been used. These examples include: "The further backward you look, the further forward you can see;" also commonly stated as: "The farther backward you can look, the farther forward you can see." Each of these quotes is commonly attributed to Churchill—even by H. M. The Queen in her 1999 Christmas Message to the British Commonwealth. What Churchill actually said was, "The longer you can look back, the farther you can look forward."

[47] Strauss, Howe, *The Fourth Turning*, 21.

[48] Guinness, *The Story of the China Inland Mission*, 451.

[49] Ibid., 452.

Chapter Three: Passion for the Glory of God

[1] Charles H. Spurgeon, "Daniel: A Pattern For Pleaders" (sermon, Metropolitan Tabernacle, Newington, September 25, 1870), Blue Letter Bible, no. 3484, published November 4, 1915, https://www.blueletterbible.org/Comm/spurgeon_charles/sermons/3484.cfm.

[2] Isaiah 26:12.

[3] John Weinlick, *Count Zinzendorf: The Story of His Life and Leadership* (Interprovincial Board of Comm, 1989).

[4] "The Rich Young Ruler Who Said Yes," *Christian History Magazine* 1, Zinzendorf & the Moravians (1982), https://www.christianitytoday.com/history/issues/issue-1/rich-young-ruler-who-said-yes.html.

[5] The author's interview with Coretta Christy, March 12, 2018.

[6] The author's interview with Mike Falkenstine, March 12, 2018.

[7] The author's interview with Bevin Ginder, March 12, 2018.

[8] Loren Cunningham, Janice Rogers, *Is That Really You, God?: Hearing the Voice of God* (YWAM Publishing: 2001), 32.

[9] "About Us," Youth With A Mission, accessed March 4, 2018, https://www.ywam.org/about-us/.

[10] David Sitton, "Don't Complicate the 'Missionary Call,'" *Desiring God*, July 27, 2011, https://www.desiringgod.org/articles/don-t-complicate-the-missionary-call.

[11] A. J. Lewis, *Zinzendorf, The Ecumenical Pioneer: A Study in the Moravian Contribution to Christian Mission and Unity* (SCM Press, 1962).

[12] John Piper, *Desiring God: Meditations of a Christian Hedonist* (Multnomah, 2011), 18.

[13] Nikolaus Zinzendorf, "The Servants of Christ," *The Liturgy and Hymns of the American Province of the Unitas Fratrum* no. 725 (1876): 553.

[14] *Student Mission Power: Report of the First International Convention of the Student Volunteer Movement for Foreign Missions* (William Carey Library, 1979), 12.

[15] Brian Howell, "Roots of the Short-Term Missionary 1960-1985: A brief History of Short-Term Mission in America (Part 1)," *Christianity Today*, 2006, http://www.christianitytoday.com/pastors/2006/march-online-only/rootsmissionary.html.

[16] Howell, "Roots."

[17] Charles H. Spurgeon, "A Sermon and a Reminiscence" (sermon, Metropolitan Tabernacle, Newington, early in the year 1873), Metropolitan Tabernacle Pulpit, sermon #3112, published October 1, 1908, http://www.spurgeongems.org./vols52-54/chs3112.pdf.

[18] "Count Zinzendorf quotes," sermonindex.net, accessed March 22,2018, http://www.sermonindex.net/modules/articles/index.php?view=article&aid=32366.

[19] Denny Spitters, Matthew Ellison, *When Everything Is Missions* (Pioneers-USA & Sixteen:Fifteen, 2017), Introduction.

[20] Ed Stetzer, "Involving All of God's People in All of God's Mission, Part 2," *Christianity Today*, June 2010, http://www.christianitytoday.com/edstetzer/2010/june/involving-all-of-gods-people-in-all-of-gods-mission-part-2.html.

[21] C. Gordon Olson, *What in the World Is God Doing: The Essentials of Global Missions: An Introductory Guide* (Branches Publications,1989), 12.

[22] Spitters, Ellison, *When Everything Is Missions*, Introduction.

[23] "51% of Churchgoers Don't Know of the Great Commission," *Barna Group*, March 27, 2018, https://www.barna.com/research/half-churchgoers-not-heard-great-commission/.

[24] C. Gordon Olson, "Part 1, His Word: The Biblical Dimension, 1: Dispelling the Fog" in *What in the World is God Doing?: An Introduction to World Missions* (Branches Publications, 1989).

[25] Dr. David Platt, "Mission Precision: Defining Missionary," *Radical*, June 12, 2017, http://www.radical.net/resources/sermons/defining-missionary-missionary-team.

[26] J. Herbert Kane, *Christian Missions in Biblical Perspective* (Baker Book House, 1976).

[27] Acts 1:8 (New International Version).

[28] Edmond Ng, "Reaching Across Cultures," *Living Water*, April 15, 2011, http://livwater.blogspot.com/2011/04/reaching-across-cultures.html.

[29] Matthew Ellison, "When Everything is Missions, Episode One," When Everything is Missions podcast, December 3, 2017, https://www.wheneverythingismissions.com/podcast/2017/12/3/when-everything-is-missions-episode-one.

[30] Denny Spitters, "When Everything is Missions, Episode One," When Everything is Missions podcast, December 3, 2017, https://www.wheneverythingismissions.com/podcast/2017/12/3/when-everything-is-missions-episode-one.

[31] Ralph D. Winter, Steven C. Hawthorne, *Perspectives on the World Christian Movement: A Reader* (William Carey Library, 1999), John R. W. Stott, "The Living God is a Missionary God," 9.

[32] The author's interview with Scott Fletcher, March 12, 2018.

[33] The author's interview with Scott Fletcher, March 12, 2018.

[34] David Platt (sermon, Urbana 15, December 30, 2015), InterVarsity, https://vimeo.com/150364821.

[35] Saint Augustine of Hippo, Confessions, Lib 1,1-2,2.5,5: CSEL 33, 1-5, https://faculty.gordon.edu/hu/bi/ted_htildebrandt/spiritualformation/texts/augustine_confessions.pdf.

[36] St. Irenaeus of Lyons, Against Heresies, Lib. 4, 20, 5-7; SC 100, 640-642, 644-648.

[37] Piper, *Desiring God*.

[38] Colossians 1:27 (The Message Translation).

[39] 2 Corinthians 3:18 (New Living Translation).

[40] Revelation 5:9-10 (New International Version).

[41] Revelation 5:11-14 (New International Version).

[42] J. Taylor Hamilton, *A History of the Missions of the Moravian Church During the Eighteenth and Nineteenth Centuries* (Bethlehem, PA, Times Publishing Company, 1901), 4.

[43] 1 Corinthians 9:19, 22-23 (New International Version).

[44] Levin Theodore Reichel, *The Early History of the Church of the United Brethren, Commonly Called Moravians, in North America, A. D. 1734-1748* (The Moravian Historical Society, 1888), 93.

[45] David Platt, "Urgency of Missions," YouTube, December 23, 2010, https://youtu.be/01QnPDZ7Ab4.

[46] A. W. Tozer, "The Self-sufficiency of God," in *The Knowledge of the Holy* (1961), Chapter 6.

[46] J. E. Hutton, "Chapter VI, The Foreign Missions and Their Influence" in *History of the Moravian Church* (Kessinger Publishing, 2004). http://www.ccel.org/ccel/hutton/moravian.v.vi.html.

[47] Paris Reidhead, "Ten Shekels and a Shirt" (sermon, Bethany Fellowship, Bloomington, Minnesota, 1965), http://www.parisreidheadbibleteachingministries.org/pdf/Ten_Shekels.pdf.

[48] "John R. W. Stott quotes," Goodreads, accessed March 17, 2018, https://www.goodreads.com/author/quotes/14919141.John_R_W_Stott.

Chapter Four: The Internal Monologue

[1] John S. Moffat, *The Lives of Robert and Mary Moffat* (London: T. Fisher Unwin, 1886), 153.

[2] Moffat, *The Lives of Robert and Mary Moffat*, 155.

[3] "Clifton Strengths," Gallup, accessed March 17, 2018, https://www.gallupstrengthscenter.com/.

[4] Tom Rath, *Strengths Finder 2.0* (Gallup Press, 2007), 55.

[5] The author's interview with Luke Gilbert, February 25, 2018.

[6] Steven Furtick, *Crash the Chatterbox: Hearing God's Voice Above All Others* (Multnomah, 2014), 12.

[7] Amy Carmichael, "Chapter 14" in *Gold Cord: The Story of a Fellowship* (London: Society for Promoting Christian Knowledge, 1932).

[8] Faith Hassett, *The Mind of a Missionary Survey*, submitted February 25, 2017.

[9] Chase McNorton, *The Mind of a Missionary Survey*, submitted February 26, 2017.

[10] Hannah Lim (a pseudonym), *The Mind of a Missionary Survey*, submitted March 2, 2017.

[11] Steve Jennings, *The Mind of a Missionary Survey*, submitted February 27, 2017.

[12] Katie Cavanaugh, *The Mind of a Missionary Survey*, submitted February 25, 2017.

[13] 2 Corinthians 10:5 (New International Version).

[14] Philippians 4:7, New International Version.

[15] Leaf, *Switch On Your Brain*, 50.

[16] Leaf, *Switch On Your Brain*, 55.

[17] Leaf, *Switch On Your Brain*, 33.

[18] Leaf, *Switch On Your Brain*, 13.

[19] Moffat, *The Lives of Robert and Mary Moffat*, 153.

[20] Ibid., 154.

[21] Ibid., 154.

[22] Jeremy Blakley, *The Mind of a Missionary Survey*, submitted February 25, 2017.

[23] Anonymous missionary, *The Mind of a Missionary Survey*, submitted February 25, 2017.

[24] Moffat, *The Lives of Robert and Mary Moffat*, 158.

[25] Ibid., 289.

[26] Furtick, *Crash the Chatterbox*, 65.

[27] Colossians 3:1-3 (New International Version).

[28] Frazier, *Mission Smart*, 130.

[29] Ibid., 84.

[30] Letter from Mother Teresa to Archbishop Périer, December 18, 1960.

[31] Mother Teresa, from the Mediterranean Sea to Blagovijest (the local Catholic magazine in Skopje), March 25, 1929.

[32] Brian Kolodiejchuk, *Mother Teresa: Come Be My Light: The Private Writings of the Saint of Calcutta* (The Crown Publishing Group, 2009), 1.

[33] Mother Teresa to Father Joseph Neuner, S.J., undated, most probably written during the retreat of April 1961.

[34] Malcolm Muggeridge, *Something Beautiful for God* (New York: Harper & Row, 1971), 18.

[35] Kolodiejchuk, *Mother Teresa*, 4.

[36] Leaf, *Switch On Your Brain*, 72.

[37] Furtick, *Crash the Chatterbox*, 107.

[38] J. H. Morrison, *The Missionary Heroes of Africa* (New York: George H. Doran Co., 1922).

[39] H. K. W. Kumm, *African Missionary Heroes and Heroines* (New York: The MacMillan Company, 1917), 173.

[40] Moffat, *The Lives of Robert and Mary Moffat*, 161; Reverend Henry Grey, Reverend W. Lindsay Alexander, Reverend Dr. Brown (thanksgiving addresses delivered to Dr. Robert Moffat, Broughton Place Church, November 3, 1842).

[41] John Snow, Robert Moffat, *Missionary Labours and Scenes in Southern Africa* (Paternoster-Row, 1842), 191.

[42] J. E. Chambliss, *The Life and Labors of David Livingstone* (Hubbard Bros., 1875), 313.

[43] Kumm, *African Missionary Heroes and Heroines*, 190-191.

[44] Ibid., 191.

Chapter Five: Social Influence

[1] Luke 9:23.

[2] John 6:66.

[3] Matthew 10:38 (New International Version).

[4] Galatians 2:20 (English Standard Version).

[5] Jackie Pullinger, "Dying" (sermon, Church of Our Saviour, Singapore), https://youtu.be/fKFq_RS6bdw.

[6] Charles Goddard, "The Clearance" in *City of Darkness: Life in Kowloon Walled City* (Watermark, 1999), 208–11.

[7] "Social Influence: Crash Course Psychology #38," Crash Course, November 11, 2014, https://thecrashcourse.com/courses/psychology Navigate to "normative social influence," 5:31, YouTube, https://youtu.be/UGxGDdQnC1Y?t=5m31s See also https://en.wikipedia.org/wiki/Normative_social_influence.

[8] Social Influence: Crash Course Psychology #38," Crash Course, November 11, 2014, https://thecrashcourse.com/courses/psychology Navigate to "conformity," 3:53, YouTube, https://youtu.be/UGxGDdQnC1Y?t=3m53s See also https://en.wikipedia.org/wiki/Conformity.

[9] Social Influence: Crash Course Psychology #38," Crash Course, November 11, 2014, https://thecrashcourse.com/courses/psychology Navigate to "groupthink," 8:06, YouTube, https://youtu.be/UGxGDdQnC1Y?t=8m6s See also https://en.wikipedia.org/wiki/Groupthink.

[10] Solomon E. Asch, "Opinions and Social Pressure," *Scientific American* 193, no. 5 (November 1955), https://www.scribd.com/doc/249982831/Asch-1955.

[11] Romans 12:2 (New International Version).

[12] The author's interview with Jacob Bennett, June 6, 2018.

[13] John 17:14, 16.

[14] David Mathis, "Let's Revise the Popular Phrase 'In, But Not Of,'" *Desiring God*, August 29, 2012, https://www.desiringgod.org/articles/lets-revise-the-popular-phrase-in-but-not-of.

[15] John 17:14-18 (English Standard Version).

[16] Mathis, "Let's Revise."

[17] 1 Peter 2:9.

[18] Jackie Pullinger, *Chasing the Dragon: One Woman's Struggle Against the Darkness of Hong Kong's Drug Dens* (Hodder and Stoughton, 1980), 36.

[19] Dan Nosowitz, "Life Inside The Most Densely Populated Place On Earth [Infographic]," *Popular Science*, April 19, 2013, https://www.popsci.com/technology/article/2013-04/life-inside-most-densely-populated-place-earth-infographic.

[20] Elizabeth Sinn, "Kowloon Walled City: Its Origin and Early History," *Journal of the Royal Asiatic Society Hong Kong Branch*, vol. 27 (1987).

[21] Goddard, "The Clearance."

[22] Nosowitz, "Life Inside."

[23] Diana Preston, *The Boxer Rebellion* (Bloomsbury Publishing, USA, 2000), 370; Claude MacDonald, the British representative during the convention, picked a ninety-nine-year lease because he thought it was "as good as forever."

[24] Peter Wesley Smith, *Unequal Treaty 1898-1997: China, Great Britain, and Hong Kong's New Territories* (Oxford University Press, 1998), 12.

[25] Pullinger, *Chasing the Dragon*, 38.

[26] Ibid., 39.

[27] Ibid., 44.

[28] Ibid., 40.

[29] Jackie Pullinger, *Crack In the Wall: Life and Death in Kowloon Walled City* (London: Hodder & Stoughton, 1989), 16.

[30] Pullinger, *Chasing the Dragon*, 48.

[31] This is attributed to Pierre Teilhard de Chardin in *The Joy of Kindness* (1993), by Robert J. Furey, 138; but it is attributed to G. I. Gurdjieff in *Beyond Prophecies and Predictions: Everyone's Guide To The Coming Changes* (1993) by Moira Timms, 62; neither cite a source. It was widely popularized by Wayne Dyer, who often quotes it in his presentations, crediting it to Chardin, as does Stephen Covey in *Living the 7 Habits: Stories of Courage and Inspiration* (2000), 47.

[32] Colossians 3:2.

[33] "51% of Churchgoers," *Barna Group*.

[34] "Is Evangelism Going Out of Style?" *Barna Group*, December 17, 2013, https://www.barna.com/research/is-evangelism-going-out-of-style/.

[35] The author's interview with Todd Tillinghast, June 7, 2018.

[36] Norman P. Grubb, *C. T. Studd: Athlete and Pioneer* (1933), 196.

[37] Frazier, *Mission Smart*, 130.

[38] John 15:5.

[39] Matthew 6:33.

[40] The author's interview with Steve Schirmer, April 15, 2018.

[41] Ibid.

[42] Sarita Hartz, "The Need for a New Missions Paradigm," *Sarita Hartz*, September 29, 2015, http://www.saritahartz.com/the-need-for-a-new-missions-paradigm/.

[43] John 13:35 (The Message Translation).

[44] Pullinger, *Chasing the Dragon*, 45.

[45] José Luis González-Balado, *Mother Teresa: In My Own Words* (Liguori Publications, 1997), 23.

[46] Matthew 13:31-32.

[47] Pullinger, *Chasing the Dragon*, 83.

[48] Ibid., 56-57.

[49] Annie Le Blanc, "Chinese Triads Part 2," *WebCite*, cached October 19, 2009, https://www.webcitation.org/5keWc8Z47?url=http://www.geocities.com/leixiaojie/Triads2.

[50] Pullinger, *Chasing the Dragon*, 86.

[51] Ibid., 105.

[52] Ibid., 246.

[53] Staff Reporter, "Work to Start on Slum Area, *South China Morning Post*, March 19, 1993, http://www.scmp.com/article/22682/work-start-slum-area.

[54] Staff Reporter, "Walled City's Transformation Sparks Hopes for Other Sites," *South China Morning Post*, December 23, 1995, http://www.scmp.com/article/143914/walled-citys-transformation-sparks-hopes-other-sites.

[55] Joannes, *The Space Between Memories*, 4.

[56] "Our Story," St. Stephen's Society, accessed June 10, 2018, http://www.ststephenssociety.com/en/story.php The original Hang Fook Camp (in English, "House of Blessing") was a collection of tin huts on a plot of land in the poorest part of Hong Kong. Many of the hundreds of addicts who withdrew from drugs in various homes all over Hong Kong later came to live with Jackie at the camp.

[57] Jacob Baynham, "Hong Kong Missionary Uses Intensive Prayer to Help Heroin Addicts," *SFGate*, December 14, 2007, https://www.sfgate.com/news/article/Hong-Kong-missionary-uses-intensive-prayer-to-3235012.php.

[58] Pullinger, *Chasing the Dragon*, 237.

[59] "Jackie Pullinger's Jubilee Year in Hong Kong," St. Stephen's Society, accessed June 10, 2018, http://www.ststephenssociety.com/en/jubilee.php.

[60] Pullinger, *Chasing the Dragon*, 56.

Chapter Six: A Posture of Expectancy

[1] The Oxford American College Dictionary is the definition provider for Google Dictionary.

[2] Eugene Peterson, *A Long Obedience in the Same Direction* (Downers Grove, IL: InterVarsity, 1980/2000), 144.

[3] Bradley Bell, "Expectations vs. Expectancy: The Fine Line of Missionary Attrition," *International Mission Board*, September 20, 2017, https://www.imb.org/2017/09/20/expectations-vs-expectancy-fine-line-missionary-attrition/.

[4] Psalm 119:166 (The Message Translation).

[5] Psalm 130:5 (The Living Bible).

[6] Roman 8:24-25 (The Voice).

[7] Andrew Marshall, *The Trouser People: Burma in the Shadows of the Empire* (River Books, 2002), Kindle locations 3567-3568.

[8] Patrick Winn, "Myanmar: Ending the World's Longest-Running Civil War," *Pittsburgh Post-Gazette*, May 13, 2012, http://www.post-gazette.com/world/2012/05/13/Myanmar-ending-the-world-s-longest-running-civil-war.

[9] Jane Li, "Who and What Are Behind Myanmar's Long-Running Civil War on China's Doorstep?" *South China Morning Post*, November 21, 2016, http://www.scmp.com/news/china/diplomacy-defence/article/2047966/who-and-what-are-behind-myanmars-long-running-civil-war.

[10] Ivan Watson, Javed Iqbal, Manny Maung, "Myanmar's Hidden War," *CNN*, November 11, 2015, https://edition.cnn.com/2015/11/11/asia/myanmar-shan-rebels-civil-war/index.html.

[11] Winn, "Myanmar."

[12] "David Eubank on War Zone Ministry," *Fuller Studio*, January 22, 2018, http://www.freeburmarangers.org/2018/01/22/fuller-studio-david-eubank-war-zone-ministry/.

[13] "Global Day of Prayer for Burma," *Free Burma Rangers*, 2017, http://www.freeburmarangers.org/wp-content/uploads/2017/01/2017-DOP-LowRes.pdf.

[14] "David Eubank on War Zone Ministry," *Fuller Studio*.

[15] "Vision, Mission," Who We Are, Free Burma Rangers, accessed May 24, 2018, http://www.freeburmarangers.org/who-we-are/.

[16] Tegan Taylor, "The Man Who Willingly Takes His Family to War," *ABC Australia*, September 4, 2017, http://www.abc.net.au/news/2017-09-04/david-eubank-man-who-willingly-takes-his-family-to-war/8867792.

[17] "Free Burma Rangers," Wikipedia, accessed May 24, 2018, https://en.wikipedia.org/wiki/Free_Burma_Rangers.

[18] "Free Burma Rangers, A Feature Documentary Film," Deidox, accessed May 24, 2018, https://deidox.org/fbr/.

[19] Taylor, "The Man."

[20] "I Brought My Family With Me to Mosul," *BBC World Service*, July 16, 2017, http://www.bbc.co.uk/programmes/p058vpw5.

[21] Taylor, "The Man."

[22] "Trailblazers Series," Christian Focus Publications, accessed May 24, 2018, https://www.christianfocus.com/.

[23] Matthew 10:37 (New International Version).

[24] David Platt, "The Gospel Demands Radical Sacrifice" (sermon, September 3, 2016), https://youtu.be/XcdCPzXsI5Y.

[25] Sahale Eubank, YouTube, https://www.youtube.com/channel/UCidZ46cYu4RbGqGjnIgoUKw/featured.

[26] Sahale Eubank, "Not Alone: White Monkey in Kurdistan," YouTube, https://youtu.be/rsvNA4eXDUk.

[27] Sahale Eubank (@alaskanmonkey), Instagram, https://www.instagram.com/alaskanmonkey/.

[28] Suuzanne Eubank (@suu_eubank), Instagram, https://www.instagram.com/suu_eubank/

[29] Eubank (@suu_eubank).

[30] Taylor, "The Man."

[31] Eubank, "Not Alone."

[32] Matthew 7:12 (New International Version).

[33] Isaiah 26:3.

[34] Psalm 46:10 (New International Version).

[35] 2 Corinthians 12:9-10 (New International Version).

[36] "David Eubank on War Zone Ministry," *Fuller Studio*.

[37] Ibid.

Chapter Seven: Physical Challenges

[1] Ripken, Lewis, *The Insanity of God*, 78.

[2] Ibid., 129-130.

[3] Ibid., 130-131.

[4] Ibid., 135-136.

[5] A.J. Broomhall, "Book Four: Survivors' Pact," in *Hudson Taylor and China's Open Century* (London: Hodder and Stoughton and Overseas Missionary Fellowship, 1988), 291.

[6] Ripken, Lewis, *The Insanity of God*, 136.

[7] Brian P. Hogan, *There's a Sheep in my Bathtub: Birth of a Mongolian Church Planting Movement* (Asteroidea Books, 2008), 155.

[8] Hogan, *There's a Sheep in my Bathtub*, 151.

[9] Ibid., 250.

[10] Elisabeth Elliot, *A Chance to Die: The Life and Legacy of Amy Carmichael* (Grand Rapids, MI: Fleming H. Revell Company, 1987).

[11] David Platt, *Radical: Taking Back Your Faith from the American Dream* (Multnomah, 2010), 181.

[12] "World Watch List 2018," Open Doors, accessed May 12, 2018, https://www.opendoorsusa.org/christian-persecution/world-watch-list/.

[13] George Verwer, "Ten Reasons Why Missionaries Leave the Field and Don't Return," January 22, 2003, https://www.mrnet.org/system/files/library/ten_reasons_why_missionaries_leave_the_field.pdf.

[14] "The Sad Facts About Missionary Attrition," *Paracletos*, March 25, 2015, https://paracletos.org/the-sad-facts-about-missionary-attrition/.

[15] William Taylor, "Prologue," in *Too Valuable to Lose: Exploring the Causes and Cures of Missionary Attrition* (William Carey Library, 1997), XV.

[16] Taylor, *Too Valuable to Lose*.

[17] "Your Amazing Brain," accessed March 3, 2018, http://www.youramazingbrain.org/brainchanges/stressbrain.htm.

[18] George Lakoff, Mark Johnson, *Metaphors We Live By* (Chicago, IL: University of Chicago Press, 1980).

[19] Martin J. Gannon, "Cultural Metaphors: Their Use in Management Practice as a Method for Understanding Cultures," November 1, 2011, https://scholarworks.gvsu.edu/cgi/viewcontent.cgi?article=1065&context=orpc.

[20] Gannon, "Cultural Metaphors."

[21] Peter J. Buckley, Michael Z. Brooke, *International Business Studies: An Overview* (Blackwell Publishing, 1992), 528.

[22] Germaine W. Shames, *United Airlines Hemispheres*, February, 1995, 39–40.

[23] William D. Taylor, "Mission Frontiers' Missionary Attrition Series, Part 1," *Mission Frontiers*, July 1, 1999, http://www.missionfrontiers.org/issue/article/mission-frontiers-missionary-attrition-series-part-1.

[24] Taylor, *Too Valuable to Lose*, 96.

[25] Craig Thompson, "Is Conflict with Teammates Really the Top Reason for Missionaries Leaving the Field?" *A Life Overseas*, July 28, 2017, http://www.alifeoverseas.com/is-conflict-with-teammates-really-the-top-reason-for-missionaries-leaving-the-field/.

[26] Katie Rowe, "Closer to the Truth about Current Missionary Attrition: An Initial Analysis of Results," *A Life Overseas*, April 16, 2018, http://www.alifeoverseas.com/closer-to-the-truth-about-current-missionary-attrition-an-initial-analysis-of-results/.

[27] Rowe, "Closer to the Truth."

[28] Ripken, Lewis, *The Insanity of God*, 1.

[29] Ibid., "Prologue."

[30] Ibid., 19.

[31] Ibid., 6.

[32] Ibid., 44, 45.

[33] "Somalia," Secondary Wars and Atrocities of the Twentieth Century, Necrometrics, accessed April 25, 2018, http://necrometrics.com/20c300k.htm#Somalia.

[34] "Somalia - United Nations Operation in Somalia 1," United Nations, updated March 21, 1997, https://www.un.org/Depts/DPKO/Missions/unosomi.htm.

[35] "Security Council Resolution 794," United Nations, April 24, 1992, paragraph 3.

[36] Ripken, Lewis, *The Insanity of God*, 127.

[37] Ibid., 154.

[38] Ibid., 158.

[39] Ibid., 196.

[40] "About," Nik Ripken Ministries, accessed March 5, 2018, http://www.nikripken.com/about/.

[41] Clare Bruce, "What Aussie Christians Can Learn from Persecuted Believers," *Hope* 103.2, November 22, 2016, https://hope1032.com.au/stories/faith/2016/aussie-christians-can-learn-persecuted-church/.

[42] Ripken, Lewis, *The Insanity of God*, 198-200.

[43] Hebrew 11:14-16 (The Message Translation).

[44] Samuel M. Zwemer, *The Unoccupied Mission Fields of Africa and Asia* (Cornell University Library, 1918), 222-223.

[45] Romans 8:35-39 (New International Version).

Chapter Eight: Emotional Struggles

[1] Dr. Thomas Dow, review of *Dorothy Carey: The Tragic and Untold Story of Mrs. William Carey*, by James R. Beck, https://mafiadoc.com/the-tragic-and-untold-story-of-mrs-william-carey-bethel-college_5a13e7e71723ddb7810a8a9d.html.

[2] Basil Miller, *William Carey: The Father of Modern Missions* (Bethany House Publishers, 1985), 32.

[3] William Carey, "The Deathless Sermon" (sermon, Friar Lane Baptist Chapel, Nottingham, England, May 30, 1792).

[4] Peter Morden, *Offering Christ to the World: Andrew Fuller (1754–1815) and the Revival of Eighteenth Century Particular Baptist Life, Studies in Baptist History and Thought* 8 (Carlisle: Paternoster, 2003), 136.

[5] James R. Beck, *Dorothy Carey: The Tragic and Untold Story of Mrs. William Carey* (Baker, 1992), 112.

[6] Beck, *Dorothy Carey*, 109.

[7] Ibid., 180.

[8] Tom Payne, *The Template of Time: Our Destiny Decoded* (iUniverse, Inc., 2013), 132.

[9] Dow, review of *Dorothy Carey*.

[10] The author's interview with Deanna Fraser, March 13, 2018.

[11] The author's interview with Deanna Fraser, March 13, 2018.

[12] Sarita Hartz, "A Missionary's Story of PTSD and Healing," *Sarita Hartz*, June 29, 2017, http://www.saritahartz.com/a-missionarys-story-of-ptsd-and-healing/.

[13] Joan Carter, "Missionary Stressors and Implications for Care," *Journal of Psychology and Theology* 27, no. 2 (1999): 171-180.

[14] "The Holmes and Rahe Stress Scale," *JIBC*, http://www-files.jibc.ca/community_social_justice/pdf/cl/Life_Stress_Self_Assessment_(Holmes_and_Rahe).pdf.

[15] Dr. Ronald Koteskey, "What Missionaries Ought to Know About Burnout," *Missionary Care*, http://www.missionarycare.com/burnout.html.

[16] Koteskey, "What Missionaries."

[17] The author's interview with Deanna Fraser, March 13, 2018.

[18] The author's interview with Michelle Blackman (a pseudonym), March 12, 2018.

[19] The author's interview with Claire Henderson, March 12, 2018.

[20] Mike Pettengill, *The Mind of a Missionary Survey*, submitted February 25, 2017.

[21] Andrew Braze, *The Mind of a Missionary Survey*, submitted February 25, 2017.

[22] Cornelius Groenewald, *The Mind of a Missionary Survey*, submitted February 27, 2017.

[23] Platt, Urbana 15.

[24] Matthew 11:28 (New Living Translation).

[25] Matthew 28:18-20 (New International Version).

[26] The author's interview with Deanna Fraser, March 13, 2018.

[27] John Piper, *Andrew Fuller: Holy Faith, Worthy Gospel* (World Mission, Crossway, 2016), 15.

[28] Stephen Neill, *A History of Christian Missions* (New York: Penguin, 1964), 571.

[29] J. B. Myers, *William Carey: The Shoemaker Who Became the Father and Founder of Modern Missions* (Fleming D. Rebell Company, 1887), 98.

[30] George Smith, *The Life of William Carey, D.D.: Shoemaker and Missionary, Professor* (Edinburgh: R&R Clark), 1885), 150, Part 4.

[31] Vishal Mangalwadi, *The Legacy of William Carey: A Model for the Transformation of a Culture* (Crossway Books, 1999), 24–25.

[32] Iain Murray, *The Puritan Hope: A Study in Revival and the Interpretation of Prophecy* (Banner of Truth 1971), 140.

Chapter Nine: Spiritual Hurdles

[1] Jonathan Trotter, "The Idolatry of Missions," *A Life Overseas*, November 9, 2014, http://www.alifeoverseas.com/the-idolatry-of-missions/.

[2] Trotter, "The Idolatry."

[3] Joseph Campbell, *The Hero with a Thousand Faces* (Princeton University Press, 1949), 23.

[4] The author's interview with Jonathan Vickers, March 19, 2018.

[5] J. Hudson Taylor, "The Power of Prayer," in *A Retrospect: The Story Behind My Zeal for Missions* (Toronto: China Inland Mission, 1902).

[6] The author's interview with Jacob Bennett, March 19, 2018.

[7] Taylor, "The Power of Prayer," in *A Retrospect*.

[8] Ibid.

[9] Taylor, "The Call to Service," in *A Retrospect*.

[10] Ibid.

[11] Walter Henry Medhurst, *China; It's State and Prospects, with Special Reference to the Spread of the Gospel, Containing Allusions to the Antiquity, Extent, Population, Civilization, Literature, and Religion of the Chinese* (Crocker & Brewster, 1838).

[12] Taylor, "The Call to Service," in *A Retrospect*.

[13] Ibid.

[14] Ibid., "Preparation for Service," in *A Retrospect*.

[15] The author's interview with Kathy Balcombe, March 24, 2018.

[16] Broomhall, "Book Six: Assault on the Nine," in *Hudson Taylor and China's Open Century*, 189.

[17] Hudson Taylor, *Hudson Taylor's Choice Sayings: A Compilation from His Writings and Addresses* (London: China Inland Mission), 13.

[18] The author's interview with Kathy Balcombe, March 24, 2018.

[19] C. S. Lewis, *Mere Christianity* (San Francisco, 1952), 134.

[20] Colossians 3:2 (New International Version).

[21] Dr. And Mrs. Howard Taylor, *Hudson Taylor and the China Inland Mission: The Growth of a Work of God*, (The Religious Tract Society, 1913), 30-31.

[22] Taylor, "A New Agency Needed," in *A Retrospect*.

[23] Broomhall, "Book Five: Refiner's Fire," in *Hudson Taylor and China's Open Century*, 57.

[24] This is attributed to Pierre Teilhard de Chardin in *The Joy of Kindness* (1993), by Robert J. Furey, 138; but it is attributed to G. I. Gurdjieff in *Beyond Prophecies and Predictions: Everyone's Guide To The Coming Changes* (1993) by Moira Timms, 62; neither cite a source. It was widely popularized by Wayne Dyer, who often quotes it in his presentations, crediting it to Chardin, as does Stephen Covey in *Living the 7 Habits: Stories of Courage and Inspiration* (2000), 47.

[25] Romans 8:14.

[26] Galatians 5:25.

[27] Romans 12:1-2 (New American Standard Bible).

[28] Ephesians 6:12 (New International Version).

[29] C. S. Lewis, "Letter 12," in *The Screwtape Letters* (HarperCollins, 1996), 61.

[30] Lewis, "Letter 4," in *The Screwtape Letters*, 16.

[31] Lewis, "Letter 6," in *The Screwtape Letters*, 25.

[32] Lewis, "Letter 15," in *The Screwtape Letters*, 75.

[33] Ephesians 2:22.

[34] The author's interview with Jonathan English, March 23, 2018.

[35] The author's interview with Steve Braselton, March 22, 2018.

[36] Taylor, *Hudson Taylor and the China Inland Mission*, 279.

[37] Cao Shuji, *Zhongguo Renkou Shi [A History of China's Population]* (Shanghai: Fudan Daxue Chubanshe, 2001), 455, 509.

[38] Taylor, *Hudson Taylor and the China Inland Mission*, 90.

[39] Taylor, "Early Missionary Experiences," in *A Retrospect*.

[40] Broomhall, "Book Two: Over the Treaty Wall," in *Hudson Taylor and China's Open Century*, 362.

[41] Taylor, "Timely Supplies," in *A Retrospect*.

[42] Taylor, *Hudson Taylor's Choice Sayings*, 52.

[43] Leslie T. Lyall, *A Passion for the Impossible: The Continuing Story of the Mission Hudson Taylor Began* (London: OMF Books, 1965), 37.

[44] Taylor, *Hudson Taylor and the China Inland Mission*, 184.

[45] Ibid., 187.

[46] Ibid., 189.

[47] Charlotte Elliott, "O Holy Savior, Friend Unseen," 1836, *The Christian Life: Faith and Trust* (publication date 1929): 240.

[48] Taylor, *Hudson Taylor and the China Inland Mission*, 196.

[49] Lyall, *A Passion for the Impossible*, 5.

[50] "OMF and China Inland Mission (CIM) History," OMF, accessed June 17, 2018, https://omf.org/about-omf/history/.

[51] OMF, "History."

[52] 2 Chronicles 16:9 (New Living Translation).

[53] Broomhall, "Book Five: Refiner's Fire," in *Hudson Taylor and China's Open Century*, 350.

[54] Hudson Taylor, "The Source of Power" (speech, Ecumenical Missionary Conference, New York City, 1900).

[55] Amy Peterson, "Farewell to the Missionary Hero," *Christianity Today*, September 14, 2015, http://www.christianitytoday.com/ct/2015/september/farewell-to-missionary-hero.html.

[56] Edward M. Bounds, *Power Through Prayer* (Grand Rapids, MI: Baker, 2007), 5, 7.

Chapter Ten: Joy of the Journey

[1] Jeanne Stevenson Moessner, "Missionary Motivation," *Sociology of Religion* 53, issue 2 (July 1, 1992), 189–200, https://doi.org/10.2307/3711123.

[2] Amy Carmichael, *Candles in the Dark* (CLC Publications, The Dohnavur Fellowship, 1981), Kindle locations 901-903.

[3] "A Rendezvous with Destiny," in Chapter Two: Obedience to the Commands of Christ.

[4] Amy Carmichael, *Amma's Book: Amy's Autobiography* (in the Dohnavur library, unpublished), 13.

[5] Iain H. Murray, *Amy Carmichael: Beauty for Ashes*, A Biography (The Banner of Truth Trust, 2015), 5-6.

[6] Murray, *Amy Carmichael*, 7.

[7] Charles F. Harford, *The Keswick Convention: Its Message, Its Message and Its Men* (London: Marshall Brothers, Keswick House, Paternoster Row, EC, 1907), 4.

[8] Harford, *The Keswick Convention*, 77.

[9] Carmichael, *Candles in the Dark*, 100.

[10] Frank L. Houghton, *Amy Carmichael of Dohnavur* (Christian Literature Crusade, 1988), 44.

[11] J. (Hans) Kommers, *Triumphant Love: The Contextual, Creative, and Strategic Missionary Work of Amy Beatrice Carmichael in South India* (Cape Town: AOSIS, 2017), 102, https://doi.org/10.4102/aosis.2017.tl41.09.

[12] Kommers, *Triumphant Love*, 102.

[13] Murray, *Amy Carmichael*, 10.

[14] Broomhall, "It Is Not Death To Die!" *Hudson Taylor and China's Open Century*, 182. Here Broomhall adds: "The same Amy Carmichael was to become the 'Amma' of Dohnavur, the lifelong friend of the [China Inland Mission]."

[15] Amy Carmichael, *From Sunrise Land: Letters from Japan* (London: Marshall Brothers, 1895), 92.

[16] Carmichael, *Amma's Book*, 38-39.

[17] Kommers, *Triumphant Love*, 134.

[18] Carmichael, *Amma's Book*, 25.

[19] Amy Carmichael, *Raj, Brigand Chief: The True Story of an Indian Robin Hood Driven by Persecution to Dacoity; An Account of His Life of Daring Feats of Strength, Escapes & Tortures, His Robbery of the Rich & Generosity to the Poor, His Sincere Conversion to Christianity & His Tragic End* (London: Seeley, Service, 1927), 309.

[20] Psalm 103:7.

[21] Andrew Murray, *That God May Be All In All*, 404; see also Andrew Murray, *Andrew Murray at Keswick: Three Unrevised Talks Given in 1895* (Wamboin, Australia: Clairview House, 2014).

[22] Kommers, *Triumphant Love*, 148.

[23] TKW (1895): 46, 110; this motto, "Nothing Too Precious for Jesus," she had also fixed on the wall in her room in the Bangalore hospital; see Houghton, *Amy Carmichael of Dohnavur*, 90.

[24] Carmichael, *Amma's Book*, 41.

[25] Kommers, *Triumphant Love*, 147.

[26] Eliza F. Kent, *Converting Women: Gender and Protestant Christianity in Colonial South India* (New York: Oxford University Press, 2004), 103.

[27] Kommers, *Triumphant Love*, 166.

[28] Iain H. Murray, *The Puritan Hope: A Study in Revival and the Interpretation of Prophecy* (Edinburgh: The Banner of Truth, 1971), 140.

[29] Murray, *The Puritan Hope*, 141.

[30] Philippians 2:10-11 (New American Standard Bible).

[31] Carmichael, *Candles in the Dark*, Kindle locations 907-908.

[32] KCMMB, mission report, August 5, 1896.

[33] Peter Morden, *Offering Christ to the World: Andrew Fuller (1754–1815) and the Revival of Eighteenth Century Particular Baptist Life, Studies in Baptist History and Thought 8* (Carlisle: Paternoster, 2003), 136.

[34] Kommers, *Triumphant Love*, 160.

[35] Ibid., 180.

[36] Amy Carmichael, *The Continuation of a Story* (London : Dohnavur Fellowship, 1914), 37.

[37] This was in a time when Indian converts to Christianity had to adopt English dress, English customs, and English names. This is illustrative of the Victorian fear of "going native," which was seen as the opposite of the "civilizing" aspect of mission work.

[38] Kommers, *Triumphant Love*, 171.

[39] Kent, *Converting Women*, 224.

[40] Kumari Jayawardena, *The White Woman's Other Burden: Western Women and South Asia During British Colonial Rule* (Routledge, 1995), 94-95.

[41] Carmichael, *Amma's Book*, 45.

[42] Carmichael, *Candles in the Dark*, 102.

[43] Carmichael, *Candles in the Dark*, Kindle locations 904-906.

[44] Twenty-year-old Amy Carmichael in *Scraps*, a Carmichael family magazine, beautifully handwritten, illustrated, and published monthly for family and friends; It was Amy who proposed a family journal. The object of Scraps was "for the improvement and amusement of the members" (*Scraps*, March 18, 1887 onwards). Amy signed all her contributions with the pseudonym "Nobody." This quote is also found in *Amy Carmichael (Heroes of the Faith)* by Sam Wellman (Barbour Publishing, Inc., 2012), 32.

[45] Philippians 2:15-16 (New International Version).

[46] Amy Carmichael, *Ponnammal, Her Story* (London, 1918), 12.

47 Isabella Lilias Trotter, *A Life on Fire* (1888), quoted in B.A.F. Pigott, I. Lilias Trotter (London: Marshall, Morgan & Scott Ltd., 1930), 54.

48 Hebrews 12:2 (New American Standard Bible), italics mine.

49 Amy Carmichael, *Lotus Buds* (Morgan & Scott Ld., 1909), 249.

50 Kommers, *Triumphant Love*, 204.

51 Katherine Mayo, *Mother India* (G. A. Natesan & Co., 1927), 52.

52 Carmichael, *Lotus Buds*, 71.

53 Ibid., 257.

54 Carmichael, *Things As They Are*, 226, 229, 234.

55 Carmichael, *The Continuation of a Story*, 10.

56 Amy Carmichael, "Notes on Photographs," in *Ploughed Under: The Story of a Little Lover* (S.P.C.K., 1934), VI.

57 Amy Carmichael, *Overweights of Joy* (London: Morgan & Scott, 1906), 174.

58 Houghton, *Amy Carmichael of Dohnavur*, 114.

59 The author's interview with Andy Lepper, May 3, 2018.

60 John 3:30 (The Message Translation).

61 The author's interview with Amy Rhodes, May 8, 2018.

62 Carmichael, *Gold Cord*, Introduction.

63 Carmichael, *Overweights of Joy*, VIII.

64 Margaret Wilkinson one day visited her at Adayar in the south of Madras. The first thing that caught her attention in Laksmi's room was a small photo of Amy Carmichael hanging on her wall. Asked why that photo was there, Laksmi answered that it was "through Amma that she had first seen the temple women were a blot on her religion. After her study in Europe, she decided to seek election to the legislature in Madras. Her special concern was to see an Act passed which would really deal with the evil of the Devadasi system and put an end to the giving of children to temple houses." (Margaret Wilkinson, *At BBC Corner I Remember Amy Carmichael*, (1996), 91.)

65 Kommers, *Triumphant Love*, 212.

66 Carmichael, *Gold Cord*, 158.

67 Elliot, *A Chance to Die*, 85.

68 Carmichael, *The Continuation of a Story*, 4.

69 The author's interview with Ana Opungu, May 5, 2018.

70 Amy Carmichael, *Fragments That Remain* (CLC Ministries, 1964), 13.

71 Carmichael, *Gold Cord*, 5.

72 Ibid.

73 Murray, *That God May Be All In All*, 404.

74 Kommers, *Triumphant Love*, 356.

75 J. Hudson Taylor, "Union and Communion," in *China's Millions* (London: China Inland Mission, 1950), 24.

76 Elisabeth Elliot, "Amy Carmichael, God's Missionary," *The Elisabeth Elliot Newsletter*, May/June 2002, http://www.elisabethelliot.org/newsletters/2002-05-06.pdf.

77 Elliot, *Through Gates of Splendor*, 257.

78 Artist Ross Wilson, "Bangor Welcomes New Sculpture of Amy Carmichael," *Bangor Worldwide Missionary Convention*, 2017, https://www.worldwidemission.org/year/2017/news/bangor-welcomes-new-sculpture-of-amy-carmichael.

79 "Amy Carmichael's 'Giving Heart' Continues to Inspire," *The Irish News*, December 21, 2017, https://www.irishnews.com/lifestyle/faithmatters/2017/12/21/news/amy-carmichael-s-giving-heart-continues-to-inspire-1214155/.

80 Carmichael, *Ponnammal*, 44.

81 Philippians 4:13 (New King James Version).

82 Amy Carmichael, *Thou Givest They Gather* (CLC Ministries, 1982), 69.

83 Carmichael, *Fragments That Remain*, 143.

84 Houghton, *Amy Carmichael of Dohnavur*, 293.

85 Amy Carmichael, *Ragland, Pioneer* (Madras: S.P.C.K. Depository, 1922), 91.

86 David Hazard, *Amy Carmichael, I Come Quietly to Meet You: An Intimate Journey in God's Presence* (Bethany House, 2005), 79.

87 Carmichael, *Candles in the Dark*, 99.

88 Elisabeth Elliot, *Amy Carmichael, God's Missionary* (Christian Literature Crusade, 1997), 52.

89 The pattern of God's Garden in Dohnavur was according the plan of the earliest Quaker burial grounds which had no markers; see Michael L. Birkel, *Silence and Witness: The Quaker Tradition (Traditions of Christian Spirituality)* (Orbis Books, 2004), 111.

Chapter Eleven: Breakthrough in Ministry

1 Don Richardson, *Peace Child: An Unforgettable Story of Primitive Jungle Treachery in the 20th Century* (Regal Books, 1976), 90.

2 Ebenezer G. Vine, secretary of the Philadelphia council of Regions Beyond Missionary Union (RBMU), an international missions society (now World Team), in a message given in 1955 at Prairie Bible Institute in Alberta, Canada, where the motto was plainly and unaffectedly "training disciplined soldiers for Christ!"

3 Richardson, *Peace Child*, 81.

4 Ibid., 84.

5 Ibid., 87.

6 Ibid., 87.

7 John Piper, *Let the Nations Be Glad!: The Supremacy of God in Missions* (Baker Academic, third edition, 2010; first edition, 1999), 15.

8 Richardson, *Peace Child*, 89.

9 Ibid., 90.

10 Ibid., 34.

11 Ibid., 93-94.

12 Ibid., 96-97.

13 "Hai Tanahku Papua" is the national anthem of the Republic of West Papua (New Guinea).

14 The Morning Star flag was a flag used in a supplemental fashion on Netherlands New Guinea to the Flag of the Netherlands. It was first raised on December 1, 1961, prior to the territory coming under the administration of the United Nations Temporary Executive Authority (UNTEA) on October 1, 1962.

15 Richardson, *Peace Child*, 56.

16 Ibid., 129.

17 Don Richardson, "Cultural Compasses that Point to Jesus" (Stonebridge Church, Cedar Rapids, IA, USA, January 12, 2014), https://youtu.be/GDf3HpC9yms.

18 Richardson, *Peace Child*, 139.

19 A. Scott Moreau, *The Evangelical Dictionary of Missions* (Baker Book House, 2000), 252.

20 Richardson, "Cultural Compasses."

21 Richardson, *Peace Child*, 178.

22 Richardson, "Cultural Compasses."

23 Genesis 12:2-3.

24 Isaiah 61:3.

25 Joannes, *The Space Between Memories*, 19.

26 Romans 1:20 (New International Version).

27 John 3:14-15 (New King James Version).

28 Acts 17:22-23 (New International Version).

[29] Jiraphon Serithai, "God of the Thai: How One Movement Overcomes the Perception of a Foreign God," *Mission Frontiers* issue November-December, "The Fingerprints of God in Buddhism" (November 1, 2014), http://www.missionfrontiers.org/issue/article/god-of-the-thai.

[30] Serithai, "God of the Thai."

[31] Philip Bassham, "John 3:16 from a Thai Buddhist Worldview - Total Opposite!," *Project Thailand*, January 4, 2011, https://projectthailand.net/2011/01/04/john-316-from-a-thai-buddhist-worldview-total-opposite/.

[32] "Global Statistics," Joshua Project, accessed May 29, 2018, https://joshuaproject.net/people_groups/statistics.

[33] H. Richard Niebuhr, *Christ and Culture* (1951), is often referenced in discussions and writings on a Christian's response to the world's culture. Niebuhr provides five paradigms for understanding the relationship between Christ and culture: Christ against Culture, Christ of Culture, and Christ above Culture (a paradigm which includes the last two as subsets: Christ and Culture in Paradox and Christ Transforming Culture).

[34] For a deeper understanding of *analogia entis* or "the analogy of being," see the writings of Thomas Aquinas. Although no centralized text states Aquinas' doctrine directly and succinctly, *Summa Theologiae*, 1a.13.1-6 covers the central issues. The contemporary selection/translation by Timothy McDermott in the "World's Classics" *Aquinas: Selected Philosophical Writings* (Oxford), 214-228, can be found online here: http://www.newadvent.org/summa/1013.htm.

[35] The author's interview with Ben Fa'alafi Jones, May 14, 2018.

[36] Richardson, *Peace Child*, 192.

[37] Ibid., 192.

[38] Ibid., 206.

[39] Isaiah 9:6

[40] Richardson, *Peace Child*, 213-214.

[41] Ibid., 233.

[42] "Never The Same," Pioneers, accessed May 29, 2018, https://www.pioneers.org/connect/connect-full-view/never-the-same.

[43] Pioneers, "Never The Same."

[44] Richardson, "Epilogue," in *Peace Child*.

[45] "Sawi Progress Report," Joshua Project, accessed May 29, 2018, https://joshuaproject.net/people_groups/18881/ID.

[46] Pioneers, "Never The Same."

Chapter Twelve: The Kingdom of God on Earth

[1] Bill Johnson, *Compelled by Love*, documentary (Iris Global Films, Shara Pradhan, 2014).

[2] Heidi Baker, *Compelled By Love: How to Change the World Through the Simple Power of Love in Action* (Charisma House, 2008), 49.

[3] Matthew 5:3, 5.

[4] Together the four Gospels specifically mention God's Kingdom eighty-six times in addition to other (oblique) references to it. The remainder of the New Testament, from Acts through Revelation, mentions God's Kingdom many times.

[5] The Gospel of Matthew usually referred to "the Kingdom of God" by using the term, "the Kingdom of Heaven."

[6] Noel Hornor, "Why Don't People Understand the Kingdom of God?" *Good News Magazine*, September-October 1998, https://www.ucg.org/the-good-news/why-dont-people-understand-the-kingdom-of-god.

[7] Luke 23:2; John 19:12.

[8] John Bright, *The Kingdom of God: The Biblical Concept & Its Meaning for the Church* (Abingdon Press, 1953), 197.

[9] Isaiah 2:4; Amos 9:13.

[10] John Piper, "Book Review of 'The Kingdom of God' by John Bright," review of *The Kingdom of God*, by John Bright, *Desiring God*, February 1, 1975, https://www.desiringgod.org/articles/book-review-of-the-kingdom-of-god-by-john-bright.

[11] Bright, *The Kingdom of God*, 196.

[12] Matthew 6:10.

[13] Revelation 11:15.

[14] Matthew 25:31-46.

[15] The author's interview with Jeshua Ting, May 25, 2018.

[16] The author's interview with Jacob Bennet, May 25, 2018.

[17] Luke 12:32 (English Standard Version).

[18] 2 Peter 1:11 (New King James Version).

[19] Philippians 2:6-8 (New American Standard Version).

[20] Philippians 2:3.

[21] Harold Carl, "User-Friendly Faith," *Christian History* 55: The Monkey Trial and the Rise of Fundamentalism (1997): 20, https://christianhistoryinstitute.org/magazine/issues.

[22] D. G. Hart, "Right Jabs and Left Hooks," *Christian History* 55, The Monkey Trial and the Rise of Fundamentalism (1997): 24, https://christianhistoryinstitute.org/magazine/issues.

[23] Hartz, "Surprising Ways."

[24] Piper, "The Kingdom."

[25] Matthew 6:33 (New International Version).

[26] David Brainerd, *Jonathan Edwards, An Account of the Life of the Late Reverend Mr. David Brainerd* (Boston: D. Henchman, 1749), 185; May 22, 1746 journal entry.

[27] Rolland Baker, *Compelled by Love*, documentary.

[28] Baker, *Compelled By Love*, 9.

[29] "History," About, Iris Global, accessed June 13, 2018, https://www.irisglobal.org/about/history.

[30] Baker, *Compelled By Love*, 37.

[31] Ibid., 32.

[32] Iris Global, "History."

[33] Baker, *Compelled By Love*, 13.

[34] Psalm 139:7-12.

[35] Rolland Baker, *Compelled by Love*, documentary.

[36] Heidi Baker, *Compelled by Love*, documentary.

[37] Bill Johnson, *Compelled by Love*, documentary.

[38] Heidi Baker, *Compelled by Love*, documentary.

[39] Rolland Baker, Heidi Baker, *There Is Always Enough: The Miraculous Move of God in Mozambique* (Sovereign Publishing, 2003), 58.

[40] Baker, *Compelled by Love*, 1-2; also Heidi Baker, "Lay Down and Let Him Love You," (sermon, Show Me Your Glory Conference, Toronto Airport Christian Fellowship, March 5, 2004, recording transcribed by Jennifer A. Miskov). To read this account from Randy Clark's perspective, see Randy Clark, *There Is More!: The Secret to Experiencing God's Power to Change Your Life* (Chosen Books, 2013), 116-117.

[41] Bill Johnson, *Defining Moments: God-Encounters with Ordinary People Who Changed the World* (Whitaker House, 2016), Kindle locations 4851-4855.

[42] UN Office for the Coordination of Humanitarian Affairs, "Mozambique: Ross Mountain Praised Media's Role and International Solidarity, *Reliefweb*, March 17, 2000, https://reliefweb.int/report/mozambique/mozambique-ross-mountain-praised-medias-role-and-international-solidarity.

[43] RSMC La Reunion (Report), "Cyclone Season 1999–2000," *Meteo-France*, retrieved July 15, 2014, http://www.meteo.fr/temps/domtom/La_Reunion/webcmrs9.0/anglais/archives/publications/saisons_cycloniques/index19992000.html.

[44] Iris Global, "History."

[45] Cassandra Soars, "Heidi Baker: 'A Modern-Day Mother Teresa,'" *Charisma Magazine*, May 11, 2016, https://www.charismamag.com/spirit/evangelism-missions/26027-heidi-baker-love-like-fire.

[46] Mother Teresa, *One Heart Full of Love* (Ann Arbor, MI: Servant Publications, 1988), 87.

[47] The author's interview with Samantha Gordon, May 24, 2018.

[48] The author's interview with Brian Britton, May 29, 2018.

[49] "Official: More Than 1M Child Prostitutes in India, CNN, May 11, 2009, http://edition.cnn.com/2009/WORLD/asiapcf/05/11/india.prostitution.children/index.html; see also https://en.wikipedia.org/wiki/Prostitution_in_India.

[50] Lyle Phillips, *Compelled by Love*, documentary.

[51] John 18:36.

[52] Colossians 1:13.

[53] Zechariah 4:6.

[54] Lyle Phillips, *Compelled by Love*, documentary.

[55] Baker, *Compelled By Love*, 44.

[56] Bright, *The Kingdom of God*, 231.

[57] Bright, *The Kingdom of God*, 264.

[58] Henry Martyn, missionary to India and Persia, 1781-1812.

[59] Matthew 22:35-40.

[60] Leaf, *Switch On Your Brain*, 42.

[61] Leaf, *Switch On Your Brain*, 25.

[62] Romans 12:2.

[63] Clark, *The Missions of the Church Missionary Society and the Church of England Zenana Missionary Society in the Punjab and Sindh*, 1904. 71.

[64] Heidi Baker, *Birthing the Miraculous: The Power of Personal Encounters with God to Change Your Life and the World* (Charisma House, 2014), 38-40.

[65] 1 Corinthians 2:16.

ABOUT THE AUTHOR

David Joannes is the founder and president of Within Reach Global, which serves the advance of the Gospel in some of Southeast Asia's most difficult places. He is the author of *The Space Between Memories: Recollections from a 21st Century Missionary*. David has a love for language, culture, and creative writing, and for the last 20 years, he has witnessed God's Kingdom established in forgotten parts of the globe. David lives in Chiang Mai, Thailand with his wife, Lorna, and their daughter, Cara.

CONNECT WITH US

CONNECT WITH DAVID JOANNES ONLINE:
www.davidjoannes.com

FACEBOOK: facebook.com/davidjoannesofficial
TWITTER: twitter.com/davidjoannes
EMAIL: david@withinreachglobal.org

TO LEARN MORE ABOUT WITHIN REACH GLOBAL
OR TO BECOME A MONTHLY VISION PARTNER, VISIT US ONLINE:
www.withinreachglobal.org

FACEBOOK: facebook.com/withinreachglobal
TWITTER: twitter.com/within_reach
NEWSLETTER: withinreachglobal.org/newsletter
EMAIL: info@withinreachglobal.org

TO LEARN MORE ABOUT *The Mind of a Missionary*, VISIT US ONLINE:
www.themindofamissionary.com

⭕ within reach global

CPSIA information can be obtained
at www.ICGtesting.com
Printed in the USA
LVHW110404190821
695610LV00009B/395

9 780998 061153